GREGOR CLARK & BRENDAN SAINSBURY

Contents

PLAN YOUR TRIP

Highlights 6
Best For 12
With Kids... 14
Accessible Trails 16
Essentials.. 18
Walking in Italy 20

BY REGION

ITALIAN LAKES 26
Orrido di Sant'Anna......................30
Greenway al Lago di Como.................32
La Strada del Ponale 36
Monte Isola Loop............................38
The Slopes of Monte Grona 40
Monte Baldo:
Sentiero del Ventrar.......................42
Also Try 44

**CAMPANIA
& THE AMALFI COAST** 46
Passegiata del Pizzolungo...............50
Punta Campanella 52
Sentiero degli Dei..........................54
Valle del Sambuco.........................58
Le Tre Marine.................................60
Valle delle Ferriere 62
Santa Maria
del Castello Circuit........................64
Also Try 66

ABRUZZO 68
Santo Stefano di Sessanio
to Rocca Calascio...................... 72
Above Pescasseroli 74
Campo Imperatore Ridge 76

Rocca Ridge................................. 78
Monte Mileto..............................82
Sentiero della Libertà 86
Also Try 90

TUSCANY 92
Panzano to Radda 96
Castellina to Radda.......................98
Certaldo to San Gimignano.............100
Chianti Classico........................... 102
Tuscan Hill Crests 106
Medieval Towns & Villages 110
Also Try 114

SICILY 116
Stromboli.....................................120
Necropoli di Pantalica 122
La Rocca di Cefalù 124
Riserva Naturale dello Zingaro 126
Oasi Faunistican di Vendicari 130
Fossa di Vulcano 132
Punta Troia 134
Also Try 136

DOLOMITES & STELVIO 138
Hans & Paula Steger Weg.............. 142
Passo Gardena to Vallunga 144
Sassolungo Circuit............................148
Tre Cime di Lavaredo 150
Alpe di Fanes..............................152
Pragser Wildsee 156
Percorso delle Segherie 158
Adolf Munkel Weg 160
Also Try 162

SARDINIA 164
Cala Goloritzé 168
Gola di Gorropu 170
Tiscali 172
Cala Sisine to Cala Luna 176
Monte Corrasi...............................178
Also Try 180

UMBRIA & LE MARCHE 182
Passo del Lupo...................................186
Gola dell'Infernaccio......................188
Monte Subasio................................190
Around the Pian Piccolo 194
Bosco di San Francesco 196
Also Try 198

LIGURIA 200
Levanto to Monterosso...................204
Portofino to San Fruttuoso 206
Manarola to Corniglia 208
Sentiero Azzurro 210
Porto Venere to Riomaggiore 214
Also Try 216

**WESTERN
& MARITIME ALPS** 218
Tour du Mont Blanc.......................... 222
Sella-Herbetet Traverse 226
Gran Balconata del Cervino 228
Vallone di Grauson 232
Rifugio Garelli 234
Also Try 236

LANGUAGE............................... 238
BEHIND THE SCENES 240
BY DIFFICULTY............................241
INDEX 242
OUR WRITERS 248

The country that gave the world Michelangelo and the Pantheon might not be everyone's first choice for a walking holiday. But, *escursionismo* (hiking) is one of the latent delights of the *bel paese* (beautiful country) better known as Italy. With enough trails to ring the globe, and diverse landscapes that oscillate between stark volcanoes, cleaver-sharp alpine ridges and gentle Tuscan hills, the walking potential here is unlimited – and surprisingly untapped. While Venice and Rome heave with tourists, the beech forests of Abruzzo and the balmy coastal enclaves of Sardinia are invariably 'hear-a-pin-drop' quiet. Adding to the feeling of detachment are semi-abandoned mountain villages, off-the-radar family-run restaurants, and rutted country lanes where farmers in old Fiats nod a cursory *buongiorno*. Welcome to Italy, uncensored, uncrowded and devoid of tourist trimmings. It's all yours, if you're happy to undertake a bit of footwork.

Highlights

TOUR DU MONT BLANC, WESTERN & MARITIME ALPS

Explore the Italian side of Europe's highest peak on this one-day segment of the legendary 170km Tour du Mont Blanc. p222

MONTE MILETO, ABRUZZO

From ancient beech woods to high mountain meadows in a land once roamed by medieval hermits, this is rural Italy at its best. p82

STROMBOLI, SICILY

Join a sunset climb to the summit of Sicily's favourite volcanic island and get a close-up look at its eternal fireworks. p120

CHIANTI CLASSICO, ♂
TUSCANY

From vine to winery, this oenological voyage through the dells and swells of the Tuscan countryside has the making of an all-time classic. **p102**

CALA SISINE TO CALA LUNA, SARDINIA

Immerse yourself in the stunning beauty of Sardinia's coastline on this adventurous jaunt between two remote coves. **p176**

GREENWAY AL LAGO DI COMO, ITALIAN LAKES

Advertising the true essence of the Italian Lakes amid the finely manicured gardens and villas of Lago di Como. **p32**

PASSO GARDENA TO VALLUNGA, DOLOMITES & STELVIO

Thread your way through the Dolomites' rocky spires, traversing the wild highlands of Parco Naturale Puez-Odle and descending into an idyllic green valley. **p144**

ALPE DI FANES, DOLOMITES & STELVIO

Cross through the ethereal high country of Parco Naturale Fanes-Sennes-Braies, setting for many a Ladin legend. **p152**

PORTOFINO TO SAN FRUTTUOSO, LIGURIA

A wild coastal trail linking a swanky Riviera resort with a tiny monastic beach hamlet. **p106**

SENTIERO DEGLI DEI, CAMPANIA & AMALFI COAST

The scent of lemons, the braying of cliff-side goats, the distant sparkle of the Mediterranean: Italy's most famous day walk contours the splendid Amalfi Coast. **p54**

Best For...

DADO DANIELA/GETTY IMAGES ©

JACKBOLLA/SHUTTERSTOCK ©

HISTORY & CULTURE

Beyond historical heavyweight Rome lie smaller but equally compelling snippets of Italy's past.

MEDIEVAL TOWNS & HAMLETS, TUSCANY
Peel off medieval layers in this rustic rollercoaster of tiny settlements (San Gimignano pictured) that embellish the landscape. p110

NECROPOLI DI PANTALICA, SICILY
Explore this honeycomb of 5000 prehistoric chamber tombs cut into the limestone canyon walls. p122

SENTIERO DELLA LIBERTÀ, ABRUZZO
Re-enact the exploits of escaping Allied prisoners as they forged a path across the Appennines. p86

MONTE SUBASIO, UMBIRA & LE MARCHE
Make a pilgrimage to this mountain hermitage near Assisi, a favourite spiritual retreat for St Francis in the 13th century. p190

TISCALI, SARDINIA
Climb to a mysterious abandoned village in a collapsed mountaintop cave in Sardinia's rugged Supramonte region. p172

SPECTACULAR COASTLINES

Italy's most famous trails contour the precipitous segments of its coastline, revealing traditional villages that practice geography-defying methods of agriculture.

SENTIERO DEGLI DEI, CAMPANIA & THE AMALFI COAST
The 'path of the gods' is indeed a heavenly experience, traversing crags, grottoes and terraces. p54

SENTIERO AZZURRO, LIGURIA
This ancient path is a heady melange of terraced gardens, medieval fishing villages and sparkling sea. p210

PASSEGGIATA DEL PIZZOLUNGO, CAMPANIA
Capri's top hits packed into 4km of paved paths, tree-draped staircases and coastal splendour. p50

RISERVA NATURALE DELLO ZINGARO, SICILY
Weave along the supremely scenic shoreline (pictured) in Sicily's original nature reserve. p126

CALA GOLORITZÉ, SARDINIA
Descend past ancient oaks to the blue-green waters of this idyllic cove. p168

JENIFOTO/SHUTTERSTOCK ©   QQ7/GETTY IMAGES ©   WWW.TONNAJA.COM/GETTY IMAGES ©

 QUAINT VILLAGES

Atmospheric *borghi* (hamlets) and villages abound.

MANAROLA TO CORNIGLIA, LIGURIA
Cliff-clinging medieval villages unchanged by modernism. **p208**

GRAN BALCONATA DEL CERVINO, WESTERN & MARITIME ALPS
Wander through hamlets and glimpse the Matterhorn. **p228**

GREENWAY AL LAGO, ITALIAN LAKES
Follow an old Roman road along the shore of Lago di Como. **p32**

LA ROCCA DI CEFALÙ, SICILY
Gaze down over the alleys of this seaside village (pictured). **p124**

SANTO STEFANO DI SESSANIO TO ROCCA CALASCIO, ABRUZZO
Wander between two villages undergoing an eco-inspired renaissance. **p72**

AVOIDNG THE CROWDS

It's possible to go an entire day without seeing a single person.

MONTE MILETO, ABRUZZO
It's peaceful amid the peaks. **p82**

TUSCAN HILL CRESTS, TUSCANY
You'll have these rural trails all to yourself **p106**

AROUND THE PIAN PICCOLO, UMBRIA & LE MARCHE
Commune with animals on this solitary odyssey. **p194**

PUNTA TROIA, SICILY
Escape to the turquoise seas of Marettimo. **p134**

PORTO VENERE TO RIOMAGGIORE, LIGURIA
The less crowded extension of popular Sentiero Azzurro (Riomaggiore pictured). **p214**

MOUNTAIN VIEWS

Some of the highest and most handsome mountains in Europe.

SELLA-HERBETET TRAVERSE, WESTERN & MARITIME ALPS
View the Alps from Parco Nazionale Gran Paradiso. **p226**

CAMPO IMPERATORE RIDGE, ABRUZZO
Marvel at Corno Grande. **p76**

TRE CIME DI LAVAREDO, DOLOMITES & STELVIO
Circumnavigate this magnificent massif. **p150**

THE SLOPES OF MONTE GRONA, ITALIAN LAKES
Exhilarating taste of the Italian pre-Alps (pictured). **p40**

SASSOLUNGO CIRCUIT, DOLOMITES & STELVIO
Watch hang gliders soar. **p148**

With Kids

THE BASICS

Many Italian families enjoy walking together. Some carry babies in specially designed backpacks and it's not unusual to see children as young as six skipping around happily at high levels. However, it you have never taken your child walking before, don't expect the introduction to be trouble-free. It may take some time and it demands lots of patience to 'train' a child to go on walks of any duration.

If you're bringing along inexperienced youngsters, choose areas where it's easy to find short, undemanding walks, such as Tuscany, Liguria, the Amalfi-Sorrento area and parts of the Italian Lakes. It may also help if you make your trip multifarious, interspersing a day or two of walking with time spent pursuing more traditional sightseeing. The Amalfi is within easy striking distance of Naples with its ruins, interesting street life and world-class pizza. Tuscany is adjacent to Florence and Siena. The Italian Lakes have an abundance of villas, castles and botanical gardens to explore.

For slightly older kids of 10 and up, it's worth injecting a bit of adventure into proceedings. Staying in a *rifugio* (hostel) halfway up a mountain in the Dolomites is a great way to embrace the great outdoors, meet other families and enjoy basic comforts while still feeling like you're living a little apart from the rest of civilisation. Most *rifugio* accept children. Some have family rates and special kids activities. All count on direct access to numerous trails.

In flatter climes, consider staying in an *agriturismo* or farmstay where kids may be able to interact with farm animals, wander the grounds, and – in the posher places – enjoy swimming pools or cooking classes. Tuscany is blessed with a wide variety of *agriturismi*.

CHOOSING A TRAIL

Italy isn't Alaska. There is little true wilderness and wild animals (chamois, ibex) are invariably an interesting distraction rather than a dangerous menace. Additionally, you're never far from a village or hamlet with a least one basic bar, deli or restaurant, along with a communal fountain dispensing potable water.

Choosing a trail largely depends on your kids' age, walking experience and interests.

Kids of two and under can be carried in a 'baby-carrier' by a fit adult. At the other end

Other Outdoor Activities

Kids can quickly tire of walking, so it pays to choose an area where you can diversify your trip with some alternative outdoor activities.

Aeolian Islands Seven tiny volcanic islands off Sicily with everything from spewing lava to black-sand beaches. **p118**

The Dolomites Cycle through orchards and farmland on family-friendly trails in Val Venosta and Val Pusteria. **p138**

Lago Maggiore & Lago di Garda Lakeside beaches, water sports, climbing, mountain biking, canyoning (from Riva del Garda; pictured), swimming, horse riding and kilometres of cycling paths. **p28**

Abruzzo Take to central Italy's first **zipline** (☎366 7279724; www.zipline majella.com; Piazza del Popolo 13; single ride €40-45; ⏱10am-6.30pm daily, Sat & Sun only Sep-Jun) for a thrilling ride over the village of Pacentro in the Parco Nazionale della Majella. Kids can use it if their parents agree and they're over 35kg. **p82**

Best Walks with Kids

Adolf Munkel Weg Work out the wiggles in a wide-open meadow and munch on Kaiserschmarren (sweet South Tyrolean pancakes) at an alpine hut. **p160**

Orrido di Sant'Anna Short, flat walk with a natural pool for swimming en route. **p30**

Percorso delle Segherie Watch the workings of a water-driven sawmill and stop for a trailside playground break in the verdant Val di Rabbi. **p158**

---

of the age scale, growing teenagers can usually endure the same physical rigours as their parents. For the in-betweeners, err on the side of caution by picking short trails with scheduled stops and other potential points of interests en route. Castles and beaches are ideal (and abundant in Italy). And who hasn't 'bribed' their wilting offspring with a post-hike ice cream from one of Italy's ubiquitous gelaterias? Older and fitter kids might get a kick out of climbing the smouldering volcanoes of Stromboli and Vulcano in the south.

With younger kids, avoid 'expert' trails labelled EE that sometimes incorporate steep and exposed sections of path, but don't write off mountainous areas altogether. Italy has a broad selection of mountain trails that can be reached by cable car – an entertaining start/finish to any high-country hike. Boat access is another fun overture and/or finale to a day of walking. Plenty of trails in Liguria, the Amalfi Coast and the Italian Lakes are accessible by boat.

EATING OUT & PICNICS

Eating is one of the joys of travelling in Italy and kids are welcome pretty much everywhere, especially in the kind of casual, family-run trattorias that populate the less-touristed towns and villages located close to trail networks. These places are usually pretty informal with friendly, indulgent waiters and menus of simple pasta dishes and grilled meats. Pizzerias are another option, offering food that's easy to eat, quick to arrive and beloved by children the world over.

Italian families eat late and few restaurants open their doors much before 7.30pm or 8pm. Some serve a *menu bambino* (child's menu), but if not it's perfectly acceptable to order a *mezzo porzione* (half-portion) or a simple plate of pasta with butter or olive oil and Parmesan. High chairs (*seggioloni*) are occasionally available, but if your toddler needs to be strapped in, bring your own portable cloth seat.

Picnics are half the essence of an elongated day-walk. *Pizza al taglio* (sliced pizza), *panini* from delicatessens, and gelato are perfect on-the-walk snacks. And markets everywhere burst with salami, cheese, olives, bread, fruit and other inspiring picnic supplies. Some of the more popular hiking paths in coastal areas and natural parks have picnic areas – if not, there are always the beaches.

Accessible Trails

CHOOSING A TRAIL

To the surprise of many, Italy has a huge network of efficiently organised trails, most of them clearly waymarked and lightly trammelled. The almost total lack of dangerous wild animals along with the abundance of towns, villages and *rifugi* (mountain huts) en route mean that day or multi-day hiking is safe, easy to plan and anxiety-free (a hot cappuccino or cold beer is refreshingly close at hand at the end of most hikes). Public transport in Italy is similarly comprehensive and even the most obscure hikes to the most out-of-the-way villages have regular rural bus and/or train connections.

Trails maintained by the Club Alpino Italiano are marked with red-and-white signposts or blobs of paint emblazoned on rocks,

walls or trees. Point-to-point journeys are usually defined by duration (hours), rather than distance (kilometres). While trails fan out countrywide, they are more ubiquitous and better-marked in the north of the country.

Trails labelled as 'expert' or EE (Escurionisti Espert) can be challenging and exposed, with scrambling sections and cables provided for balance and support. Walkers who are prone to dizziness or unsure of foot should not attempt these trails.

Older footpaths in coastal regions – particularly Amalfi and Cinque Terre – often include hundreds of stone steps which can be debilitating in hot weather (avoid July and August).

Outside of big cities, wheelchair accessible paths are hard to find. For walkers looking for

relatively gentle terrain on wide gravel or paved roads, Tuscany makes a good starting point.

On occasion, due to adverse weather conditions and lack of maintenance, key signposts can be missing. If you go for over 15 minutes without seeing a trail marker, retrace your steps to the last marker and re-evaluate. It is wise to always carry a map.

GETTING TO & FROM THE TRAILS

Italy has an excellent pubic transport system and almost all the trails in this book are accessible without a car. However, due to the sometimes sporadic nature of local transport in more emote villages, it's wise to plan ahead.

TRAIN

Trains in Italy are relatively cheap compared with other

Agencies for Accessible Travel

Accessible Italy (www.accessibleitaly.com) A San Marino–based nonprofit company that runs guided tours and provides services for people with disabilities.

Rome & Italy (www.romeanditaly.com/tourism-for-disabled) A mainstream travel agency with a well-developed accessible tourism arm that offers customised tours, including walking tours of Volterra and San Gimignano.

Sage Traveling (www.sagetraveling.com) A US-based accessible-travel agency that offers tailor-made tours to assist mobility-impaired travellers in Europe.

Best Trails

Greenway al Lago Straight-forward lakeside ramble through a string of beautiful villages. **p32**

Oasi Faunistica di Vendicari Enjoy a leisurely afternoon amidst the flamingo-rich wetlands of this Sicilian coastal nature reserve. **p130**

Pragser Wildsee Explore the shores of a sparkling emerald lake (pictured) high in the Dolomites. **p156**

Castellina to Radda Tuscan hike that's 90% on gravel or paved roads with easy gradients. **p98**

European countries and the better categories of train are fast and comfortable. Trenitalia (www .trenitalia.com) is the partially privatised, state train system that runs most services. There are several types of trains. Some stop at all or most stations, such as *regionale* or *interregionale* trains. Intercity (IC) trains are fast services that operate between major cities. Eurocity (EC) trains are the international version.

All tickets on *regionale* trains must be validated before boarding by punching them in the yellow or green and silver machines at the entrance to train platforms. If you don't validate, you risk an on-the-spot fine.

Visit the information page of Trenitalia (www.trenitalia.com/en/purchase/info_contacts/disabled_passengers.html) for full details of services offered to

the elderly, pregnant women or people with disabilities.

If travelling by train, you can arrange assistance through SalaBlu (https://salabluonline.rfi.it) online or by calling 800 90 60 60 (from a landline) or 02 32 32 32 (from a landline or mobile).

BUSES
Within Italy, bus services are provided by numerous companies and range from local routes linking small villages to fast, reliable intercity connections, making it possible to reach just about any location throughout the country. Buses can be a cheaper and faster way to get around if your destination is not on a main train line.

Bus timetables for the provincial and intercity services are usually available online. For smaller local services, you

may have to enquire at the local tourist office or bus station.

In some smaller towns and villages, tickets are sold in bars – ask for *biglietti per il pullman* – or on the bus.

Many urban buses are wheelchair-accessible; however some of the stops may not be – ask before you board.

BOAT
Navi (large ferries) service the islands of Sicily and Sardinia; all vessels carry vehicles. Ferries and hydrofoils ply the waters of the three big lakes in the Lake District, and offer a relaxing alternative to buses or cars as you move around the area. There are also popular passenger ferries serving towns on the Amalfi and Ligurian coasts and providing access to many of this book's walks.

Essentials

MAPS

Despite plenty of trail signage, it is surprisingly easy to get lost in Italy. The sheer density of the trail network, plus the abundance of wonderfully distracting views have led many a walker gallivanting down the wrong path. While you'll rarely be lost for long, adding an extra kilometre to the 5km you've already walked can be a frustrating experience. Hence, it is always beneficial to carry a local trail map.

The best places to buy maps in Italy are newsagents, bookshops and *tabaccherie* (tobacconists). Major city bookshops (such as those of the Feltrinelli chain) have map sections but the range is usually limited.

The most useful walking maps are the 1:25,000 scale series; they contain an enormous amount of detailed information, including waymarked paths, although the numbering may not be entirely accurate or up to date. Different publishers specialise in different parts of the country. Austrian publisher, Kompass, has the most comprehensive selection.

SAFETY & PRE-PLANNING

• Allow plenty of time to accomplish a walk before dark, particularly when daylight hours are shorter.

• Don't overestimate your capabilities. Study the route carefully before setting out, noting the possible escape routes and the point of no return (where it's quicker to continue than to turn back).

• Monitor your progress during the day against the time estimated for the walk, and keep an eye on the weather.

• It's wise not to walk alone. Always leave details of your intended route with someone responsible before you set off.

• Before setting off, make sure you have the relevant map and a compass. You should also make sure you know the weather forecast for the area for the next 24 hours.

CLOTHING & EQUIPMENT

You don't need to spend a fortune on gear to enjoy walking, but you do need to think carefully about what you pack to make sure you're comfortable and prepared for an emergency.

The gear you need will depend on the type of walking you plan

When to Go

- Walking in Italy is possible all year round, though the months from April to October are the most reliable.
- Due to snowfall and fickle weather, the hiking season in the Alps and Apennines is relatively short. The best time to tackle these mountainous areas is from late June to late September. These months usually have the best weather and longer hours of daylight. It is also when the nation's comprehensive network of *rifugi* (mountain huts) are open for business.
- The cooler months of spring and autumn (April, May, September and October) are good times to consider visiting the coastal and lowland areas of Liguria, Tuscany, Campania, Sicily and Sardinia.
- August is Italy's most crowded month, when the whole country goes on holiday.

Resources

www.stanfords.co.uk Website of the famous London-based travel book/map store.

www.omnimap.com Order maps online out of the US.

www.cai.it/andare-in -montagna/rifugi-e -bivacchi List of all Club Alpino Italiano–run mountain huts (in Italian) with links to individual websites.

to do. For day walks, clothing, footwear and a backpack are the major items; you might get away with runners, a hat, shorts, shirt and a warm pullover.

The secret of comfortable walking is to wear several layers of light clothing, which you can easily take off or put on as you warm up or cool down. Most walkers use three main layers: a base layer next to the skin, an insulating layer, and an outer, shell layer for protection from wind, rain and snow.

The ideal specifications for a rain jacket are a breathable, waterproof fabric, a hood which is roomy enough to cover headwear but still allows peripheral vision, a capacious map pocket and a good-quality, heavy-gauge zip protected by a storm flap.

Your footwear will be your friend or your enemy, so choose carefully. The first decision you

will make is between boots and shoes. Runners or walking shoes are fine over easy terrain but, for more difficult trails and across rocks and scree, most walkers consider that the ankle support offered by boots is invaluable.

For day walks, a day-pack of 30L or less will usually suffice. Load it with emergency snacks, extra clothing, maps and a re-usable water bottle. Water from *sorgenti* (fountains) in towns and villages, and from taps over troughs in the countryside is safe to drink, unless a sign stating *'acqua non potabile'* tells you that it isn't.

RIFUGI (MOUNTAIN HUTS)

Italy has a vast network of *rifugi* mostly located in mountainous areas, especially the Alps and the Apennines. They are usually

only open from June to late September. While some are little more than rudimentary shelters, many *rifugi* are more like alpine hostels. Accommodation is generally in dormitories, but some of the larger *rifugi* have doubles. Many *rifugi* also offer guests hot meals and/or communal cooking facilities. Though mattresses, blankets and duvets are usually provided, most *rifugi* will require you to bring your own sleeping bag or travel sheet. Some places offer travel sheets for hire or purchase.

The price per person (which typically includes breakfast) ranges from €20 to €30 depending on the quality of the *rifugio*. A hearty post-walk single-dish dinner will set you back another €10 to €15.

The Club Alpino Italiano (www.cai.it; p25) owns and runs many of Italy's mountain huts.

Walking in **Italy**

From the lofty *vie* (paths) of the Dolomites to the ancient pilgrims' routes of Tuscany, this is a country where every track, trail and country lane hides an intriguing story. Kiss goodbye to Roman piazzas, choose a rural path and see where the route takes you.

A HISTORY OF HIKING IN ITALY

When Roman emperor Hadrian trudged his way to the summit of Sicily's Mt Etna in AD 125 to watch the sun rise he, arguably, became the world's first recreational hiker. It wasn't long before his fellow countrymen were tramping reverently in his footsteps. Utilising the empire's well organised network of *vie,* Roman citizens regularly travelled on foot around the Italian peninsula, stopping off at various *mansiones* (large villas offering refreshment and accommodation) en route. One of the oldest surviving *vie* in Italy is the Appian Way or *reginaviarum* (queen of roads) begun by Roman censor, Appius Claudius Caecus in 312 BC to link Rome with Brindisi in the southeast. Frequented by such biblical luminaries as St Peter and St Paul, this sturdily built highway was constructed to support Roman legions marching south towards the Adriatic and Greece.

Another path with its roots in antiquity was the Via Francigena, a long-distance pilgrims' route that joined Canterbury in England to the religious sites of Rome. A 1700km walking path that zigzagged between various way stations and abbeys, the Via Francigena was first mentioned in the 8th century by an Anglo-German bishop. By the Middle Ages it had become one of the most heavily hiked pilgrims' paths in Europe. In the last decade, it has enjoyed – rather like Spain's Camino de Santiago – a Renaissance, with new markings and recognition from Unesco as a 'cultural route'.

In the days before mass transportation and annual holidays for workers, hiking was more a necessity than a hobby, though there were some notable exceptions. In 1336, Tuscan poet Francesco Petrarch climbed to the top of Mont Ventoux in southeast France and recorded the event in his diary. A century and a half later, Leonardo da Vinci is known to have ascended to a snowfield on Monte Rosa to undertake some scientific experiments. One mountain with an early recorded ascent date is Monte Rochemelon in Piedmont, scaled by a Teutonic knight, Bonifacius Rotarius, in 1358; Rotarius carried a metal replica of the Virgin Mary to the summit, which he offered as thanks for having survived the crusades.

By most reckonings, the modern era of hiking was inaugurated in 1786 when two Frenchmen ascended Mont Blanc. But it wasn't until 70 years later – in 1857 – that the founding of the Alpine Club of London ushered in what became known as 'the golden age of alpinism'. It was during this period

that parties of mainly British climbers undertook successful first ascents of numerous Italian peaks, including Gran Paradiso (1860), Marmolata (1864) and the Matterhorn (1865).

Italy's home-grown alpine club, the Club Alpino Italiano (CAI), was founded in Turin in 1863 and quickly adopted an all-inclusive policy that opened membership to all. By 1913, the club had expanded to 7500 members and by 1939 this figure had increased ten-fold to 75,000, making it the second-largest alpine club in Europe (a position it still enjoys).

Italy's earliest *rifugi* (mountain huts) date from the late 18th century when gold miners in the Alps constructed basic shelters on the slopes of Monte Rosa to protect them from the inclement weather. With the birth of the CAI and the ensuing 'golden age of alpinism', several more *rifugi* were built to link trails and accommodate the pioneering mountaineers who were gradually working their way through a long list of unclimbed alpine summits. The Dolomites gained its first *rifugio* in 1877 and, with the inauguration of Italy's first national park, Gran Paradiso, in 1922, old lodges formerly used by hunters were gradually upgraded into hostel-style accommodation.

A early alpine *rifugio,* the Capanna Regina Margherita, was named after the then Italian queen, Margherita, who tore up royal protocol and traversed several glaciers to attend the *rifugio's* opening ceremony in 1893 in a heavy 19th-century ankle-length dress with half-a-dozen ladies-in-waiting in tow.

Elsewhere, new trails were slowly being created and laid out, while those that had existed for centuries, such as the inter-village paths in the Amalfi and Cinque Terre, were numbered and given proper signage. *Vie ferrate* (fixed-protection climbing routes) were pioneered in the Dolomites in the 1930s, while long-distance paths in the Alps were industriously charted in the 1960s.

By the 1980s, the Himalayan heroics of Italy's greatest mountaineering icon, Reinhold Messner, had woken many ordinary Italians to the joys and possibilities of hiking. In 1983, with the backing of the CAI, a group of outdoor enthusiasts proposed the development of Italy's first cross-country footpath, the Sentiero Italia (Grand Italian Trail). The idea became reality in 1995 when a group set out from Trieste in the northeast to walk the 6166km to Santa Teresa Gallura in northern Sardinia.

WILDLIFE

Italy is more famous for its heavyweight historical monuments than its fearsome fauna, but while lions and elephants may be restricted to the peninsula's zoos, a more innocuous quintet of wild animals can be found roaming in numerous national and regional parks.

Marsican Bears Critically endangered and critically misunderstood, the Marsican bear has always trodden a shaky line with the vastly more territorial human species. The 50 or so remaining Marsicans are concentrated in the Apennines – more specifically Abruzzo, Lazio and Molise National Park – and, aside from small pockets in the Pyrenees and Cantabrian Mountains in France and Spain, they are the only bears left in Western Europe.

Italian Wolves A protected species in Italy, current reports suggest that there are up to 1800 individuals living in the wild, primarily in the Apennines. While the population is increasing overall, wolves still regularly fall prey to poachers and road accidents.

Ibex On the verge of extinction in the early 19th century,

the Alpine ibex's (pictured left) survival was assured after the inauguration of the Parco Nazionale Gran Paradiso in 1922 and its installation of a vigorous ibex revival programme. Characterised by their large curved ridged horns, the animals have spread to numerous other alpine locations as far south as the Maritimes.

Chamois The goat-like chamois are extremely agile and can ascend 1000m in 15 minutes over mountainous terrain if disturbed. Well-established populations can be found in the Alps and around the Corno Grande region in the Apennines.

Marmots You'll hear the whistles of these noisy but highly sociable wild rodents all over Italy's northern mountains warning their brethren of your imminent approach. Marmots are essentially large squirrels that live in burrows like rabbits and hibernate during the winter months.

ITALIAN NATIONAL PARKS

Italy's 25 national parks protect approximately 5% of the country's total land mass and thousands of kilometres of its finest trails. The oldest, Gran Paradiso in the Valle d'Aosta, established in 1922 to protect the Alpine ibex, was something of a pioneer created a good 20 years before national parks took root in the UK and Germany. Other early Italian parks included Stelvio (1935) in the northeastern Alps which linked up with an already existing park in Switzerland, and Abruzzo, Lazio and Molise (1923) in the Apennines revered for

Tour du Mont Blanc

The first documented circumnavigation of Mont Blanc was by botanist Horace-Benedict de Saussure in 1758. Twenty-eight years later in 1786, the mountain was scaled vertically by daring French climbers Jacques Balmat and Michel-Gabriel Paccard.

Officially waymarked since 1952, the modern Tour du Mont Blanc (TMB) is a 173km romp around the base of Western Europe's highest mountain through Italy, France and Switzerland.

Over time it has become one of the continent's most iconic walks incorporating some staggering beautiful scenery. The nexus for the hike in Italy is the Valle d'Aosta town of Courmayeur, though many hikers begin the seven to 10 day excursion in Chamonix in France before proceeding to walk in an anticlockwise direction up 12,000m of combined ascent.

Upping the stakes in what is already a difficult walk, the TMB hosts Europe's most prestigious mass-participation trail run, the Ultra-Trail du Mont Blanc (UTMB), which takes place every August.

its expansive beech forests and small population of Marsican bears.

The national park system had a checkered early history. During the Mussolini era some of the inaugural parks actually lost their protected status – albeit temporarily – at the expense of dubious development projects while, in the lean financial years of the 1950s, deforestation and the construction of ski resorts regularly infringed upon biodiversity and wildlife.

Miraculously, the 1990s heralded a new beginning in Italy's approach to environmental management and, over the last three decades, the park system has more than quadrupled in size with notable new additions in the Apennines and Sardinia. Many of today's parks have extensive trail networks, including Gran Paradiso and Stelvio in the Alps, Cinque Terre in Liguria, and the four interconnecting parks – Majella, Monti Sibillini, Gran Sasso and Abruzzo – that cover a broad sweep of land across the Apennines in central Italy.

ICONIC TRAILS

Though Italy's natural landscapes can't compete size-wise with the boreal forests of North America or the outback of Australia, the country's position at the crossroads of feuding empires for over 3000 years has left deep fissures on its landscape. Preserved in ancient hilltop villages and steep vineyards, the imprint of human history is everywhere here; yet nowhere has its juxtaposition with the natural environment appeared as harmonious as on its iconic trails.

Placed end to end, Italy's walking paths would stretch around the world – easily. The 'pantheon' of day walks is the Senteiro degli Dei (path of the gods), a coastal extravaganza that weaves over ingeniously cultivated cliff-sides and farm terraces, and links several historic fishing villages. Mirroring it to the north is the Sentiero Azzirro (blue path), a history soaked mule path that bisects Liguria's Cinque Terre (five villages). Due to its popularity, it is one of the few paths in Italy you must pay to enter.

But, Italy's real heavyweight hikes are its long-distance trails. Some of these multifarious paths follow ancient pilgrim routes; others circumnavigate huge mountain massifs, while one – the marathon Sentiero Italia (SI) – tackles the whole elongated peninsula knee to toe. While the trails themselves are generally old, their amalgamation into various routes and circuits is usually a more modern creation. The *alte vie* (high routes) in the Dolomites

are a post-war invention, the SI was conceived in the 1990s, while the magnificent Tour du Cervino (Matterhorn) is less than two decades old.

VIE FERRATE

During WWI while the British and French were bogged down in trench warfare in the Flanders mud, their Italian allies were engaged in an equally terrifying conflict against the Austrians along a battlefront that cut across the lofty arc of the Dolomites from Passo di Monte Croce in the east to Marmolada in the west.

But hidden in the swirling mountain mist were two far more foreboding enemies: the freezing winter weather and the precipitous terrain.

In order to maximise ease of movement across the rugged peaks, the two armies attached ropes and ladders over seemingly impregnable crags, giving birth to a series of fixed-protection climbing paths known as *'via ferrata'* (plural *'vie ferrate'*) or 'iron ways'.

Upgraded with steel rungs, iron bridges and heavy-duty wires after the war, *vie ferrate* took on a more recreational role. Armed with basic equipment and a sense of adventure, non-mountaineers could engage in an activity that blended standard hiking with full-blown rock climbing and enabled ordinary mortals access to areas hitherto out of bounds.

To tackle one of these trails, you'll first need to acquire a climbing harness and a *via ferrata* kit. The kit has two specially designed carabiners tied on either end of a length of dynamic (shock-absorbing) rope, commonly referred to as a lanyard. This rope passes through a simple, but extremely important, energy-absorbing device, which in turn is attached to the harness with a locking carabiner.

You don't need mountaineering experience to use *via ferrata* equipment, though proper attention to safety and technique is essential. Though the trend has spread worldwide in the 21st century, the best and most historic trails still reside in the Dolomiti heartland. The small towns of Madonna di Campiglio and Cortina d'Ampezzo are the gateways to some of the more spectacular routes, including the legendary Via Ferrata delle Bocchette, first pioneered in the 1930s.

OPPOSITE PAGE: MONT BLANC (P23, P222)

Club Alpino Italiano

The unseen friend to all walkers in Italy, the Club Alpino Italiano (www.cai.it) is the country's premier alpine club with over 320,000 members devoted to mountaineering, hiking and other related outdoor activities. Formed in 1863, it once aided Italian climbers Achille Compagnoni and Lino Lacedelli in their first successful human ascent of K2, the world's second highest mountain.

Closer to home and more relevant to casual walkers, the CAI is the benevolent overseer of much of Italy's formidable trail network, identifying, maintaining and waymarking up to 60,000km of paths, tracks, roads and routes. The organisation, which is split into 450 local chapters, also manages over 600 *rifugi* (mountain huts) that are open to all and ideal for walkers planning longer overnight or multi-day excursions. Alternatively, *rifugi* are great places to decamp for a mid-walk snack or drink.

ITALIAN LAKES

01 **Orrido di Sant'Anna** Short valley circuit on the Piedmontese shores of Lago Maggiore. **p30**

02 **Greenway al Lago di Como** A 'best of' Lago di Como's villages, incorporating villas, gardens and ancient Roman lanes. **p32**

03 **La Strada del Ponale** Spectacular path cut into the cliffs above Lago di Garda. **p36**

04 **Monte Isola Loop** Get to know the largest lake island in southern Europe. **p38**

05 **The Slopes of Monte Grona** Short, sharpish ascent to a refuge perched above Lago di Como, with options to continue higher. **p40**

06 **Monte Baldo: Sentiero del Ventrar** A wild botanical 'garden' hidden on the exposed slopes of Lago di Garda's sentinel ridge. **p42**

Explore
ITALIAN LAKES

The Lakes! Where Germanic precision meets Italian passion and gothic alpine peaks collide with the colours and cacophony of the Mediterranean. This is a land of posh yachts and placid fishing harbours, extravagant villas and hill-hugging villages, well-combed gardens and wild mountain slopes. Choose your lake – historic Maggiore, deluxe Como, or sporty Garda (or perhaps the smaller Iseo or Orta) – and choose your path. Trails fan out in all directions and, unlike most things in this lavishly decorated region, you don't have to pay wads of euros to use them.

LAGO DI COMO

Set in the shadow of the snow-covered Rhaetian Alps and hemmed in on both sides by steep, verdant hillsides, Lago di Como is perhaps the most spectacular of the three major lakes. Shaped like an upside-down Y, measuring around 160km in squiggly shoreline, it's littered with villages, including exquisite Bellagio and Menaggio. Where the southern and western shores converge is the lake's main settlement, Como, an elegant, prosperous Italian city that echoes with history.

LAGO MAGGIORE

Lago Maggiore is the most demure of the three main lakes. While Lago di Garda hosts theme parks and Como breeds billionaires, tourism is much less pervasive here – you'll see people going about their everyday lives, growing vegetables, cutting grass, and coppicing chestnut trees. There are mountains too, less dramatic than Como's stash, but eye-catching all the same with their steep tree-covered slopes extending well into Switzerland on the lake's northern extremity.

Maggiore's best walks cover its western Piedmontese slopes, departing from quiet Cannobio (the entrance to the Valle Cannobina and a network of age-old paths) and handsome Stresa, whose grand belle-époque buildings recall an age of bygone decadence.

LAGO DI GARDA

Poets and politicians, divas and dictators, they've all been drawn to captivating Lago di Garda. In fact, 7% of all tourists to Italy head for the lake's shores, taking to its wind-ruffled waters in the north and village- and vineyard-hopping in the south. Surrounded by three distinct regions – Lombardy, Trentino Alto-Adige and the Veneto – the lake's cultural diversity attracts a cosmopolitan crowd. Mitteleuropeans colonise northern resorts such as Riva del Garda and Torbole, where restaurants serve air-dried ham and Austrian-style *carne salada* (salted beef), while in the south, French and Italian families bed down in Valtenesi farmhouses and family-friendly

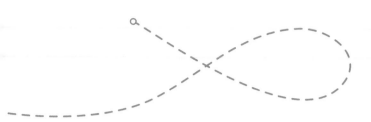

spa towns such as Sirmione and Bardolino.

LAGO D'ISEO

Less than 100km from both Bergamo and Brescia, Lago d'Iseo (aka Sebino) is one of the least known Lombard lakes. Shut in by soaring mountains, it's a magnificent sight. About halfway along the lake, a mountain soars right out of the water forming the hump-backed island of Monte Isola, nexus for the region's best trails.

The gateway to the area is the eponymous town of Iseo on the lake's eastern shore with fast train links to the city of Brescia. From here, boats depart multiple times daily for Monte Isola.

 **WHEN TO GO**

May to September is the Lakes' best weather window, when the temperature is mild to warm and the forecast is most likely to be settled. July and August are usually hot, and the area is very crowded with tourists. Whatever the weather, lake ferry services are substantially reduced in autumn and winter.

 **TRANSPORT**

The Italian Lakes are all best accessed through the northern Italian hub city of Milan. Efficient and regular trains run from Milan to the southern lake shores of Maggiore, Como and Garda. From here, you're better off travelling by bus or, better still, boat. Public ferries run on all three main lakes, although services are cut back between October and April.

 **WHERE TO STAY**

The Lakes have a good range of accommodation. In summer, you should book at least a month in advance, and in popular places such as Como and Bellagio a minimum two-night stay may be required. The best-value accommodation is in B&Bs and some of the more luxurious versions border on boutique hotels. For the flush, the region is renowned for its exclusive lakeside villas turned five-star hotels.

Stresa is a good gateway town for Lake Maggiore, Como (city) anchors Lago di Como. From a

Resources

Gestione Navigazione Laghi (www.navigazionelaghi.it) Covers ferry services on the three main lakes (Maggiore, Como and Garda). The website includes timetables and pricing.

www.360gardalife.com Information portal for activities around Lago di Garda including a full list of walks on Monte Baldo.

walking perspective, Riva del Garda is the best base on Lago di Garda.

 **WHAT'S ON**

Rockmaster Festival (www. rockmasterfestival.com) Arco, near the tip of Lago di Garda, is one of Europe's most popular climbing destinations and is the location of the Rockmaster festival and climbing competition in late summer.

Settimana del Tulipano In the last week of April, tens of thousands of tulips erupt in magnificent multicoloured bloom in Verbania's Villa Taranto on the shore of Lago Maggiore.

01

ORRIDO DI SANT'ANNA

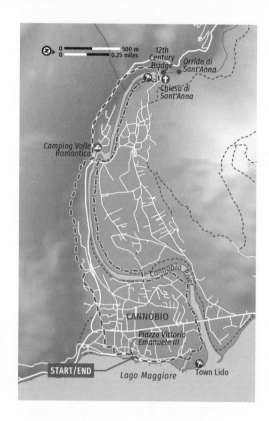

DURATION	DIFFICULTY	DISTANCE	START/END
2hrs	Easy	5km	Cannobio

TERRAIN	Flat riverside paths and paved roads

The walk to Orrido di Sant'Anna is a perfect excuse to decamp to Cannobio (pictured), home of Lake Maggiore's most splendorous waterfront esplanade. Sitting on the cusp of the forested Valle Cannobina, the Orrido itself is a narrow gorge guarded by a medieval church above a diminutive beach and pool ideal for summer swimming.

From Cannobio's unusual lake-facing main square, **Piazza Vittorio Emanuele III**, stroll north passing waterside bars and restaurants until you reach a roundabout near the town *lido*.

Pick up a paved walking path behind the *lido* which goes under a road bridge and follows the Cannobino River inland. Cross the river at the second bridge (a bouncy pedestrian-only suspension bridge), and take the well-marked trail along the northern bank.

This skirts woodland (meandering paths lead closer to the rushing mountain stream), and finally to tranquil shallows at the base of a cliff topped by a small church, the **17th-century Chiesa di Sant'Anna**.

The pebbly beach here makes a fine spot for a dip on warm days. Just past the church is the **Orrido di Sant'Anna**, a tight ravine where the rushing water has carved a path through the mountains on its descent to the lake. The gorge is crossed by two stone bridges, one dating from the 12th century.

From here, loop back to Cannobio by taking the road on the opposite side of the bridge. You'll quickly merge with a wider road (SP75). Follow it for 1km before veering right onto a **cycling trail** near the Camping Valle Romantica. Follow this trail through suburban streets back to the southern end of Cannobio.

02

GREENWAY AL LAGO DI COMO

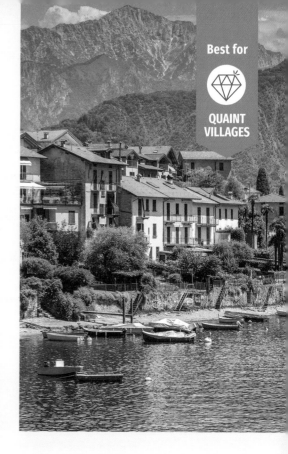

Best for

QUAINT
VILLAGES

DURATION	DIFFICULTY	DISTANCE	START/END
3hrs	Easy	10km	Colonno/ Cadenabbia

TERRAIN	Quiet paved roads and lanes through lakeside villages

Following the Strada Regina, an old Roman road that linked Milan and Switzerland, this refreshingly well-signposted path winds its way along Lago di Como's western shore between Colonno and Cadenabbia, avoiding the traffic-choked highway and dipping into plenty of *bella* villages along its course.

The trail meanders along lakeside esplanades draped in wisteria and cobbled lanes empty save for the odd cat. Minor climbs are rewarded with Como-esque views over red-tiled roofs and distant villas.

GETTING HERE

The **ASF** (www.asfautolinee.it) bus C10 from Como will get you to the start of the walk in Colonno. It runs roughly hourly throughout the day.

STARTING POINT

Begin on the main lakeside road at the south entrance to the village of Colonno. Next to the bus stop, a green sign pointing up Via Cappella marks the start of the Greenway.

01 Walk up Via Cappella, following it around a tight bend before forking right into Via Civetta. The street descends into the medieval heart of Colonno, crossing a stream and exiting the red-roofed settlement on an old cobbled Roman road, the Via Vecchia Regina. Running roughly parallel to the main SS340 below, the narrow lane heads north, past olive terraces and private gardens to the adjacent village of **Sala Comacina**.

02 Forking left onto a cobbled path just past the **San Rocco chapel**, the Greenway descends to the main road just north of Sala

Comacina. As you head down you can admire the **Isola Comacina** (pictured p18), Lago di Como's only island, shimmering below. Once the site of a Roman fort and medieval settlement, it today protects the ruins of two **Romanesque churches**.

03 Walk briefly along the main road past the **San Giacomo church** before turning left up Via Santuario and entering **Ossuccio** (pictured), a tiny village with a few Romanesque vestiges and an archaeological museum hiding in its narrow lanes. For those seeking some extra exercise and a little spiritual enlightenment, it's worth making a diversion to the **Sacro Monte di Ossuccio** (the Sacred Mountain of Ossuccio), a chapel-lined walking route that has been a pilgrimage destination for centuries. The church at the top, the **Santuario della Madonna del Soccorso**, was built over various periods from 1537 until 1719, and its ceiling is swirling with richly hued frescoes depicting the coronation of the Virgin Mary and her assumption into heaven. To reach it, continue straight (away from the lake) on Via Sanctuario. It's a 1.5km one-way walk.

04 Otherwise, turn right off Via Sanctuario around 200m from the lakefront onto Via Castelli, cross a roundabout and cut right at a T-junction by a church to rejoin the SS340 by the impressive entrance to the stately **Villa Balbiano** (p27).

05 Here the path veers off the main road again, crosses a bridge, snakes past a campground and the entrance to the glorious **Villa Balbianello** (worth an elongated side trip; see p35) to dispense you on the lakeshore at **Lido di Lenno** where ice cream awaits. It's worth lingering awhile on this deluxe promenade with its **11th-century church** and **free-standing octagonal baptistery** complemented by a **tiny artificial beach**.

⚜ Villa Carlotta

The star of the show on a lake shore not bereft of elegant touches, the **Villa Carlotta** (www.villacarlotta.it; Via Regina 2; adult/reduced €10/8; ⏱9am-6.30pm Mar-Sep, to 5.30pm Oct, 10am-4pm Nov & Dec) is a fusion of neoclassical architecture and harmonious garden design. The botanic gardens are filled with colour: orange trees are interlaced with pergolas next to rhododendrons, azaleas and camellias. The 8-hectare gardens also contain a fern valley, a bamboo grove, a rock garden, cedars and a lookout.

The 17th-century villa adds a human touch to the surroundings, with bright rooms embellished with sculptures, paintings and tapestries.

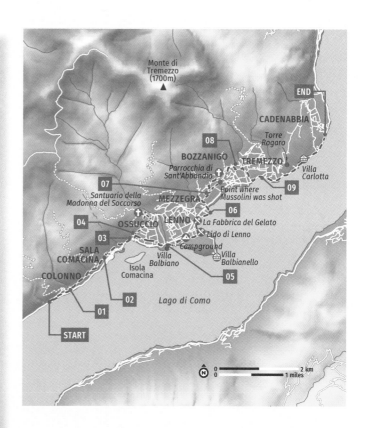

06 Continue along the lakeshore, crossing a stream and turning left up an alleyway to bring you back to the SS340. Cross the road and head uphill on Via della Piana to a four-way junction where a right turn puts you on Via Pola in the village of **Mezzegra** perched on the hill slopes overlooking the lake.

07 After 300m, veer left at a fork into Via Pola Vecchia (if you continue on Via Pola for another 300m, you'll come to the spot where Mussolini was shot by Italian partisans in April 1945, marked by a black cross). Turn right at a T-junction, pass the **Chiesa di San Giuseppe** and, after veering left at a second junction, you'll reach the much larger **Parrocchia di Sant'Abbondio**. From here there are extra-special lake views over towards Bellagio and the so-called Larian Triangle.

08 After curving through the narrow streets of the hamlet of **Bozzanigo** and its **17th-century Brentano palaces**, pitch downhill, turning left into Via delle Gere, right into Via Fabio Sala and left again into Via Monte Grappa to descend back to the lakeside on the western edge of **Tremezzo**. The ritzy town sits opposite Bellagio on the villa-lined Riviera della Tremezzina at the point where the three arms of Lago di Como meet. Recalling older more combative times is the **Torre Rogaro**, a medieval watchtower that once formed part of an elaborate lakeside defence system.

CERI BREEZE/SHUTTERSTOCK ©

Villa Balbianello

A 1km walk along the partially wooded lake shore from Lenno's main square, **Villa Balbianello** (www.fondoambiente. it; Via Comoedia 5, Località Balbianello; adult/reduced villa & gardens €20/10, gardens only €10/5; ⊙ gardens 10am-6pm, villa 10am-4.30pm Tue & Thu-Sun mid-Mar–mid-Nov) has cinematic pedigree: this was where scenes from Star Wars Episode II and the 2006 James Bond remake of *Casino Royale* were shot. The reason? It is one of the most dramatic locations anywhere on Lago di Como, a genuinely stunning marriage of architecture and lake views.

Though the grounds (pictured) are lovely, it's well worth joining a guided tour to view the villa's interior.

09 From Tremezzo it's a straightforward, but hugely attractive, lakeside walk alongside the main SS340 (equipped with a protected pavement) to the ferry dock at Cadenabbia. Along the way you'll pass **grand hotels**, **handsome Liberty facades** and the crème de la crème of Como's stately houses, the art-packed **Villa Carlotta.** From Cadenabbia, regular ferries will take you back to Como.

 **TAKE A BREAK**

The word *fabbrica* (factory) takes on a whole new meaning when you stick the words 'ice cream' after it. Out go thoughts of smoky factories and in come ideas of artisan gelato served in generous dollops right on Lenno's waterfront. On busy summer days, the owners at **La Fabbrica del Gelato** (☎340 916 83 25; Piazza 11 Febbraio 14; gelato from €2; ⊙11am-9pm) dispense cones from a cute little ice-cream van that looks like a polished relic from a black-and-white Fellini movie.

03

LA STRADA DEL PONALE

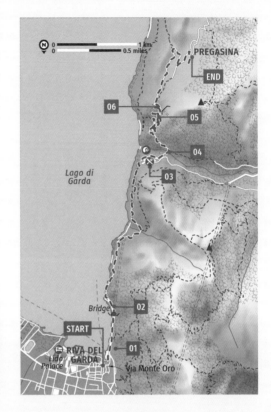

DURATION	DIFFICULTY	DISTANCE	START/END
2½hrs	Moderate	6.5km	Riva del Garda/ Pregasina
TERRAIN	Gently ascending old road – a mixture of dirt, gravel and asphalt		

Once the main (and only) road linking Riva del Garda with Limone, the Ponale has been reborn as a dedicated cycling and walking path (pictured) that cuts into the cliff face like a horizontal crevasse close to Lago di Garda's northern tip. From a distance it looks like a *via ferrata,* but up close it's wide enough for mountain bikers and hikers to share the road.

GETTING HERE
Riva del Garda is accessible by ferry from most points around Lago di Garda

STARTING POINT
Get orientated at the boat dock of Tyrolean flavoured red Riva del Garda on the windy northern tip of Lago di Garda.

01 Head south from **Riva del Garda's waterfront** using the pavement that parallels the main lakeside road (SS45). Pass a hydroelectric plant and, after around 700m, veer left where the SS45 disappears into a long tunnel. In another 50m, turn right, go under a bridge and turn right again to circle back over the same bridge.

02 You're now – as various signboards and markers will announce – on the **Strada del Ponale**. Mostly unpaved in its early stages, the vehicle-wide track ascends gently past old WWI emplacements and through numerous tunnels dynamited out of the rock. Much of the road is split in two with separate lanes for cyclists and walkers, but you'd still be wise to watch out for fast-moving mountain bikes that come hurtling around blind curves. Etched into Lago di Garda's massive cliffs, the views from the Ponale are extravagantly expansive (and a little vertigo-inducing).

A Palace to Stay

If you're flush with euros, Riva's captivating **Lido Palace** (☎ 0464 02 18 99; www.lido-palace.it; Viale Carducci 10; d/ste from €300/450; P ✳ @ 🛜 ≋) is the place to offload them. The exquisite building dates back to 1899 when it opened as a resort for holidaying Austrian royalty.

A renovation means super-modern bedrooms with muted colour schemes now embellish the grand Liberty-style villa, offering peerless views over lawns and lake.

GORILLAIMAGES/SHUTTERSTOCK ©

03 The first main stop and turnaround point, comes after 3km at **Ponale Alto Belvedere**, a spectacularly sited bar-restaurant where a couple of nearby waterfalls are visible from the deck.

04 Around 250m past the Belvedere, the now paved (but car-free) road splits. A right turn – the Strada del Ponale proper – takes you inland, zigzagging up the slopes of the Valle di Ledro to a car park just outside Biacesa. It's more rewarding to take the **left fork** which crosses a gully and snakes back towards the coast en route to the village of Pregasina (532m).

05 While still offering fabulous **lake views**, the road soon begins to switchback through tight hairpin bends as it climbs 300 vertical metres up the cliff side with trees offering sporadic shade.

06 The car-free strada ends just north of Pregasina where it joins a main road at the mouth of a tunnel. Turn sharp left (away from the tunnel) and you'll soon be in **Pregasina** where you can replenish your appetite before heading back on foot – or by catching bus B214 – to Riva.

TAKE A BREAK

Perched high above Lago di Garda on the La Strada del Ponale, the **Ponale Alto Belvedere** (☎ 0464 56 73 21; Molina di Ledro; ⊙9am-6pm) lures in large consortiums of walkers and cyclists either because they're too knackered to go any further, or because they can't resist the view. There's been a bar here for over a century, but the current incarnation comes equipped with a modern wooden deck offering views over the lake and two nearby waterfalls.

04

MONTE ISOLA LOOP

DURATION	DIFFICULTY	DISTANCE	START/END
3hrs	Moderate	11km	Peschiera Maraglio

TERRAIN	Hill paths, mule tracks and a flat paved section at the end

Hiking (or biking) is practically obligatory on Monte Isola, an island in Lago D'Iseo where cars are mercifully banned, so you might as well go the whole hog and aim to conquer the island's highest point, crowned by the beautifully weathered Santuario Madonna della Ceriola (pictured right).

GETTING HERE

Trains from Brescia run to the lakeside town of Iseo (€3.30, 30 minutes, one to two hourly). Ferries operated by **Navigazione sul Lago d'Iseo** (☏ 035 97 14 83; www.navigazionelagoiseo.it) run over half-a-dozen times daily between Iseo and Peschiera Maraglio (one-way/return €3/5) on Monte Isola.

STARTING POINT

Peschiera Maraglio is an attractive lakeside village on the southeastern shores of Monte Isola. A sign-posted trail starts behind the information centre.

01 After climbing some stairs and crossing a paved road, a well-defined hill path leads steeply out of Peschiera Maraglio and winds up through woodland. Following an abrupt ascent, the trail levels off and contours around the south side of the island. As the trees thin out you'll get fabulous views of the **southern part of Lago d'Iseo**.

02 Within around 2.5km you'll reach the hamlet of Cure set high on the hillside. Here the path forks, presenting two options to reach the Ceriola sanctuary. We recommend the longer route accessed by turning right just before you enter the village. A mule path switches back south, passes a house and then curves north, finishing with a series of steps that ascend to the **Santuario Madonna della Ceriola** (pictured) perched at the island's highest point (600m).

Monte Isola

The towering island at the south end of Lago d'Iseo is easily the lake's most striking feature, its beauty magnified by the lack of any four-wheeled traffic (cars are banned). With a population a little under 2000 spread over 11 separate hamlets, the island has been furnished with the EU-sponsored EDEN award for sustainable tourism.

The erstwhile Duke of Milan, Francesco Sforza, granted the people of Monte Isola special fishing rights in the 15th century. Its people, whose ancestors may have lived here in Roman times, became known for their handmade fishing nets. Nets and hammocks are still made here in smaller numbers, while locally caught lake fish are hung out in the sun to dry.

BRENDAN SAINSBURY/LONELY PLANET ©

03 At the top, you can admire the heady lake views, genuflect before the chapel's surprisingly ornate **altarpiece** and grab a toasted *panino* from an industrious gentleman who operates a small cafe adjacent to the church.

04 From the church, descend past 15 chapels dedicated to the rosary to a pleasant mule track that snakes through olive groves and fields down to the hamlet of **Massa** on the island's northern slopes.

05 In Massa, proceed past the village **church of San Rocco**, turn right in the square and then right again onto a paved road signposted Olzano.

06 The paved road quickly ends in the hamlet of **Olzano**, from where a well-used path descends lake-ward to a cluster of houses known as Nocelle, 1km below. From here steps drop down to the larger lakeside settlement of **Carzano**.

07 From Carzano, it's a sedate 2.7km stroll along a **car-free lakeside esplanade** back to Peschiera Maraglio. The flat paved path runs the full eastern length of the island and is popular with cycling tourists and the odd local on a moped.

 TAKE A BREAK

The Soardi family has been serving up local dishes at **Locanda al Lago** (📞 030 988 64 72; www.locandaal lago.it; Località Carzano 38; meals €27-37; ⏱ noon-2.30pm & 7-9pm Wed-Sun) in Carzano since 1948, perfecting deceptively simple treatments of lake fish. It means you can sit on the waterside terrace and feast on fish lasagna or the day's catch combined with *trenette* (a flat pasta) and lashings of extra virgin Monte Isola olive oil.

05

THE SLOPES OF MONTE GRONA

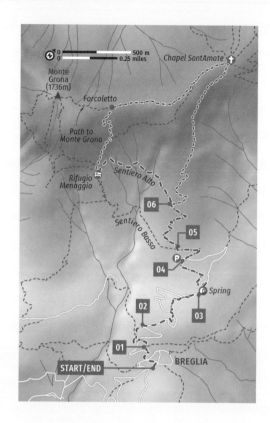

DURATION	DIFFICULTY	DISTANCE	START/END
5hrs	Hard	8km	Breglia

TERRAIN	Mostly on mountain paths with some steep ascents

Steep-sided Monte Grona glowers like a craggy faced old man above the town of Menaggio and Lago di Como. While its tree-filled lower reaches are innocuous enough, the rocky upper sections are precipitous and narrow. This walk to the idyllically located Rifugio Menaggio is relatively straightforward, while easy passage to the lonesome Sant'Amate chapel can be enjoyed by continuing along a grassy ridge.

GETTING HERE

Breglia can be reached on bus C10 from Menaggio (25 minutes, nine daily). Menaggio has regular ferry service to other towns on Lago di Como, including Como itself (€10.60, 2½ hours).

STARTING POINT

Breglia is a small mountain village situated 7km from and 550 vertical metres above Menaggio. This walk starts at the main bus stop.

01 Walk up the **narrow paved road** marked Rifugio Menaggio. After a couple of bends, turn right and ascend a path signposted to the *rifugio*.

02 The path soon rejoins the paved road, crosses it and ascends a track for 50m before turning right by an electricity pylon. Within minutes you'll join the road again. Follow it up for approximately 300m before turning left by a **red and white marker**.

03 Climb up past some small houses and meet the road twice more. On the first occasion cross it; on the second, turn right into an

Side Trip: Sant'Amate

Directly above the rifugio, prominent red and yellow signs indicate the way up to a rugged saddle called Forcoletto and, above it, Monte Grona. Ignore the Grona signs and head north towards Sant'Amate, along a clear path along a smooth ridge. The simple stone chapel stands on a grassy windswept ridge at 1623m with romantic views over two lakes – Como (pictured) and Lugano – and two countries (Italy and Switzerland). From the chapel, take the descent path, signposted to Breglia. It crosses the steep grassy eastern flank of the ridge. About 30 minutes walk brings you back to the path you took up to the rifugio. Head downhill for Breglia.

COLOMBO NICOLA/SHUTTERSTOCK ©

Best for

MOUNTAIN VIEWS

open area replete with **sorgente** (spring) and picnic tables. A sign behind the *sorgente* directs you uphill on a path that crosses the contact zone between greyish crystalline rocks and the smooth, grey-white limestone (dolomite).

04 After reaching a rough parking area at the end of the narrow road, take the path to the **rifugio** leading off to the left (uphill).

05 A path junction soon after gives an option of two routes to the refuge: the *sentiero basso* (low path) and the *sentiero alto* (high path). Weather permitting, take the *sentiero alto* that sallies upwards as **lake views** unfold like a widescreen cinema epic below you.

06 Within 15 minutes, you'll come to a junction where the return path from Sant'Amate rejoins the main route. Keep left and the path will soon leave the spur and make a fine rising contour around a valley, up to the **Rifugio Menaggio** (1¼ to 1½ hours from Breglia) where you can relax, drink and even stay over.

TAKE A BREAK

Magnificently set amid the rocky heights at 1383m, the **Rifugio Menaggio** (☎ 0344 3 72 82; www.rifugiomenaggio.eu; Località Mason del Fedel, Plesio; dm €15, with breakfast/half-board €20/45; ⏲ Sat, Sun & holidays mid-Jun–mid-Sep) makes a fine base camp with its clean, simply set rooms and sweeping views. If you're stopping by during a hike, you can refuel on hearty mountain meals, including vegetable soup and plates of polenta with meat or cheese (meals around €20).

06

MONTE BALDO: SENTIERO DEL VENTRAR

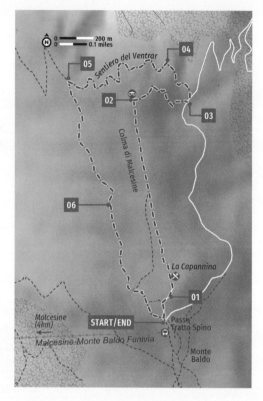

DURATION	DIFFICULTY	DISTANCE	START/END
2hrs	Hard	5km	Tratto Spino

TERRAIN	Mostly on mountain paths with some mildly exposed sections with cable support

The high grassy meadows and narrow ridgelines of Monte Baldo dominate the northeast shores of Lago di Garda and engender a true top-of-the-world feeling. Accessible by cable car from the lakeside town of Malcesine, the ethereal domain hides plenty of high-country surprises, including this exhilarating cliff walk amid a botanical array of mountain flora.

GETTING HERE

Malcesine is on the northeastern shores of Lago di Garda. Regular express ferries connect to Desenzano and towns on the lower lake. A cable car heads up to Tratto Spino.

STARTING POINT

The *funivia* (cable car) deposits you at Passo Tratto

Spino (pictured), a saddle atop the Monte Baldo ridge where numerous trails converge.

01 Exit the upper station of the *funivia*, turn left and head uphill towards La Capannina restaurant. Pass the restaurant building on your right and follow the narrow trail (path 651) across the smooth grassy ridgetop of **Colma di Malcesine**. Fabulous viewpoints open up on both sides. The ridge is a popular launch site for paragliders utilising the thermals that caress the exposed slopes on this part of Lago di Garda.

02 After around 2km, the path reaches a **belvedere** (viewpoint) where the ridgeline ends. To the north and northwest, the tip of Lago di Garda plunges like a knife into the Trentino region with the Brenta Dolomites in the background. The mountain immediately to the north is Altissimo di Nago (2079m), part of the Monte Baldo range. From

 Monte Baldo

Monte Baldo is the name of a long mountain ridge rather than an individual peak. Ironically, the name doesn't refer to its baldness (although the upper slopes are treeless), rather, it comes from the German word 'wald' meaning forest. Monte Baldo reaches its highest point at Cima Valdritta (2218m), one of five significant summits that punctuate the ridge.

Baldo is a hiking paradise thanks to a combination of lake views, well-maintained trails and easy access to high alpine terrain via the Monte Baldo cable car located at 1760m. It is also intensely popular with mountain bikers who revel in the tumbling single-track descents that head down towards the base terminus in Malcesine.

STEFFI GNOTKE/EYEEM/GETTY IMAGES ©

the *belvedere,* the path swings to the right and heads steeply downhill to meet a road.

03 From the road, path 3, aka the **Sentiero del Ventrar,** veers off to the left. Though not particularly steep or technical, the trail has narrow and exposed sections that wrap around the gullies and rock-walls at the north end of the Colma di Malcesine. Cables are provided in places for safety and support. It's not recommended for vertigo sufferers.

04 As you progress along the ledges and bluffs,

you'll notice both long-range and short-range views. Omnipresent in the background is the Alpine majesty of Lago di Garda and its surrounding peaks. Adorning the crags and ledges at close range is a botanical bonanza of flowers and plants, including the red and pink **dwarf alpenrose** and the haunting **devil's claw** (pinky-blue with black tips).

05 The end of the main section of the 1km-long Sentiero del Ventrar is marked by a **signboard**. Turn left on narrow trail 16 that ascends on a long diagonal back south along the Colma di Malcesine.

06 The return trail cuts lightly into the grassy hillside and will eventually deposit you back at the **upper funivia station**.

 TAKE A BREAK

Several eating options are available at the upper station of the cable car. Arguably, the best is freshly renovated **La Capannina** located around 200m north of the main buildings. Choose from a sunny terrace with sunloungers or a woodsy alpine interior. The mountain-flavoured menu emphasises polenta, mushroom tagliatelle, strudel and the like.

Also Try...

NICK BRUNDLE/SHUTTERSTOCK ©

MONTE MOTTARONE

The 1492m-high alpine peak behind the Lago Maggiore town of Stresa is known as Monte Mottarone and can be ascended by cable car (pictured) or by a well-marked moderately graded trail labelled as L1. Thanks to the cable car you can opt to either hike up or down – or both!

Trail L1 starts near Stresa's train station and ascends up through the attractive villages of Somerano and Levvo to the Alpina botanical garden at the cable car halfway station. It's worth stopping at this four acre site to view more than 1000 species of subalpine plants. From here, it's a fairly straightforward ascent through woodland and, later, grassland to Mottarone's summit, home to a winter ski area and a summer amusement park. There are superb views of Lago Maggiore's Borromean Islands with their privately owned palaces and meticulously manicured gardens below.

DURATION 4hrs
DIFFICULTY Moderate
DISTANCE 11km

SASS CORBÉE

A medium-length walk with historical twists, this easy-ish urban-rural ramble near Lago di Como incorporates the popular resort of Menaggio, the villa-sprinkled domain of Loveno, plus a brief foray into the Senagra River valley with its broad-leafed foliage and rather interesting milling history.

The walk is relatively straightforward save for an energetic scramble up a small gorge on the north side of Sass Corbée (steps and some hand-rails are provided). The section along the river is well-trammelled and furnished with a number of interactive signs that provide explanations on the various local sights, including a mill, a chapel, an old lime kiln and a former nail-making factory.

From Piazza Garibaldi in Menaggio, take Via Calvi inland through the villages of Loveno and Pianure to the Val Sanagra Park. From here the path loops back round via the village of Barna to Pianure.

DURATION 3hrs
DIFFICULTY Moderate
DISTANCE 10km

CRISTIAN PUSCASU/SHUTTERSTOCK ©

CANNOBIO–CARMINE SUPERIORE

This combo of paths and lanes meanders to the semi-abandoned hamlet of Carmine Superiore, perched 100m above Lago Maggiore (no road access).

Take Via Cuserina followed by Casali Bagnara to link with the path south out of Cannobio. It ascends through chestnut woods, briefly joins a road and winds past old farmhouses on its way to the hamlet of Mulinesc (Mollineggi). From here, follow the path down to the lakeside eagle's perch of Carmine Superiore with its 14th century Romanesque church.

DURATION 1½hrs
DIFFICULTY Moderate
DISTANCE 3.5km

ORTA SAN GIULIO

Overlooking the banks of shimmering Lago d'Orta, the village of San Giulio (pictured) has abundant allure.

The village and the adjacent hill topped by the Sacro Monte di San Francesco occupies a kidney-shaped peninsula and can be circumnavigated on a series of delightful walking paths. You'll be close to the water for two-thirds of the route, ambling through the cobbled streets of Orta San Guilio and along a narrow waterside esplanade that creeps past lake-lapped gardens, family vegetable plots and private fishing jetties.

DURATION 1hr
DIFFICULTY Easy
DISTANCE 3km

MONTE BOLETTONE

The Dorsale of the Triangolo Lariano is a 31km ridge walk that zigzags between the upper reaches of Lago di Como and Bellagio above dazzling Lago di Como.

It takes about 12 hours in one hit, but for those with less time it's possible to undertake a quicker clamber to the grassy hump of Monte Bolettone (the first peak on the Como side), 5km northeast of the upper funicular station in Brunate. Take the cable car from the lakeside in Como and factor in time to visit the hilltop Faro Voltiano (lighthouse) for 360-degree views en route.

DURATION 4hrs
DIFFICULTY Moderate
DISTANCE 10km

CAMPANIA & THE AMALFI COAST

07 **Passeggiata del Pizzolungo** Capri's greatest hits are squeezed into 4km of coastal splendour. **p50**

08 **Punta Campanella** Admire a protected marine reserve on the rugged tip of the Sorrento peninsula. **p52**

09 **Sentiero degli Dei** The 'Path of the Gods' is one of Italy's most heavenly trails. **p54**

10 **Valle del Sambuco** Ruined mills, fat lemons, hidden hamlets and a medieval convent atop a forested hillcrest. **p58**

11 **Le Tre Marine** A coast-hugging extravaganza linking three contrasting Amalfi coves. **p60**

12 **Valle delle Ferriere** A shady sojourn through a coastal river valley speckled with waterfalls. **p62**

13 **Santa Maria del Castello Circuit** Spectacular climb above Positano to an ancient mountain crossroads. **p64**

Explore
CAMPANIA &
THE AMALFI COAST

Looked at through the prism of its often frenetic travel industry, Italy's most densely populated region can sometimes feel more like a tourist conveyor belt than a temple to history and art. But the outward mayhem belies a curious inner calm.

Away from the busy towns and cities, Campania hides a parallel universe of ancient stone stairways and deserted trails crowned by the steep-sided Amalfi Coast, an irresistible melange of terraced gardens and plunging escarpments dotted with priceless medieval heirlooms.

A MAZE OF TRAILS

The Amalfi Coast is laced with ancient footpaths, many of them dating back to the 10th and 11th centuries and the era of the *ducato* (independent city state). Until the coastal road was built in the 1850s, the trails were the primary means of getting around. Today, they're still frequented by a mix of hikers on holiday and locals who use them to access their terraced lemon groves and outlying farm buildings.

Italy's main hiking body, the CAI (Club Alpino Italiano), maintains a list of 124 numbered trails in the region, all marked with distinctive red-and-white paint. Between them, they measure out a total distance of 530km. The longest trail is the arterial **Via dei Monti Lattari** (trail 300), a 70km west–east romp that's rarely done in its entirety. The most popular by far is trail 327, aka the Sentiero degli Dei (Path of the Gods), a lofty cliffside traverse between the villages of Bomerano and Nocelle with unbroken coastal views.

With the coastline mainly made up of plunging cliffs and craggy mountains, the paths are notorious for their steps (there is little flat ground in these parts). Additionally, some of the narrower, higher trails are mildly exposed. If you're out of shape and/or acrophobic, plan your route carefully before setting out.

Although the area is heavily populated and the paths well used, it's wise to take a map. The complexity of the trail network and often erratic signage can hinder navigation. While you'll rarely be lost for long, needlessly adding 500 steps to the 1000 you've already scaled can weaken the steeliest resolve.

AMALFI

Pretty little Amalfi, with its sun-and-shade piazzas and diminutive beach, was once a maritime superpower that ruled over a de facto independent state. Today, the tightly packed coast-hugging community is significantly smaller but continues to exude plenty of history and culture, spearheaded by its oversized

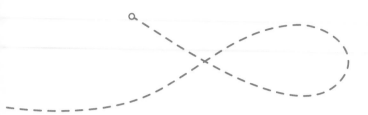

Byzantine-influenced cathedral and unusual Paper Museum.

Amalfi gets congested with tourists in season, but – fear not, solitude-seeking hiker – 95% of visitors rarely leave the town's compact medieval grid, meaning the surrounding trails are gloriously serene.

SORRENTO

A small resort with a big reputation, Sorrento is a town of lemons, high-pedigree hotels and plunging cliffs that cut through the heart of the historical core.

The town's longstanding popularity stems from its proximity to Naples and location at the western gateway to the Amalfi. Tourism has a long history here. It was a compulsory stop on the 19th-century 'Grand Tour' when a long line of holidaying literary geniuses – including Byron, Goethe, Dickens and Tolstoy – came to sample the Sorrentine air. The romance persists.

 WHEN TO GO

The Amalfi Coast is strictly seasonal, with the majority of hotels, restaurants and bars pulling down their shutters from late October to Easter.

April to June and October are less crowded periods, with June usually offering proper summer heat. The best time for hiking is April and May, when colourful wildflowers bloom and the weather is pleasantly temperate, albeit occasionally wet.

 TRANSPORT

Campania is easily accessible from most other parts of Italy via Naples, its biggest city. Trains connect Naples with Sorrento and Salerno, but the rest of the Amalfi region is only accessible by bus.

 WHERE TO STAY

If you're planning on exploring beyond the coast, Sorrento has the best transport connections, making it a convenient base. Positano, Amalfi and Ravello offer some of the most atmospheric and sophisticated accommodation in Italy, ranging from sumptuous *palazzi* (mansions) to humbler B&Bs with knockout coastal views. Always book ahead in summer and remember that most hotels close over the winter.

 WHAT'S ON

Settimana Santa (Holy Week) Sorrento's holy week is famed throughout Italy for its atmospheric processions of robed and hooded penitents on Holy Thursday and Good Friday.

Ravello Festival (www.ravellofestival.com) In July and August, the Ravello Festival – established in 1953 – turns much of the town centre into a stage. Events range from orchestral concerts and chamber music to ballet performances, film screenings and exhibitions.

07

PASSEGGIATA DEL PIZZOLUNGO

DURATION	DIFFICULTY	DISTANCE	START/END
1hr	Moderate	4km	Capri Town

TERRAIN	Paved pathway with ascending and descending steps

This fine walk can be done as a circuit from the centre of Capri Town. It's spectacular even by Capri standards, taking in a necklace of west-coast sights including the Arco Naturale, Faraglioni and several grottoes and *belvederes* (lookouts). Most of the path is paved and there are quite a few steps, though it is not inordinately difficult.

Head east out of Capri Town on the Via Le Botteghe and the Via Matermàina to the **Arco Naturale**, a curious eroded-limestone arch dating back to the Paleolithic era and formed by millennia of natural wear and tear.

At the end of Via Matermàna, backtrack to **Le Grottelle restaurant** and take the set of stairs beside it (Passeggiata del Pizzolungo). About halfway down you'll pass the **Grotta di Matermània**, a giant natural

cave used by the Romans as a *nymphaeum* (shrine to the water nymph). You can still see traces of the mosaic wall decorated with shells.

At the bottom, continue down the path as it follows the rocky coastline south. The striking flat-roofed red villa you eventually see on your left, on the Punta Massullo promontory, is **Villa Malaparte** (pictured), the former holiday home of Tuscan writer Curzio Malaparte (1898–1957).

Carrying on, the sea views become increasingly impressive as the path continues westward around the lower wooded slopes of **Monte Tuoro**. A few hundred metres further along you will arrive at a staircase on your right, which leads up to the **Belvedere di Tragara**, a prime viewing point for the pointed **Isole Faraglioni**. From here, follow Via Tragara back to the town centre.

08

PUNTA CAMPANELLA

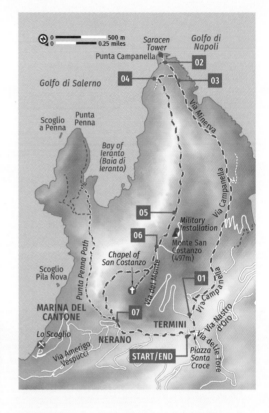

DURATION	DIFFICULTY	DISTANCE	START/END
3hrs	Moderate	8km	Termini

TERRAIN	Good paved path juxtaposed with a moderate hillside ascent over stonier ground

Sorrento has seduced many an enamoured North European visitor and this hike on a rocky uncultivated peninsula with spectacular views across the Bay of Naples to the island of Capri will do little to sully its lofty reputation.

GETTING HERE

SITA Sud (www.sitasudtrasporti.it) runs buses roughly hourly to Termini from the Circumvesuviana train station in Sorrento.

STARTING POINT

Get your bearings in the diminutive Piazza Santa Croce in the village of Termini, 8km southwest of Sorrento.

01 From the Piazza, follow Via Campanella to the left as it zigzags downhill, following signs for Punta Campanella. The minor road soon becomes a wide track and takes you all the way to the **headland.**

02 Punta Campanella makes a spectacular endpoint for the peninsula with **magnificent views** of Capri westwards and across the Bay of Ieranto to the mountains beyond. The modern light beacon stands close to the crumbling ruins of a Saracen tower dating from the 1300s, about 250m beyond the one and only fork in the path (where you keep right).

03 Walk back along the track to the junction and turn right following the stone path up and across the steep slope to the **ridge crest.**

04 Here you turn sharp left onto an indistinct but relatively well-marked path that ascends steeply close to the **ridge**, through thick, low scrub and rock outcrops.

Baia di Ieranto

A spectacular beach at the tip of the Punta Penna peninsula just southeast of Punta Campanella, the Baia di Ieranto is reached via a path that starts in the village of Nerano about three-quarters of the way around this hike. The walk takes about 45 minutes one way and there are several steep downhill sections to negotiate. The small pebbly beach with crystalline water is sheltered by headlands and perfect for swimming, but can get crowded in summer.

LAURADIBIASE/GETTY IMAGES ©

05 The building at the summit of **Monte San Costanzo** (497m) is a fenced-off military installation. The path (pictured) skirts the southwestern (right) side of the compound just shy of the summit and then descends to a minor road on a bend; turn right.

06 About 50m just past the bend at a small parking bay on the right, turn off and follow the widest path through a pine grove. From the far (eastern) edge of the pines, go up steps to the plain white **chapel of San Costanzo**, another superb viewpoint.

07 Retrace your steps from the chapel (200m) and go down to the left at the edge of the pine grove on a faint path diagonally across a grassy slope. Contour the slope past a vegetable garden and a stone hut on the right. Then swing left to pass a deep cleft on the right and almost immediately, at the corner of a stone wall, turn diagonally right along a path and descend (hands required) through woodland. Eventually, two flights of steps take you down to the cobbled **Punta Penna** path; turn left to reach the village of **Nerano**.

08 From the Via Rotabile di Nerano in Nerano go

up beside Olga's *alimentari* and pass between **houses and olive groves** back to Termini.

TAKE A BREAK

If you're passing through Nerano, it's practically obligatory to try the local pasta dish, *spaghetti alla Nerano* (with fried courgettes and cheese), as well as the seafood. The best restaurants hug the seafront in Marina del Cantone, 1.5km from Nerano, and include **Lo Scoglio** (☏081 808 10 26; www.hotelloscoglio.com; Piazza delle Sirene 15, Marina del Cantone; meals €60; ⊙12.30-5pm & 7.30-11pm).

09

SENTIERO DEGLI DEI

Best for

COASTAL SCENERY

DURATION	DIFFICULTY	DISTANCE	START/END
3½hrs	Moderate	9km	Bomerano/Positano

TERRAIN	Narrow hillside paths, some paved sections, lots of (downhill) steps towards the end

Sentiero degli Dei translates as 'Path of the Gods' and this high-level coastal hike certainly has a celestial quality. This is by far the best-known walk on the Amalfi Coast, and for good reason. Not only is it spectacular from start to finish, but unlike most Amalfi treks, it doesn't involve Olympian amounts of stair-climbing.

GETTING HERE

Take a SITA Sud (www.sitasudtrasporti.it) bus from Amalfi town up to the village of Bomerano.

STARTING POINT

The walk starts in the main square (Piazza Paolo Capasso) in the village of Bomerano (a subdivision of Agerola), where several cafes supply portable snacks.

01 Follow the **red-and-white signs** southwest along Via Pennino. Pass under a bridge and, within a minute or two, you'll come to a signboard directing you right over a wooden bridge and up a staircase to a paved road. Turn left.

02 The start of the walk proper is marked by a **monument** inscribed with quotes by Italo Calvino and DH Lawrence. Views of terraced fields quickly open out as the path contours around a cliff-face and passes beneath the overhanging **Grotta del Biscotto** (Biscuit Cave).

03 From here, the trail continues its traverse of the mountainside with some minor undulations. Periodically it dips into thickets of trees and sometimes you'll be required to negotiate rockier sections, but, in the main, the going is relatively easy.

04 The first main landmark after the *grotta* is a path junction at **Colle Serra**. Just below Colle Serra, a path from the Sentiero degli Dei's alternative start in Praiano joins the main trail. Bear in mind that starting in Praiano involves a thigh-challenging climb up 1000 steps before you reach the trail proper. Here you get a choice between a low route or a high route. The **low route** (left turn) threads its way through vineyards and rockier sections with magnificent views of Praiano below. Roughly 800m along its course, it is possible to make a short diversion south to the San Domenico Monastery. The more popular **high route** (327a), accessed by turning right, sticks to the rocky heights with broad, sweeping vistas. Both paths are moderately exposed but not dangerous if handled with care.

05 The two paths converge at a point called **Cisternulo**, 1.5km beyond Colle Serra. After Cisternulo, the path kinks around some half-obscured *grotte* (caves) and descends into the **Valle Grarelle** before climbing back up to the official finish point in the tiny village of **Nocelle**.

06 A small **kiosk** selling cold drinks and coffee, served on a charming terrace with fresh flowers, greets you as you enter the village. Alternatively, head a little further through the village to **Piazza Santa Croce**, where a stall dispenses fantastic freshly squeezed orange and lemon juice. Although this is the end of the Sentiero degli Dei proper, it makes sense to carry on to Postiano with its beach, restaurant and transport links. Some people take the stairs (around 1500 of them!) down through the village to be deposited, via a succession of olive groves, on the coast road 2km

Nocelle

A tiny, still relatively isolated mountain village, located 2km southeast of Montepertuso, Nocelle (450m) commands some of the most spectacular views on the entire coast. A world apart from touristy Positano, it's a sleepy, silent place where not much ever happens and where the small population of residents are happy to keep it that way. The Sentiero degli Dei officially ends here.

Handy as you stumble off the Sentiero degli Dei with wobbly legs, **Villa della Quercia** (📞089 812 34 97; www.villalaquercia. com; Via Nocelle 5; d €75–85; 🕐Apr–mid-Oct; 🛜) is a delightful B&B in a former hilltop monastery. It comes armed with a tranquil garden and spectacular, goat's-eye views of the coast.

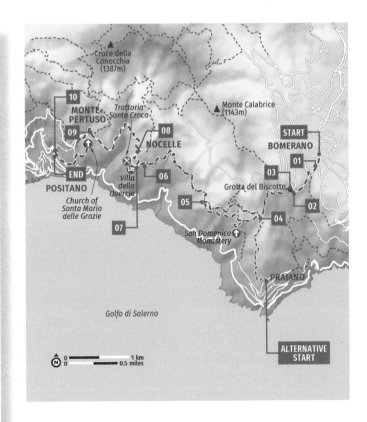

east of Positano; others catch a bus from Nocelle to Positano (minibuses run by **Mobility Amalfi Coast** depart 10 times a day). A much nicer option, especially if you're weary of steps at this point, is to continue along the path that leads west out of Nocelle towards Montepertuso.

07 Turn right off Via Pizzillo in the centre of Nocelle and follow **pedestrian Via Cercola** as it winds round to join the terminus of the village's main paved road.

08 From here, follow the quiet road for 2km as it contours around a large ravine. Don't miss the huge hole in the centre of the cliff at **Montepertuso** where it looks as though an irate giant has punched through the slab of limestone.

09 You'll know you've reached Montepertuso when you see a soccer field below. Follow the main road as it wraps around the western end of the pitch and turn left on a bend into Via Pestella that cuts below the **church of Santa Maria delle Grazie**. Just past the church continue along Via Pestella as it turns right and descends the semi-rural hillside, utilising a long narrow *scala* (stairway).

10 On the northern fringes of **Positano** (pictured), just above the town **cemetery**, the stairway pitches right and becomes Via Santa Croce. Soon after passing several impressive **villas**, you'll be deposited on SS163, the main Amalfi coast road on the eastern side

ⓘ Need to Know

The Sentiero degli Dei is not advised for acute vertigo sufferers. Although sunny days are the norm in spring and summer, it can be cloudy in the dizzy heights, but somehow that adds to the drama, with cypresses rising through the mist like dark, shimmering sword blades and shepherds herding their goats through fog-wreathed foliage. Bring a rucksack and plenty of water, and wear proper walking shoes as the going can be rough. You may want to pack swimming gear too and end the walk with a refreshing plunge into the sea.

Inclement weather and/or landslides can sometimes lead to trail closures. Check ahead. The tourist office in Bomerano can provide more guidance and details.

LUKASZ/MILENA/SHUTTERSTOCK ©

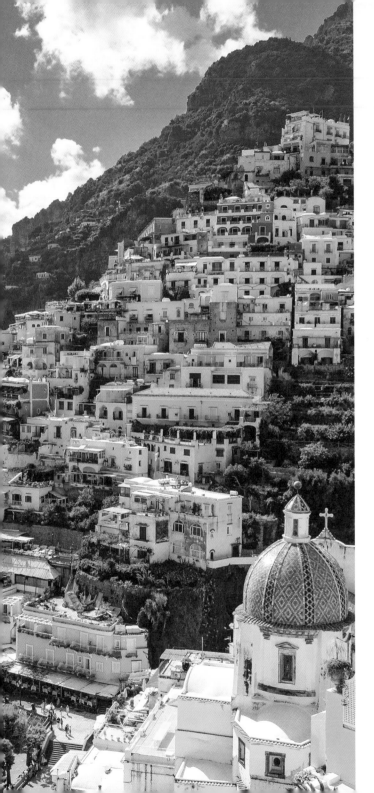

of Positano. Save a little time to explore the town with its vertiginous houses tumbling down to the sea in a cascade of sun-bleached peach, pink and terracotta. No less photo-worthy are its steep streets and steps, flanked by wisteria-draped hotels, smart restaurants and fashionable retailers. There are two beaches. Spiaggia Grande probably isn't anyone's idea of a dream beach, with greyish sand covered by legions of bright umbrellas and loungers that cost around €20 per person per day. A gentle walk west, with an acceptable number of steps (hooray!), is **Spiaggia del Fornillo**: more laid-back than its swanky neighbour and home to a handful of summer beach bars, which can get quite spirited after sunset.

 **TAKE A BREAK**

Nocelle's modest **Trattoria Santa Croce** (📞 089 81 12 60; www.ristorantesantacrocepositano.com; Via Nocelle 19; meals €22; 🕐 noon-3.30pm & 7-9.30pm Apr-Oct) has spectacular views over the coast and is located just past the 'official' finishing post on the Sentiero degli Dei in Nocelle. The menu is short and traditional, with dishes such as rustic lentil soup, *tagliatelle alla genovese* (pasta with a rich, onion-based Neapolitan sauce) and freshly caught fish with local herbs.

10

VALLE DEL SAMBUCO

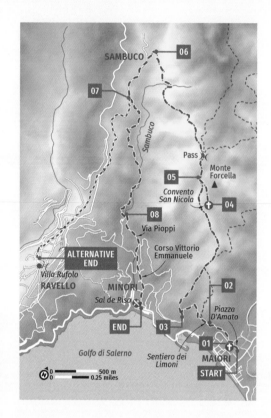

DURATION	DIFFICULTY	DISTANCE	START/END
4½hrs	Moderate	10.5km	Maiori/Minori

TERRAIN	Mix of good, clear paved and dirt paths; steps and staircases in some sections

This citrus-scented circuit explores the hills and valleys behind the Amalfi town of Minori, circum-navigating lemon groves and the ruins of old paper mills. Its peak is the 13th-century Convento di San Nicola, perched high atop the coastline amid pine and oak trees.

GETTING HERE

Maiori is linked by year-round **SITA Sud** (☎342 6256442; www.sitasudtrasporti.it; Piazza Flavio Gioia) bus-es to all other Amalfi towns. From April to October **TraVelMar** (☎089 87 29 50; www.travelmar.it) ferries also jockey between the towns.

STARTING POINT

Diminutive Piazza D'Amato is the main square in the Amalfi beach town of Maiori and is the launch site for this walk.

01 From the square, climb up the staircase to the left of the fountain to reach Maiori's main church, the 13th century **Collegiata di Santa Maria**. After admiring its bell tower and majolica-tiled dome take another stairway up to the popular paved pathway on Via Fuori Tuoro, better known as the Sentiero dei Limoni (Path of the Lemons).

02 The path heads west out of town with broad views over Maiori's **harbour**. Small terraced plots packed with lemon trees characterise the hill-sides: the plump, fragrant local lemons are known as *sfusato amalfitano*.

03 After around 700m, take the staircase on the right (CAI path 315c) signposted 'Conven-to San Nicola' and start ascending, first through **gardens** and then through **oak and pine forest**. Soon after a junction with path 315a, the trail becomes

Alternative Ending: Ravello

From Sambuco it is possible to divert via a relatively quiet paved road to the refined hilltop town of Ravello (2km).

With its weighty arts festival and luxuriant villas, Ravello has long had a metamorphic effect on artistic celebrities. This is the town that cured Richard Wagner's writer's block, provided inspiration for DH Lawrence as he nurtured the plot of *Lady Chatterley's Lover*, and impressed American writer Gore Vidal so much that he stayed for 30 years and became an honorary local.

Don't miss the **Villa Rufolo**, famed for its exquisite cascading gardens.

IGORZH/SHUTTERSTOCK ©

less steep as you traverse the hillside below the ridge of Monte Forcella with the Convento San Nicola occasionally visible.

04 To reach the **Convento San Nicola**, take a small spur trail on the right, following it for 300m to the chapel (489m), thought to date from the late 12th century, and a spectacular viewpoint.

05 Return to the main path and turn right. Within 400m, it emerges briefly from the trees and hangs left at a rocky mountain pass before heading down to the small aguricultural hamlet of **Sambuco**.

06 After passing slightly north of the village, the path crosses the **Sambuco River**, swings back around and climbs via steps, up to the paved road to Ravello. Turn left and follow this road through the village of Sambuco, branching left after 400m and taking steps down to the western side of the Sambuco river valley.

07 From here, the path parallels the river, skirting past a scattering of old **paper mills** before meeting a paved road just shy of a bend.

08 Turn left, go around the bend and continue

through the outskirts of **Minori** (pictured), finishing up on the beachfront.

TAKE A BREAK

Pasticceria? Yes. Cafe? Yes. Gelateria? Yes. **Sal de Riso** (089 87 79 41; www.salderiso.it; Via Roma 80; desserts from €4.50; 7am-1am) on Minori's seafront is all these things and more: an emporium of edible sweetness that will make your eyes pop out and your blood sugar shoot up in the same bite. The ample glass display cases are like an art gallery of avant-garde desserts crammed with delicate cheesecakes, eclairs, sponges and pastries.

11

LE TRE MARINE

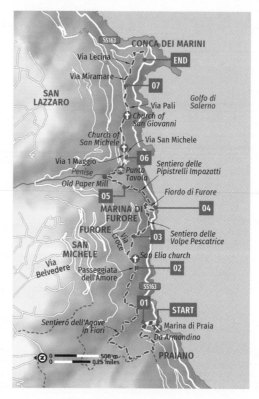

DURATION	DIFFICULTY	DISTANCE	START/END
3hrs	Moderate	7km	Marina di Praia/Conca dei Marini
TERRAIN	Narrow hillside paths, steps, some paved sections		

This coast-hugging walk incorporates three of the region's most secluded coves: Marina di Praia (pictured p47), the Fiordo di Furore and Conca dei Marini. But don't be lulled into a false sense of security by its proximity to the water: the precipitous hillsides require plenty of ascending and descending on sometimes indistinct paths. The views are rarely less than magnificent.

GETTING HERE

SITA Sud (p52) buses stop on SS163, the main Amalfi coast road, just above Marina di Praia.

STARTING POINT

The path starts just east of Praiano at Marina di Praia, the village's minuscule beach.

01 Climb up behind the beach, cross the SS163 coast road and take the path up the west side of the Vallone di Praia. As the path climbs and circumnavigates the dry, scrubby valley it becomes narrow and hard to identify before reappearing as the **Sentiero dell'Agave** in Fiori.

02 This path soon metamorphoses into the paved **Passeggiata dell'Amore**, inscribed with poetic quotes, before finally emerging opposite the **San Elia church** in Furore.

03 Take the steps heading downhill directly behind the church on what is now called the **Sentiero delle Volpe Pescatrice** to come out next to the **famous bridge** across the Fiordo di Furore.

04 Cross the bridge and take the so-called **Sentiero delle Pipistrelli Impazatti** (Path of the Crazy Bats) glued to the cliff on the east side.

Fiordo di Furore

The Fiordo di Furore (pictured), a deep and narrow cleft in the coastline 6km west of Amalfi, is a misnomer. Fjords are formed by glaciers, whereas the Furore 'fjord' is a drowned river valley carved by the Schiato stream. The mouth of the *fiordo* is crossed by an arched stone bridge, the site of an international high-diving tournament in July. A tiny beach at the bottom of the cleft, accessible by a stone staircase, is backed by a few abandoned houses.

Despite the lack of sun, this is a popular bathing and boating spot in the summer. There's a simple, seasonal bar-restaurant too.

SIMONE PADOVANI/SHUTTERSTOCK ©

Opposite you'll see the **Marina di Furore**. The tiny fishing and milling community was once a busy little commercial centre, although it's difficult to believe today. In medieval times, its unique natural position protected it from the threat of foreign raids and provided a ready source of water for its flour and paper mills.

05 Leaving the water, the path pitches inland into dense woodland. Veer left at a fork, pass some man-made water channels and you'll soon encounter an **old paper mill** (supposed home of said bats). Soon after, by a small waterfall, the path pitches right and climbs steeply out of the trees to **Punta Tavola**, a lofty viewpoint. Here it joins a paved road, the Via Maggio, on the western outskirts of **Conca dei Marini**.

06 Follow the paved path on the south side of the road, the Via San Michele, passing a **church** of the same name. The path briefly rejoins the main road before veering right again onto the pedestrian Via Pali, guarded by the vanilla-ice-cream-coloured **church of San Giovanni** clinging to the hillside.

07 Continue along Via Pali. Shortly after the church, it joins wider Via Miramare. Turn right and take the stairs down to the centre of **Conca dei Marini**.

TAKE A BREAK

Seafood lovers should head for the widely acclaimed, no-frills **Da Armandino** (☎089 87 40 87; Via Praia 1, Marina di Praia; meals €35; ⏱1-4pm & 7pm-midnight Apr-Nov) restaurant located in a former boatyard on the beach at Marina di Praia. It's great for fish fresh off the boat. There's no menu; just opt for the dish of the day – it's all excellent. The holiday atmosphere and appealing setting round things off nicely.

12

VALLE DELLE FERRIERE

DURATION	DIFFICULTY	DISTANCE	START/END
5hrs	Moderate	11km	Amalfi

TERRAIN	Mix of wooded and mountain paths with lots of stairs at the start and end

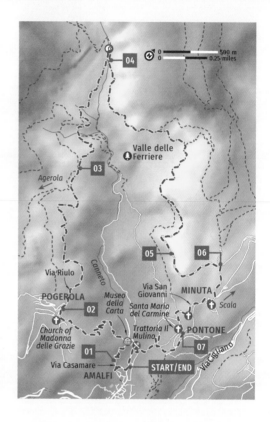

The Valle delle Ferriere is a subtropical wooded valley behind Amalfi town crossed by the Canneto river and punctuated by several waterfalls (pictured). In times of old, it hosted an ironworks *(ferriera)* and various paper factories *(cartiere)*. Today the factories are mossy ruins and the whole area has been turned into a nature reserve known for its orchids and other endemic flora.

GETTING HERE

Amalfi town is the hub of the region and linked to other coastal towns by SITA Sud (p52) buses, and from April to October by TraVelMar (p58) ferries.

STARTING POINT

The *sentiero alta* (high route) around the Valle delle Ferriere starts on the main north–south street in Amalfi Town, just south of the Museo della Carta.

01 Around 250m south of the Museo della Carta, take the Via Casamare uphill continuing as it turns into a gravelly path studded with multiple steps – thus begins a long climb to the village of **Pogerola** perched on a crag 252m above. The stairs lead directly into Pogerola's main square, overlooked by the **church of Madonna delle Grazie**.

02 From here, take the road on the right (standing with your back to the church). After 150m divert right again onto a path (Via Riulo), passing houses, fields and more steps, before entering a more forested domain. This is the Valle delle Ferriere proper, a nature reserve replete with **ferns** and a refreshing array of **waterfalls** (some up to 20m high). The mainly flat trail sets out on the

Museo ella Carta

Amalfi's **Paper Museum** (Paper Museum; ☎ 089 830 45 61; www.museodellacarta.it; Via delle Cartiere 23; adult/reduced €4/2.50; ◷ 10am-6.30pm daily Mar-Oct, to 4pm Tue-Sun Nov-late Jan) is housed in a rugged, cave-like 13th-century paper mill (the oldest in Europe). It lovingly preserves the original paper presses, which are still in full working order, as you'll see during the 30-minute guided tour (in English). The tour explains the original cotton-based paper production and the subsequent wood-pulp manufacturing. Afterwards you might be inspired to pick up some of the stationery sold in the gift shop, including calligraphy sets and paper pressed with flowers.

PROSLGN/SHUTTERSTOCK ©

wooded west side of the valley and is blissfully peaceful compared to the frenzy of the coast.

03 Veer right at the turn-off for Agerola (which heads left) and cross two steams with small cascades before arriving at the main crossing over the **Canneto River** and the largest of the waterfalls (water-flow depends on season).

04 Ford the river (there's no bridge) and return on the more open, craggy east side of the valley. Increasingly impressive **views** of Amalfi town reveal themselves as you contour the steep valley slopes.

05 After passing through a **tunnel** high above Amalfi town, the path cuts briefly north before reaching a crossroads.

06 Turn sharp right and take the steps down to the village of **Minuta**, hitting it just shy of a bend in the road to Scala. Swivel right down Via San Giovanni passing two **churches**.

07 After a left turn at a T-junction, you'll arrive at a third **church**, dedicated to Santa Maria del Carmine, in the village of **Pontone**. Take the steps to the right, cross the road and let gravity and a long staircase help you back to Amalfi.

☕ TAKE A BREAK

A TV-in-the-corner, kids-running-between-the-tables sort of place, **Trattoria Il Mulino** (☎ 089 87 22 23; Via delle Cartiere 36; pizzas €6-11, meals €20-30; ◷ 11.30am-4pm & 6.30pm-midnight Tue-Sun) is about as authentic an eatery as you'll find in Amalfi. There are few surprises on the menu, just hearty, honest pastas, grilled meats and fish. For a taste of local seafood, try the octopus cake or pasta with swordfish. It's right at the top of the town under a simple plastic awning.

13

SANTA MARIA DEL CASTELLO CIRCUIT

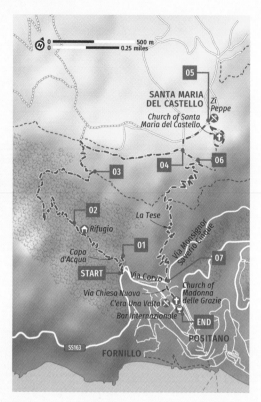

DURATION	DIFFICULTY	DISTANCE	START/END
3hrs	Moderate	9km	Positano

TERRAIN	Steep cliff paths, paved lanes, lots of stairs

For those travelling on foot, there's no real way out of Positano that doesn't involve climbing steep stone staircases – lots of 'em! The advantage of this particular circuitous route is that it enjoys a bit of shade in its early stages as you plod heavenward amid a thick and gnarly holm-oak forest.

GETTING HERE

Regular SITA buses patrol the Amalfi Coast road, connecting all the major towns and providing easy access to the start and finish points of this walk.

STARTING POINT

The walk starts on the main coast road (SS163) above Positano by a ruined building adjacent to the turnoff for Montepertuso.

01 A marked path – known locally as the **Capo d'Acqua trail** – starts beside the road, climbing steeply through ever-thickening oak trees up the mountainside.

02 Pass a rustic walk-in-only **rifugio** and continue the upward climb, utilising the steps. The oak forest gradually breaks into dryer Mediterranean scrub as you ascend high above Positano and **coastal views** open out as the path (333a) traverses the dry craggy hills above Positano, with the hulk of **Monte Sant'Angelo** standing sentinel in the background.

03 Turn left 2km up the ascent and then right at the top to join a wider trail. This track heads northeast **traversing the hillside,** passing first through scrub, then skirting the edge of a wood, before morphing into a paved road by a house with a red-tile roof.

At a Snail's Pace

Positano (pictured) is one of more than 85 towns in Italy, and over 235 worldwide, to have gained Slow City status (an extension of the Slow Food movement, established in northern Italy in 1986). In order to be considered, certain criteria must be met: towns need to have fewer than 55,000 inhabitants, no fast-food outlets or neon-lit hoardings, plenty of cycling and walking paths, and neighbourhood restaurants serving traditional cuisine with locally sourced ingredients. For more information, check www.cittaslow.org.

CHERYL RAMALHO/GETTY IMAGES ©

04 Just past the house, the track bends left by an electricity pylon, cuts up a narrow walled lane and reaches a crossroads. Turn right along another paved lane and in around 300m you'll be in the 'village' of **Santa Maria del Castello**, perched at 670m above the Mediterranean.

05 The village **church** is on the right and accessed by a short circular road. On the left is a small bar-restaurant called **Zi Peppe** that's good for a drink. Santa Maria del Castello was an ancient crossing point between Sorrento and the Amalfi Coast. A fort once stood here in medieval times. Take the narrow lane back down to the hill crest where you hiked up earlier. This time take the main path straight ahead (trail 333) by the electricity pylon.

06 The trail bends immediately to the left, proceeds around the headland and then switches right, becoming what is known as the **La Tese trail**. This path leads steeply down via a series of well-constructed staircases to Positano, visible in all its glory directly below.

07 Follow the steps down until you meet the main Positano–Montepertuso road (Via Corvo). Cross the road and head down narrow Via Chiesa Nuova. After circumnavigating the **church of Madonna delle Grazie**, you'll be deposited on the SS163 coast road next to the **Bar Internazionale** in upper Positano.

 **TAKE A BREAK**

Calling like a siren to any cash-poor budget traveller who thought Positano was for celebs only, **C'era Una Volta** (089 81 19 30; Via Marconi 127; meals €20-30; noon-3pm Wed-Mon, 6-11pm daily) is an authentic trattoria at the top of town specialising in honest Italian grub. No need to look further than the *gnocchi alla sorrentina* (gnocchi in a tomato and basil sauce) and Caprese salad. Pizzas start at €4.50; beer €2.

Also Try...

MAZERATH/SHUTTERSTOCK ©

MONTE EPOMEO

For anyone of average fitness, an ascent of the slumbering volcanic peak on the island of Ischia is practically obligatory.

The quickest way to climb Epomeo is from the village of Fontana, on the mountain's southern flank. The route (signposted from a bend in the road where the CS and CD buses stop) weaves up a paved road, diverts onto a track and finishes on a steepish path. For a more gradual and pleasant ascent, opt to start in the village of Serrara Fontana, 2km south of Fontana, where a road/track winds up through vineyards, terraced fields and scrubby brush.

Just shy of the summit there's a lovely rustic restaurant, behind which you can climb a steep tower of volcanic rock to reach the actual 789m peak (aided by steps and railings), beneath which lies a 15th century chapel.

DURATION 1hr
DIFFICULTY Moderate
DISTANCE 2.5km (one way)

CROCE DELLA CONOCCHIA

This is the westernmost peak (1314m) on the long, dramatically rugged chain of huge lumps of limestone called Sant'Angelo a Tre Pizzi – the highest part of the Amalfi's Monti Lattari Range.

Unlike the main summits, it's easily accessible from the coast. Take the step-aided path 329 (steep at first before easing) from the village of Montepertuso up to Caserma Forestale, a stone forestry barracks and major path crossroads. From here, waymarked CAI path 300 ascends north through woodland and out into open ground with stunning views of cliffs and the coast. Croce's crucifix-topped summit is easily gained, although the waymarked path bypasses it to the left in hazel woodland. The view embraces the sprawling city of Naples, Vesuvius, the isles of Ischia and Capri and mountains to the northwest. Descend via the same route.

DURATION 6hrs
DIFFICULTY Hard
DISTANCE 12km

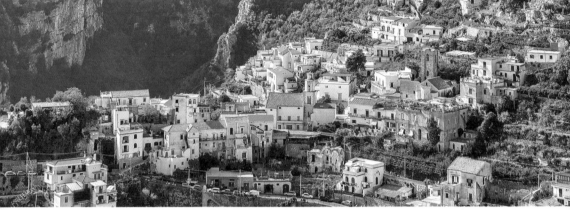

ROMAN BABAKIN/SHUTTERSTOCK ©

SENTIERO DEI FORTINI

Snaking its way along Capri's oft-overlooked western coast, the Sentiero dei Fortini (Path of the Small Forts; pictured left) is a wonderful if somewhat arduous walk that's about as remote as the island gets.

Named after the three coastal forts (Pino, Mèsola and Orrico), the path starts at Punta dell'Arcera near the Grotta Azzurra and heads south to Punta Carena at the island's southwestern tip, where it is possible to go for a refreshing swim. Along the way, it passes through some of Capri's most unspoilt countryside. Carry plenty of water.

DURATION 3hrs
DIFFICULTY Moderate
DISTANCE 5.25km

ATRANI–RAVELLO–MAIORI

Ravello is a beautiful old town (pictured), clustered on a narrow plateau rising steeply between Atrani and the coastal town of Maiori.

The town can provide the focus for an easy day out from Atrani or can be one of the highlights in a moderate walk from Atrani up to Ravello, then down to the coast again at Minori (the site of an ancient Roman coastal resort) and on to Maiori. The 6km route follows old paths and laneways through olive and citrus groves and quiet villages with extensive coast and mountain vistas.

DURATION 2½hrs
DIFFICULTY Moderate
DISTANCE 6km

FIORDO DI CRAPOLLA

From the village of Sant'Agata sui Due Golfi, with its two-way view of the Gulfs of Naples and Salerno, it is possible to walk down a deep cleft in the cliff-side known as the Fiordo di Crapolla to a secluded beach guarded by a ghostly abandoned fishing hamlet.

Leave Sant'Agata on Via Pigna and follow the path down. The final descent comprises 700-plus steps and passes a tiny cliffside chapel. Take plenty of food and water: there are no facilities, but the place feels wonderfully remote.

DURATION 3½hrs
DIFFICULTY Hard
DISTANCE 5km

ABRUZZO

14 **Santo Stefano di Sessanio to Rocca Calascio** A historic hike between two recently reinvigorated medieval villages. **p72**

15 **Above Pescasseroli** Short, steep but sweet climb above national park hub. **p74**

16 **Campo Imperatore Ridge** A close-up look at the imposing peaks atop Abruzzo's high mountain plateau. **p76**

17 **Rocca Ridge** Contrasting mix of ancient beech forests and breezy mountain ridges. **p78**

18 **Monte Mileto** A spirit-reviving circuit around the ethereal Majella mountain massif. **p82**

19 **Sentiero della Libertà** Track the course of an erstwhile WWII escape route. **p86**

Explore
ABRUZZO

Aruzzo's spinal mountains, the Apennines, are also its least crowded. Indeed, at times, a visit here feels like a trip back to the 1950s; a world of wheezing trains, buzzing Vespas (motor scooters), ruined farmhouses and fields splashed with blood-red poppies. All this is good news for prospective hikers who share the region's ample trails with sheep dogs, mountain goats, abundant birdlife and the odd – rarely sighted – human being. A major national park building effort in the 1990s has created an almost unbroken swathe of protected land across Abruzzo, protecting rare wildlife and Italy's highest mountains outside the Alps.

L'AQUILA

From tragedy springs hope. More than a decade after a powerful earthquake killed 308 of its citizens and toppled copious historic buildings, L'Aquila is – just about – back in business. It's certainly ready to welcome a new wave of out-of-town travellers, not just to admire the durability of its churches and fountains, but to study the meticulous renovation work that has returned many of them to their former glory – and in some cases even surpassing it.

SULMONA

An underappreciated city of traditional trattorias, narrow medieval streets and half-discovered mountain magic, Sulmona sits strategically on a plateau surrounded by three national parks, making it the ideal base for outdoor excursions in Abruzzo. It's easy to reach from Pescara or Rome, and simple to navigate once you arrive (trails fan out from the city limits). The city can trace its history back to the Roman town of Sulmo, where the poet Ovid (of *Metamorphoses* fame) was born in 43 BC. It is also known within Italy for its *confetti* – the almond sweets, not the coloured paper scattered at weddings.

PARCO NAZIONALE D'ABRUZZO, LAZIO E MOLISE

Italy's second-oldest national park is also one of its most ecologically rich. Established by royal decree in 1923, it began as a modest 5-sq-km reserve that, little by little, morphed into the 440-sq-km protected area it is today. The evolution wasn't easy. The park was temporarily abolished in 1933 by the Mussolini government. It returned to the fold in 1950, only to face further encroachment from housing construction, road building and ski developers.

The park has managed to remain at the forefront of Italy's conservation movement, reintroducing and protecting wild animals such as the Abruzzo chamois, Apennine wolf, lynx, deer and – most notably – Marsican bear (the park has Italy's largest surviving enclave of these threatened animals).

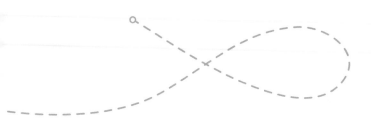

Resources

The following three maps cover all the hikes in this region and will help immensely with navigation. All are 1:25,000.

Gran Sasso D'Italia – Carta dei Sentieri (Club Alpino Italiano)

Parco D'Abruzzo – Carta Escursinistica (Iter Edizioni)

Majella – Carta Escursionistica e Scialpinistica (Il Lupo)

Today the park extends over three regions, with more than half of it covered in thick beech forest.

PARCO NAZIONALE DEL GRAN SASSO E MONTI DELLA LAGA

About 20km northeast of L'Aquila, the Gran Sasso massif is the centrepiece of the Parco Nazionale del Gran Sasso e Monti della Laga, one of Italy's largest national parks. The park's predominant feature is its jagged rocky landscape, through which one of Europe's southernmost glaciers, the Calderone, cuts its (increasingly narrow) course. It's also a haven for wildlife, home to an estimated 120 wolves, 1000 chamois and 11 pairs of golden eagles.

PARCO NAZIONALE DELLA MAJELLA

History, geology and ecology collide in 750-sq-km Parco Nazionale della Majella, Abruzzo's most diverse park, where wolves roam in giant beech woods, ancient hermitages speckle ominous mountains, and 500km of criss-crossing paths and a handful of ski areas cater to the hyperactive. Monte Amaro, the Apennines' second-highest peak,

surveys all around it from a lofty 2793m vantage point.

 WHEN TO GO

Fickle weather in the Apennines can bring both early- and late-season snow – although the region enjoys a slightly longer walking season than the Alps. It's best not to attempt the higher mountains before mid-June. The first snows often arrive in late September. Lower level trails are generally good from mid-May to mid-October.

 TRANSPORT

Buses and trains link the hub cities of Sulmona and L'Aquila with Rome and Pescara. Buses also provide links to the smaller villages in the national parks including Pacentro, Pescasseroli and Fonte Cerreto. TUA (www.tuabruzzo.it) runs the most extensive bus services.

 WHERE TO STAY

All of these hikes can be done out of bases in the cities of L'Aquila and Sulmona. L'Aquila has recently recovered from the de-

bilitating 2009 earthquake and is adding new accommodation options all the time. Sulmona excels in charismatic *locandas* (inns) and *alberghi diffusi* (diffused accommodation; generally with one central reception).

 WHAT'S ON

Giostra Cavalleresca di Sulmona (www.giostrasulmona.it) On the last weekend in July, gaily caparisoned horse riders gallop around Sulmona's Piazza Garibaldi.

Sentiero della Libertà Every year in early May, hundreds of people partake in a three-day mass communal hike along the 60km 'Freedom Trail' between Sulmona and Casoli.

14

SANTO STEFANO DI SESSANIO TO ROCCA CALASCIO

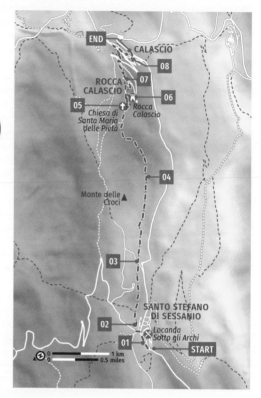

DURATION	DIFFICULTY	DISTANCE	START/END
2hrs	Moderate	7km	Santo Stefano di Sessanio/ Calascio

TERRAIN	Firm country paths, short grassy ascents

For a relatively benign introduction to the rugged ridges and peaks of the Gran Sasso mountains, look no further than this short but very attractive romp between the two historical bookends of Santo Stefano di Sessanio and Rocca Calascio.

GETTING HERE

There are four TUA buses a day running between L'Aquila bus station and Santo Stefano di Sessanio (€3, 50 minutes), but none on Sundays.

STARTING POINT

The walk starts on the western edge of the village of Santo Stefano di Sessanio on the road between Barisciano and Campo Imperatore.

01 From the car park on the west side of the once semi-abandoned, but now rejuvenated Abruzzan village of Santo Stefano di Sessanio, take the road down towards a small **lake**. At a road junction by a small chapel, turn left and then veer immediately right, following the road around a bend.

02 A trail (signposted Rocca Calascio Ruta Pan-oramica) leads off to the right just before the 'Arrivederci Santo Stefano' sign. Follow the single-track path as it winds around a small grassy hill with **fine views** back over Santo Stefano di Sessanio. Several cranes are still busy rebuilding the village and its emblematic **Medici tower** damaged in the 2009 earthquake.

03 The path subsequently widens and descends to a quiet paved road. Cross the road and make the steep ascent up the grassy slope on the other side.

04 At the top of the ascent, the path flattens out and starts to traverse beneath the southern

A Village Revived

Known as Sextantio in Roman times, the somnolent but haunting village of Santo Stefano di Sessanio (pictured) has a commanding position overlooking two valleys. The settlement flourished in the 16th century under the rule of the Medici family, whose coat of arms can still be seen on the entrance portal to the main piazza. Subsequently left behind by history, Santo Stefano lost most of its people to emigration and was falling into oblivion when it was 'rediscovered' by Swedish eco-restorer Daniele Kihlgren in 1999. Since then, Kihlgren and others have purchased many of the town's old buildings and turned them into lodgings and restaurants that maintain their attractiveness of yore.

Best for

QUAINT VILLAGES

crest of the smooth-topped **Monte delle Croci**. At this point, the distinctive silhouettes of the castle and chapel of Rocca Calascio come dramatically into view.

05 Contouring around the hill slopes, the path reaches the **Chiesa di Santa Maria delle Pietà**, an octagonal late-16th-century church with a baroque portal built to give thanks for victories over local brigands.

06 From here, it's a short climb up to the **ruined castle**, which at 1460m is the highest fortress in the Apennines. The movie *The Name of the Rose* was filmed here.

07 After visiting the castle, descend back to the chapel and take the path behind down to the small hillside *borgo* of **Rocca Calascio** (pictured p69), with its narrow alleys and half-restored buildings.

08 From **Piazza della Chiesa** at the bottom of the *borgo,* a signposted path starts to descend, short-cutting around the bends of the paved road. It will ultimately deliver you to the Piazza della Vittoria in the larger village of **Calascio**. From here, descend to the main road, where you can catch a bus back to Santo Stefano di Sessanio.

 **TAKE A BREAK**

Santo Stefano is noted for its lentils, grown by only 12 farmers on the slopes around the town. To sample, them step into the arched, 16th-century dining room of **Locanda Sotto gli Archi** (☎ 0862 89 91 16; http://santostefano.sextantio.it; Via degli Archi; meals €32-38; ⏱7.30-11pm Wed-Mon, plus 12.30-3pm Sat & Sun). Furniture and crockery here are designed to re-create the austere quality of bygone times and the excellent food uses time-honoured ingredients and techniques native to the region.

15

ABOVE PESCASSEROLI

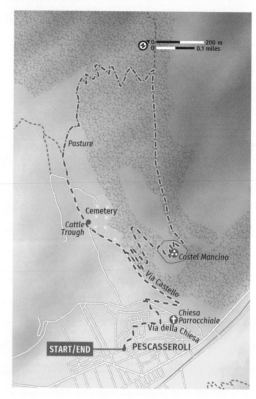

DURATION	DIFFICULTY	DISTANCE	START/END
2½hrs	Moderate	6km	Pescasseroli

TERRAIN	Village streets, forest paths, one steep descent

This short circuit above the national-park hub of Pescasseroli visits a ruined castle and provides excellent views over the town and the uncluttered countryside.

From the main square in Pescasseroli, follow Via della Chiesa north. Just before you reach the impressive **Chiesa Parrocchiale** turn sharp left up a narrow alley with steps labelled 'Salita Dott. Ciolli'. The alley almost immediately joins a paved road; turn left here and then right into Via Castello. Follow the paved road to a walled cemetery and cut diagonally down a steep bank beyond it to join a track next to a cattle trough.

Follow this track away from the town. Within five minutes, bear right off the main track on a fainter path marked by a fence on the right. When the fence runs out, cut diagonally across a **sloping pasture** and pick the clear path on the opposite side. Parallel the edge of the meadow before turning right at a junction just before a river gully. The path now steepens and plunges into the forest, zigzagging up the slope. At the first fork, veer left. At the second by a signpost, turn right and start to traverse the slope.

Before long you'll reach the splayed 11th-century ruins of **Castel Mancino** (pictured), built during the Logobard era in an almost impregnable position on the crags above town. Pines that had grown up around the castle were cut down in the 1920s, resulting in some weather-inflicted damage, but the spooky remains are still strangely evocative. A fairly clear path zigzags down steeply through the ruins back to the town visible below.

16
CAMPO IMPERATORE RIDGE

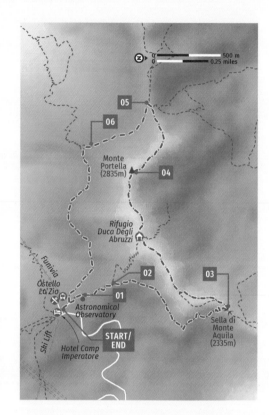

DURATION	DIFFICULTY	DISTANCE	START/END
2½hrs	Moderate	6km	Upper cable-car station, Campo Imperatore

TERRAIN	Single-track mountain paths, some narrow but not overly exposed ridge walks

To enjoy a spine-chilling 'top of the world' feeling without having to scramble on all fours up precipitous rock walls, come to Italy's aptly named 'Little Tibet' and partake in this peak-punctuated ridge walk above Campo Imperatore.

GETTING HERE

There are several daily buses from L'Aquila's main bus station to the cable-car base station at Fonte Cerreto. From here, the Gran Sasso Funivia (June to early October) will zip you up to Campo Imperatore.

STARTING POINT

Nexus for numerous high plateau hikes, the 2128m-high upper station of the *funivia* (cable car) at Campo Imperatore is where this walk starts and finishes.

01 From the top of the *funivia* station next to the Hotel Campo Imperatore (currently closed), walk towards the **domed astronomical observatory**. Built in 1965, the venerable space-gazing establishment specialises in the research and detection of 'near-Earth' asteroids and comets. Behind it, a clear, well-used path zigzags up a steep, treeless slope.

02 After five minutes of climbing, turn right at a junction following signs to Corno Grande and Monte Aquila. The single-track path (101) climbs gradually in a smooth diagonal up the southeast face of the **Serra di Monte Aquila** with **fabulous views** of the vast Campo Imperatore plateau on the right.

03 After scrambling across a couple of rocky sections, the path delivers you to a saddle, the **Sella di Monte Aquila** (2335m), where the Corno

The Gran Sasso Raid

Following his capture in 1943 during WWII, Mussolini was briefly imprisoned in the Hotel Campo Imperatore. Only weeks into his incarceration, he was rescued by the Germans in the so-called Gran Sasso Raid headed up by Otto Skorzeny, a stealthy commander in the Waffen SS. Skorzeny organised for German paratroopers to crash-land a dozen gliders into Gran Sasso Mountain on the high plateau adjacent to the hotel where Mussolini was being held. Recklessly storming the hotel with his paratroopers, the commander subsequently disabled the radio operator and the radio, and within 10 minutes had freed a flabbergasted Mussolini without a shot being fired.

BRENDAN SAINSBURY/LONELY PLANET ©

Best for

MOUNTAIN VIEWS

Grande trail heads north. Turn sharp left here and follow path 161 as it traverses beneath the north side of the ridge before swapping back to the south side and descending to the ridge-top **Rifugio Duca degli Abruzzi** (open June to September), with its spectacularly sited sundeck.

04 Continue along the narrow but not overly exposed ridge (now on path 100) to the top of **Monte Portella** (2835m) and a smaller subpeak around 800m further on. The views to the north reveal the rocky majesty of the Campo Pericoli and its deceptively gentle slopes recently repopulated with chamois, a goat-antelope native to Europe.

05 From the subpeak, descend to a saddle where a signposted trail junction will direct you along path 102, doubling back around the lower southwest skirts of **Monte Portella.** The path contours the grassy mountain slopes with little change in elevation.

06 Ignore a right-hand turn at Paso del Lupo (which leads down to the *funivia* base station) and continue along the well-defined **mountain path** back to Campo Imperatore and the start point.

 **TAKE A BREAK**

The venerable **Ostello Lo Zio** (☎ 349.8110032; www.ostellocampo imperatore.com; sandwiches €5; ☼7am-7pm) hostel at the top of the *funivia* has a small bar offering coffee and cakes as well as a casual sit-down restaurant cooking up pasta, soups and sizeable mains, or – if you're in a hurry – doorstep-sized cheese and ham sandwiches.

17

ROCCA RIDGE

DURATION	DIFFICULTY	DISTANCE	START/END
6-7hrs	Hard	19km	Pescasseroli

TERRAIN	Forest tracks, mountain-ridge paths, some paved roads

Limestone ridges, rustling beech woods, flowery meadows full of grazing sheep and perhaps even a distant bear sighting; the Rocca Ridge dominates the skyline as you look west from Pescasseroli and is the 1924m highpoint of the Parco Nazionale D'Abruzzo, Lazio e Molise.

GETTING HERE

TUA buses serve Pescasseroli from either Avezzano (linked to L'Aquila and Rome by train) or Castel del Sangro (linked to Sulmona by bus).

STARTING POINT

Initiate proceedings in the main square in the small national-park town of Pescasseroli, which has several cafes, a water fountain and a shop selling local maps.

01 From the town hall in the centre of Pescasseroli, walk south along the Viale S Lucia and continue over a crossroads onto the Via Fontana della Difesa. This leads to a fork in the road by the Hotel Iris – follow the road to the right. The pavement soon ends and the road becomes a gravel track, passing some farm buildings before delving into open country. You'll likely see or hear large white Maremma sheepdogs around here. They may bark at you, but, fear not, they'll generally leave you alone as long as you don't encroach on their territory (stay on the path!). The track soon delivers you to a **spring** below the park-owned **Rifugio della Difesa**. This is the official start of the route, around 3km from the town centre.

02 A painted sign indicates the start of path C3, which leads left off the track at the spring and climbs past the *rifugio*. Relatively well marked with red-and-white paint, it winds up through a mixture of forest and more open areas. After approximately 45 minutes, the path mounts a steep, rocky section and meets the gravel track again. Cross the track, passing a roofed plaque in a clearing, before plunging back into the trees. The gravel track is crossed several more times before steeper terrain forces the path into a series of tight switchbacks which snake up to the isolated **Santuario di Monte Tranquillo** (1600m), a dowdy chapel built on a bluff. This is the end of the gravel road.

03 A faint farm track continues up open hillside ahead. Follow this and climb

beneath the northern slopes of **Monte Tranquillo**. Pass **Rifugio di Monte Tranquillo**, a privately owned hut in a hollow, and continue up the rocky slope to join the ridge itself.

04 The **ridge** marks a junction of paths; turn right (northeast) to follow path C5 along the ridgeline. The route drops down briefly to the east, skirting around a small copse before returning to the ridge at a saddle. The ridge line is now followed for 5km. If you lose the path among the limestone outcrops, return to the ridge and continue uphill, and you will soon pick it up. The crest you are

following marks the boundary between the two Italian regions of Abruzzo (east) and Lazio (west). Despite the national park's tri-region name, 80% of it lies within Abruzzo.

05 The first cairn, around 1km onto the ridge, marks the summit of **Monte Pietroso** (1876m). Beyond the peak, the path continues to climb to the large pile of stones at the top of **La Rocca** (1924m), where the park views are panoramic – craggy ridges and forested valleys fall steeply on either side, with Pescasseroli visible far below to the east. From here you'll be looking down on

🐦 National Park Visitor Centre

The **Centro di Visita di Pescasseroli** (📞 0863 911 32 21; www.parcoabruzzo.it; Viale Colli dell'Oro, Pescasseroli; adult/reduced €6/4; ⏰10am-5.30pm) has an Apennine garden and a clinic for rescued animals who can no longer live in the wild on their own. Accommodated on site are two Marsican bears and a wolf (the only ones you're likely to see, unless you're extremely lucky). It also acts as an information portal and small museum with exhibits covering archaeology, flora, caves and a short video on bear conservation.

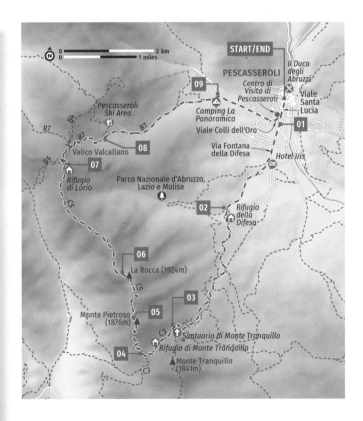

the extensive beech forests that cover 60% of the park's total area and inhabit the mountainsides up to 1800m.

06 The ridge narrows to the north of La Rocca but the path is better defined, and the terrain is largely level as the trail either follows the ridge top or contours just below it. Snow can linger here into late June, by which time an extensive array of **wild flora** will be beginning to bloom. Look out for gentians, lilies, orchids and wild herbs.

07 The **Rifugio di Lorio** soon becomes visible on the ridge to the north. Forget late-night shots of grappa and spirited sing-songs around the hearth. The Lorio is a tiny mountain hut and usually locked. Continue along the ridge past the *rifugio* for around 150m, before dropping down to the right (east) on a stone path that zigzags down the **Valico Valcallano** pass. Turn right here and pick up path R5 that plunges downhill into thick beech forest.

08 Around 1km later the forest path joins a vehicle track (B1); turn right and descend past two ski tows. On the slopes opposite is **Pescasseroli ski area**, one of Abruzzo's (and Italy's) smallest, with 8km of trails and a 585m vertical drop. Beyond the ski lifts, the track ultimately joins a paved road just north of **Camping La Panoramica**.

09 Turn right along the road and follow it to a roundabout, taking the second left along the Viale Colli dell'Oro.

Guided Walks in the Park

Bivouacked in a small shop in the national park hub of Pescasseroli, **Ecotur** (☎0863 91 27 60; www.ecotur.org; Via Piave 9, Pescasseroli; 🕘9am-1pm & 4-7.30pm) organises treks, bike rides and various other excursions in the area. Notable treks include 'On the Tracks of the Wolf' (a three-hour evening jaunt; €20) and 'Weekend with the Bear' (two days spent on the trail of the Mariscan bear (pictured p78), staying at a mountain *rifugio*; from €120). It's probably your best opportunity of spotting one of the park's elusive wild animals.

This will lead back to the Viale S Lucia and the centre of **Pescasseroli**. It's worth exploring the town after you've imbibed a drink or two. During medieval times it was an important stop on the bi-annual sheep flock migration, or *transumanza,* that headed south to Puglia. Later on, it became popular with the European aristocracy who came here to hunt bears. These days it acts as the main headquarters for the national park and is frequented mainly by Italian tourists.

TAKE A BREAK

The handsome **Il Duca degli Abruzzi** (☎0863 91 10 75; Piazza Duca degli Abruzzi 5; meals €25-30; ⏱7.30-10.30pm Fri & Sat, 1-3.30pm Sun) located on a quiet square in Pescasseroli's historic centre is a little more gourmet than your average salt-of-the-earth village trattoria, but doesn't shirk on the rustic charm either. Everything is homemade and utterly delicious: try the truffle pasta, follow up with grilled pork and wash it down with Montepulciano d'Abruzzo.

18

MONTE MILETO

Best for

AVOIDING
THE CROWDS

DURATION	DIFFICULTY	DISTANCE	START/END
7hrs	Hard	19km	Pacentro

TERRAIN	Steep but firm mountain paths, stony 4WD tracks

A steep but safe ascent to the domed summit of Monte Mileto through ancient beech woods and the spiritually soaked slopes of the Monte Morrone. The walk starts and finishes in beguiling Pacentro (pictured), situated just inside the boundary of Majella National Park, a historic village still recovering after years of abandonment following WWII.

GETTING HERE

Regular buses operated by TUA run the 10km between Sulmona and Pacentro.

STARTING POINT

Orientate yourself in the main square (Piazza del Popolo) in the spectacularly sited national park village of Pacentro. From here climb up behind the triple-towered castle and head out of town on the road (SR487) to Caramanico Terme.

01 Around 300m after joining the road, leave it on a signposted path that cuts up behind a restaurant next to a **spring**. The path climbs a slope, passes under the launch site for Pacentro's **valley-spanning zipline** (p15) and quickly rejoins the road. Follow the road for 20m before veering left on a continuation of the path as it climbs up past a farmhouse to meet the road a second time. On this occasion, turn left and follow the road uphill, past a picnic area and around two hairpin bends. On the third hairpin, path Q5 branches off to the left.

02 After just 50m, at the end of a wall, Q5 turns sharply and steeply uphill. Climb through fire-damaged pines alongside a gully on your left. After around 30 minutes, the tough climb eases slightly and the sometimes indistinct path veers left and enters a mix of meadow and sporadic pine and beech glades. Eagle-eye **views** of Pacentro's rooftops and towers unfold below. As the forest thickens, the path steepens again and zigzags beneath thick mature beech trees with crunchy dead leaves underfoot. After some effort, you'll finally emerge into **beautiful high mountain meadows** as the ascent gradually peters out.

03 Soon after, a track merges with the path from the right. Follow the track as it veers left through ever lusher meadows into a grassy hollow called **Valle Dentro**, guarded by a **ruined shepherd's hut**. The ridge to your left (west) reaches its apex at **Morrone di Pacentro** (1800m) and you can hike up to it from the hollow if you have the time and inclination for superb views of Sulmona and the Valle Peligna (there's no clear path, just aim for the ridgeline). Otherwise, from the hollow, take the clear path straight ahead (northwest) and push on up to a saddle on the opposite side where you'll encounter a signposted path junction.

04 Take Q6 (right) and within minutes you'll be on the grassy ridge behind Morrone di Pacentro, punctu- ated with dwarf mountain pine trees. The meadows and high pastures here abound with **seasonal orchids, wild roses, junipers and peonies**. The Morrone mountains acquired a special spiritual significance in the 13th century as a place of refuge and prayer for hermits and ascetics. The most notable figure was the monk Pietro da Morrone, who founded a religious order called the Morronites (aka Celestines) in 1244. Pietro and his fellow hermits built several hermitages in the mountains, utilising them for extended periods of prayer, fasting and meditation. The saintly monk later briefly went on to become Pope Celestine V

Corsa degli Zingari

Undertaken on rugged paths immediately surrounding the village of Pacentro, the Corsa degli Zingari is a barefoot running race that has been going on for more than 550 years. Its origins are the subject of conjecture. Some claim it evolved from an old hunting rite practised by Italic tribes; others suggest it was part of a medieval military initiation.

Held on the first Sunday in September, the race starts atop a stony escarpment on the hillside opposite Pacentro. Runners hurtle down a steep path and athletically ford a river before climbing another slope into the village. The finish line is the diminutive baroque Chiesa della Madonna di Loreto, where participants – their feet by now a bloody mess – collapse in front of the altar.

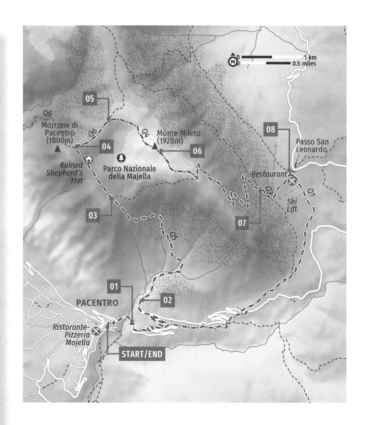

before resigning after just five months in office in 1294. His legacy has left a heavy mark in Sulmona and the Morrone Mountains, which are still dotted with a handful of medieval hermitages.

05 Continue along the rounded ridge to a second junction, which appears just as the **Valle d'Orta** on the eastern side of the Morrone massif comes into view. Take Q4 (right) and descend to a saddle and then track up grassy slopes to the rounded summit of **Monte Mileto** (1920m). From this vantage point, the views are sweeping, particularly those to the east dominated by the barren rocky summit of **Monte Amaro**, the second-highest mountain in the Apennines at 2793m.

06 From the summit, head SE to a sub-peak and then make a steep descent to a 4WD track visible below. Continue descending on the track, taking a shortcut on the first hairpin that rejoins the track in a beech wood further down. Passo San Leonardo and its peculiarly shaped restaurant are now clearly visible below.

07 The track continues descending and eventually reaches a junction with path Q3; turn right and head through the lower beech forest to the bottom of a ski lift. From here, descend through meadows to **Passo San Leonardo** and its restaurant luring you like a dislodged lighthouse. The pass marks the border between Majella National Park's two main mountain

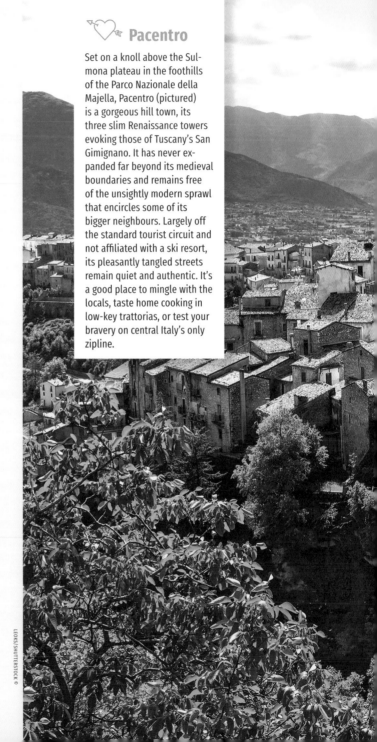

Pacentro

Set on a knoll above the Sulmona plateau in the foothills of the Parco Nazionale della Majella, Pacentro (pictured) is a gorgeous hill town, its three slim Renaissance towers evoking those of Tuscany's San Gimignano. It has never expanded far beyond its medieval boundaries and remains free of the unsightly modern sprawl that encircles some of its bigger neighbours. Largely off the standard tourist circuit and not affiliated with a ski resort, its pleasantly tangled streets remain quiet and authentic. It's a good place to mingle with the locals, taste home cooking in low-key trattorias, or test your bravery on central Italy's only zipline.

LEOKS/SHUTTERSTOCK ©

ranges: the smooth-topped Morrone and the more rugged Majella. The restaurant, known locally as **Rifugio Celidonio**, is usually open for drinks and light meals.

08 Turning right outside the restaurant, follow path Q1 across a field to the bottom of a ski lift. From here the path meanders through fields, past an old stone building and along an even older rock-strewn lane. Within around 40 minutes it hits the main Pacentro road. Turn left, walk for 50m on the tarmac and take a path that plunges downhill to the right. You'll cross the road three more times as you meander back to Pacentro and the start point. If you have time, it's worth checking out the town's mostly 14th-century **Caldora Castle** with its three famous towers, the mannerist-meets-baroque **Chiesa Santa Maria della Misericordia**, and a slew of **grand nobles' houses** that beautify the lanes between Piazza del Popolo and Piazza Umberto I.

TAKE A BREAK

You could easily walk right past Pacentro's **Ristorante-Pizzeria Majella** (📞 0864 77 33 91; Via Santa Maria Maggiore 146; meals €25-35; 🕐 11.30am-3pm & 7-11pm Tue-Sun, 6-11pm Mon): it doesn't brag about its existence. Instead, its reputation is carried by word of mouth – which in small-town Pacentro travels fast. The menu apogee is the *arrosticini*, an old Abruzzo classic comprising lamb skewers wrapped in foil and served in a sloping ceramic pot.

19

SENTIERO DELLA LIBERTÀ

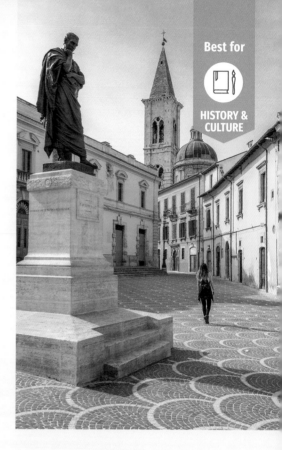

DURATION	DIFFICULTY	DISTANCE	START/END
10hrs	Hard	31km	Sulmona/ Palena

TERRAIN	Dirt roads, mountain paths and several short paved sections

Mixing the call of the wild with the call of freedom, the Sentiero della Libertà (Freedom Trail) follows in the footsteps of escaping Allied prisoners as they forged a path across the Apennines in the winter of 1943–44, fleeing German-occupied Sulmona to liberated Palena and beyond.

The full trail runs for 60km. This walk tackles the more scenic first half, crossing Majella National Park from west to east.

GETTING HERE

Sulmona is easily accessible by train or bus from Rome's Tiburtina station. Sulmona's train station is 2km from the city centre.

STARTING POINT

The walk starts 2km southeast of central Sulmona in a car park beside a cemetery on the road to Pacentro. A large signboard maps out the route and describes its highlights in Italian and English.

01 Take the paved path (marked with an 'L' for Libertà) that zigzags up the slope behind the **cemetery**. It quickly turns into a dirt vehicle track before becoming a single-track path. At a junction, fork right (ignoring signs to Grascio). Pass a **wooden bench** (from where you can look admiringly back over Sulmona and the Valle Peligna) and gradually enter scrubby mountain terrain punctuated with thorny bushes.

02 Contour around the western slopes of **Colle Savente** (pictured p88) and traverse the plateau that stretches across to **Colle Mitra**, whose summit is marked by a tall cross. Ignore all turn-offs as you pitch southeast around the skirts of Colle Mitra until you come to **Fonte Pacile** (spring) nestled in a small glade.

03 Look carefully for red-and-white markers here as you climb briefly up to a junction on a **grassy saddle**. At the saddle, turn left and start to descend on the other side of the Mitra plateau, following a vehicle-wide track down through mixed forest.

04 As the descent flattens out, a sign announces

a sharp right turn, just before a second spring, the **Fonte Sulmonita** (if you pass the spring, you've gone too far). Follow an overgrown track under gnarly trees until it comes out in a **gorgeous meadow** where a signpost points sharply to the left. After about 200m, the trail forks again, this time heading sharply to the right on the edge of a field. This turning is unsignposted so look carefully for the red-and-white markers in the bushes.

05 The now indistinct path meanders alongside an old stone wall and through overgrown pasture to an **arched**

railway bridge. Go under the bridge and descend to a paved lane where a right turn will deliver you to the busier SR55 opposite a cemetery on the edge of the village of **Cansano**.

06 Turn left, go down the road for around 300m and take the lane on the right (signposted). Bear right, follow the lane to a T-junction and turn right again. The road turns into a vehicle track, goes past a farm and meanders along sedately to another railway arch (pass underneath) and the **Fonte Ramarozzo**, where you can top up on water.

Long Walk to Freedom

With the help of sympathetic local partisans, many ex-prisoners from Campo 78 fled east across the Apennines Mountains to Casoli in the winter of 1943–44, forging a rough trail as they went. Casoli had been liberated by Allied soldiers a few months previously and, throughout that long winter as the Allied advance was temporarily halted by German troops along the 'Gustav Line', it became the hallowed end point of the so-called Sentiero della Libertà, an escape route that led east from German-occupied Sulmona to freedom.

The Sentiero's most celebrated escapee was future Italian president Carlos Azeglio Ciampi, who was in a group of 60 soldiers who walked for 25 hours through a blizzard in March 1944.

07 Continue along the flat track for another 20 minutes through verdant farmland until a sign directs you to turn sharp left across an open field.

08 After around 600m, just before reaching an **equestrian school**, go right (this crucial turn is bizarrely unsignposted) where a grassy path curves into trees and starts heading diagonally uphill. As it narrows, the path crests the modest **Serra Carpineto** ridge, where you'll encounter a set of **farm buildings** nestled in a hollow.

09 Go right here then immediately left and take a path down though pine trees to a set of railway arches that mark the edge of the small town of **Campo di Giove**. Turn right when you hit a paved road and left at the first junction to arrive in the town centre. Here you have two choices. You can finish the hike with 22km already under your belt and catch a bus back to Sulmona, or you can carry on for another 9km to Palena. A third option would be to bed down in Campo di Giove and tackle the next section on day two.

10 Exit Campo di Giove on Via Brigata Majella. Several hundred metres after passing the **town cemetery** a path, marked by a **large stone monument**, branches off to the left.

11 This is the start of stage two of the Sentiero della

BRENDAN SAINSBURY/LONELY PLANET ©

Libertà. Head uphill, cross a road and follow the path as it continues southeast ascending diagonally across the mountainside. Pretty soon you'll enter thick beech forest with occasional peek-a-boo **views** back over Campo di Giove.

12 At a Y-junction, fork left onto the higher path (the lower path leads to a small **chapel** and soon dead-ends). Within 15 minutes you'll join a wider track at the top end of a ski chairlift. Here the trees fall away and the path ascends a grassy slope to a small **ski station** and **rifugio** at the **Guado di Coccia** (1674m). This typically small Abruzzo ski area has 10km of runs but is deathly quiet in the summer.

13 This pass marked the rough border between the German and Allied occupied zones in WWII, the so-called Gustav Line held stubbornly by the Germans until June 1944. Escapees who made it this far could practically sniff freedom. Not all were lucky. On the windswept pass a **stone monument** stands in memoriam to Ettore De Corti, an Italian partisan captured and executed by the Germans in September 1943 – an enduring symbol of the underground resistance. Keeping the dark mass of **Monte Porrara** to your right, follow the path straight over the pass and down the other side.

14 A good dirt track progresses downhill

Campo 78

Campo 78 is a still-intact Prisoner of War camp, located 5km east of Sulmona in the village of Fonte d'Amore.

Around 3000 Allied soldiers were imprisoned here in September 1943 when their Italian guards deserted their posts in the face of an approaching Anglo-American army. In the six days before the Germans arrived to take over the camp and thwart the Allied advance, many of the former detainees escaped into the surrounding mountains.

The Germans subsequently closed down Campo 78 and its remaining inmates were marched north to prison camps in Germany.

through open grassy terrain with clusters of beech trees on either side. After about 15 minutes the main track swings right and crosses a small **river** in a gully. Follow it as it zigzags down with the river on your left. The track briefly joins a paved road by a hut at the bottom of a ski lift; 200m further on you leave the road via another track on the left and head downhill towards the village of Palena below.

15 The track joins and immediately leaves another road before finally linking up with it again by the outlying houses of the small village of **Palena** (pictured p86; population around 1500). Technically, you're still only halfway along the Sentiero della Libertà, which officially finishes in Casoli, over 26km to the northeast, but many walkers call it a day here. Bus services out of Palena are poor and usually involve changing in Lanciano for Pescara or Sulmona. Check ahead with www.tuabruzzo.it.

 TAKE A BREAK

You'll be starving by the time you reach Campo di Giove and in dire need of rustic **La Scarpetta di Venere** (www.lascarpettadivenere. net; Viale Marconi 3a; meals €20-28; 11am-3pm & 6-11pm Tue-Sun), with its classic Abruzzo cuisine cooked 'Slow Food' style. Go local by opting for the lamb *arrosticini* (skewers) and the saffron and ricotta-infused *chitarra* pasta.

Also Try...

ANGELO D'AMICO/GETTY IMAGES ©

SANT'OROFRIO HERMITAGE & ERCOLE CURINO RUINS

The Morrone mountains that guard Sulmona were once a haven for hermits and spiritualists inspired, in part, by the so-called hermit-pope Celestine V.

Start the walk outside the huge Celestine Abbey in the village of Badia, taking the road (Via Badia) that leads toward the foot of the mountains. The road bends to the right and diagonally ascends the lower slopes to a small car park. From here a 300m-long path heads to Ercole Curino, a Roman-era sanctuary whose foundations cover a couple of mountainside terraces and include a preserved mosaic floor sheltered in a wooden hut.

You'll need to return to the car park to access the cliff-clinging Sant'Orofrio hermitage (pictured), former refuge of Pietro da Morrone (aka Pope Celestine V). The arched porticoes cower under a massive rock face in the Morrone mountains.

DURATION 1½hrs
DIFFICULTY Easy
DISTANCE 4.5km

CORNO GRANDE

As the highest peak in the Apennines, Corno Grande (2912m) receives a lot of attention from walkers, especially since it is so readily accessible from high-altitude starting points at either Campo Imperatore or Prati di Tivo.

The impressive rock peak has extremely steep faces and from most viewpoints looks like the preserve of climbers. However, if you're sure-footed and not afraid of heights, the summit is hikeable in good conditions.

The *via normale* (normal route) from the top of the cable-car station in Campo Imperatore is a well-marked, out-and-back route. It is relatively straightforward for most of the way, but taxing for the final short steep climb to the top, where scrambling (using hands) and good route-finding skills will come in handy. The mountain is generally climbable between late June and early October. Choose a clear windless day.

DURATION 5-6hrs
DIFFICULTY Hard
DISTANCE 9km

MATTEO GABRIELI/SHUTTERSTOCK ©

ASSERGI TO SAN PIETRO DELLA LENCA

From the medieval lanes of Assergi, 15km northeast of L'Aquila, this hike explores the Valle del Vasto in the shadow of Gran Sasso mountains (pictured).

Exit the village on Via delle Ville and head northwest toward San Pietro, passing the Grotta a Male, an impressive cave complex, en route. The sanctuary of San Pierto della Lenca in a tiny hamlet is dedicated to Pope Jean Paul II, who was a regular visitor in the 1980s and '90s. Loop back to Assergi on a vehicle track that parallels your outgoing path slightly to the north.

DURATION 4hrs
DIFFICULTY Easy
DISTANCE 11km

ORFENTO GORGE

From the salubrious spa town of Caramanico Terme in the heart of the Majella National Park, this short walk delves into a deep verdant river gorge bisected by wooden bridges that feels eerily distant from the nearby town.

From the town visitor-centre-cum-museum, take the descending path with steps down to the river where a sharp left will direct you through the narrowest and most dramatic sections of the gorge with its overhanging cliffs. On reaching a road bridge, take the zigzagging path up and head back into town along the road.

DURATION 2hrs
DIFFICULTY Moderate
DISTANCE 4km

SALINELLO GORGES

In the northeastern corner of the Gran Sasso-Laga National Park, the Salinello Gorges are one of its most spectacular areas, and a designated nature reserve.

The walk starts and finishes at the car park of the enchanting little monastery of Grotte Sant'Angelo, accessed via a signed gravel road from Le Ripe, around 7km southwest of Civitella del Tronto. This is an out-and-back route through steeply stacked woodland, and you can turn around at any stage. For the best gorge views, walk as far as the ruins of Castel Manfrino (4.8km).

DURATION 5hrs
DIFFICULTY Moderate
DISTANCE 9.5km

TUSCANY

20 **Panzano to Radda** A gentle introduction to the wine country between Florence and Siena. **p96**

21 **Castellina to Radda** Undulating rural roads linking two classic Chianti towns. **p98**

22 **Certaldo to San Gimignano** Easy walk that merges with the medieval Via Francigena pilgrim's route. **p100**

23 **Chianti Classico** Vineyards, villas, rural churches and broad bucolic views. **p102**

24 **Tuscan Hill Crests** Quintessential romp through rolling Tuscan landscapes framed by slender cypresses. **p106**

25 **Medieval Towns & Villages** Beautiful *borghi* nestled between the urban bookends of San Gimignano and Volterra. **p110**

Explore
TUSCANY

Low rolling hills, fields full of barley, elegant cypresses and silvery green olives, vines ripening in the late summer sun, an old ruined monastery, a priest careering downhill in a rusty Fiat 500, potted geraniums, cyclists in multicoloured jerseys and a rustic farmhouse reborn as an *agriturismo*. Welcome to Tuscany, fount of Florentine fashion and Sienese art, land that spawned the Renaissance, Leonardo da Vinci, Humanism, the Uffizi, Chianti and a hundred different trails – most of them refreshingly undemanding.

AGRITURISMI

With a landscape dotted with small traditional farmhouses, and a culinary tradition rooted in simple, home-grown food, Tuscany was surely invented with the concept of *agriturismi* in mind. In the circumstances, it's little wonder that these rural farm stays have become almost as popular as deluxe hotels in Florence.

For virgin agri-tourists, the idea is a simple one: ditch your pricey city hotel, learn a few words of passable Italian, and decamp to an idyllic rural farm where the cheese on your breakfast platter probably came from the sheep whose baa-ing just woke you up.

Beyond that, no two *agriturismi* are the same. Some produce olive oil, others raise cattle, and a growing contingent offer surprisingly deluxe digs with additional extras such as swimming pools and cookery classes. Notwithstanding, prices are usually very reasonable.

For hikers, there's an additional bonus: many *agriturismi* in Tuscany are situated on, or close to, major trails. However, due to their burgeoning popularity, it's advisable to book in advance. For more information and/or reservations see www.agriturismo.net or www.agriturismo.it.

CHIANTI

The vineyards in this instantly seductive part of Tuscany sandwiched between Florence and Siena produce the grapes used in namesake Chianti and Chianti Classico: world-famous reds sold under the Gallo Nero (Black Cockerel/Rooster) trademark. Vines aside, this is a glorious historical landscape where you'll encounter honey-coloured stone farmhouses and imposing stone castles built in the Middle Ages by Florentine and Sienese warlords.

Though now part of the province of Siena, the southern section of Chianti (Chianti Senese) was once the stronghold of the Lega del Chianti, a military and administrative alliance within the city-state of Florence. Chianti's northern part sits in the province of Florence (Chianti Fiorentino) and is a popular day trip from that city.

RADDA IN CHIANTI

Set like a medieval crow's nest on a hill crest with sweeping

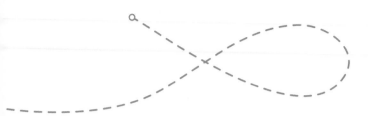

views of vineyard-striped fields, shapely trees and scattered ancient *borghi* (tiny villages), Radda is the Chianti region's most expressive lure. If you're pondering over which 'in Chianti' town to stay in, vacillate no longer. Despite its diminutive size, Radda has a varied stash of accommodation and is a crossroads for copious trails.

SAN GIMIGNANO

Originally an Etruscan village, San Gimignano had morphed into a wealthy fiefdom by the beginning of the 11th century. Flaunting their wealth, the city's powerful families built 72 towers before the plague passed through in 1348, decimating the town's population and leaving all but 14 of the towers in ruins. But the historic legacy was not lost. Today San Gimignano is one of the best-preserved medieval cities in Europe and the clustered towers have earned it the moniker of the 'Manhattan of the Middle Ages'. In summer it is crowded with tourists. But most visitors are day-trippers who rarely venture outside the town walls. After dark, San Gimi maintains a deliciously tranquil allure and the surrounding trails that fan out like a giant spider's

web from the hilltop town are only lightly trodden.

 WHEN TO GO

In spring and autumn, central Tuscany's climate is sunny and mild, and the palettes of seasonal colours are wonderful. At the beginning of October there is the *vendemmia* (grape harvest). In January and February Chianti virtually closes down; summer is the least suitable time for walking due to the sultry heat.

 TRANSPORT

Italy's fast *freccia* trains serve Florence, where you can change onto regional trains calling at Siena or Poggibonsi. To reach the smaller towns of San Gimignano and Radda in Chianti, you'll need to undertake the last leg of the journey by bus from Poggibonsi and Siena respectively.

 WHERE TO STAY

There's no shortage of quality accommodation in Central Tuscany, with San Gimignano and Radda in Chianti providing the best walking bases. Both towns have some fine *locande* (inns)

and country-style hotels. It's also worth considering the innumerable villas and *agriturismi* that dot the countryside hereabouts. Most rural accommodation only opens April to mid-October.

 WHAT'S ON

Expo del Chianti Classico (www.expochianticlassico.com) During its annual wine expo in September, Greve's central piazza is transformed into a huge wine-tasting area, attracting oenophiles from around the world. All of the major producers are represented, and ancillary events include musical performances.

Ferie delle Messi (www. cavalieridisantafina.it) San Gimignano's medieval past is evoked in the third weekend in June through re-enacted battles, archery contests and plays.

20

PANZANO TO RADDA

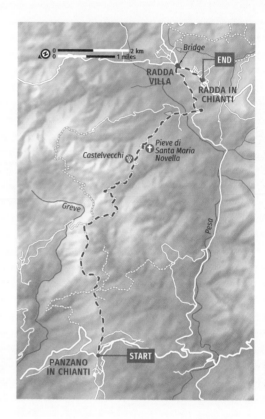

DURATION	DIFFICULTY	DISTANCE	START/END
4hrs	Easy	14.5km	Panzano in Chianti/ Radda in Chianti
TERRAIN	Undulating gravel roads with the last third on paved roads		

Mostly on gravel or paved roads, this foray through gently rolling hills between the two 'in Chianti' towns of Panzano and Radda comes with an abundance of vantage points from which to appreciate the wine-producing beauty of central Tuscany.

Take Via XX Luglio southeast out of Panzano. The road quickly turns to gravel as the houses fall away and a wide **vineyard-striped panorama** opens up to the south.

Keep on this road for the next 4km, parading through a **mixture of hill crests, woods and meadows**, ignoring all turnoffs until you reach a signposted T-junction.

Turn right, following signs to Radda, and begin a descent into mixed woodland on a good gravel road marked 'SP114 Traversa del Chianti'. After 300m, keep right at a second fork and stay left at a third. In 2.5km the wood is interrupted by craning cypresses and then thins out into some **beautiful meadows and cultivated fields**, arriving at the romantic *borgo* of **Castelvecchi** with its onsite winery.

From here a paved road twists down among **olive groves and vineyards** to the charming **Pieve di Santa Maria Novella** (pictured), which retains its original Romanesque structure of three apses.

The descent gets steeper here and reaches a fork in the road. Veer right, cross a bridge and head uphill to the main road, turning left towards Radda in Chianti. You'll need to walk 1.7km on this road until you come to a **red-brick bridge** which you pass under and then cross to put you on the final 1km climb into Radda.

21

CASTELLINA TO RADDA

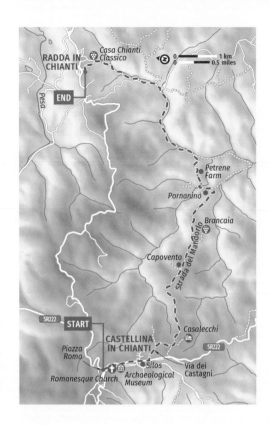

DURATION	DIFFICULTY	DISTANCE	START/END
4hrs	Easy	14km	Castellina in Chianti/ Radda in Chianti

TERRAIN	Undulating dirt and paved roads

Enjoy this relatively modest meander between two historic wine towns that stand like time-warped sentinels at either end of this placid hike.

Established by the Etruscans and fortified by the Florentines in the 15th century, **Castellina** is now a major centre for the wine industry. From the bus stop in Piazza Roma, head southeast along Via Trento e Trieste.

At the renovated **romanesque church** veer right along Via Rocca, passing an **archaeological museum** and Trattoria La Torre. Take the ramp down into Viale IV Novembre and continue south as it merges with the main SR222. Pass the **emblematic town silos** and soon after turn left into Via dei Castagni.

Follow the dirt road as it swings right and uphill, wheeling right at a fork just before a vineyard. The trail winds down to the villa of **Casalecchi**,

where a left turn puts you on a good dirt road, the Strada del Mandorlo, your friend for the next 6km to 7km.

The meandering, undulating road passes various villas like Capovento and wineries such as Brancaia before descending to a farm at **Pornanino**. Turn left here at a large shed, cross a river and take the next right up through woods and vineyards to the **Petrene farm**. From here you can cut along the house's driveway to join another dirt road heading north.

At a T-junction with a paved road, turn left and proceed for 300m before taking a path on the right alongside a river and up a slope to the outskirts of Radda. You'll be delivered next to the **Casa Chianti Classico**, a wine museum and tasting room that, by now, you've clocked enough kilometres to indulge in.

22

CERTALDO TO SAN GIMIGNANO

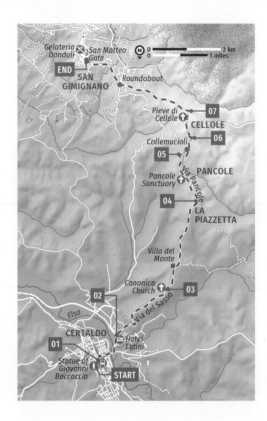

DURATION	DIFFICULTY	DISTANCE	START/END
4hrs	Easy	14km	Certaldo/ San Gimignano

TERRAIN	Mostly quiet paved backroads; the last 2km on a busier provincial road

Like a medieval sandwich with two handsome historic towns at either end and a typical Tuscan filling of mossy churches, hump-backed hills and voluptuous villas, this walk is easy on the eyes and legs.

GETTING HERE

Certaldo (pictured) is on the main train line between Florence and Siena. It is also accessible by direct bus from San Gimignano.

STARTING POINT

The walk starts in the main square of Certaldo, which is guarded by an impressive statue of native son and scribe Giovanni Boccaccio. Standing facing the Municipio building, take the road on the left: Via XX Settembre.

01 Turn left at the T-junction onto Via Giacomo Matteotti and then right into Via Trieste, following signs for San Gimignano. Cross a railway track, a bridge, a roundabout and a second bridge before turning left onto **Viale del Platani**.

02 After less than 400m, you'll see the hotel-restaurant Latini and a paved road leading to the right with a blue sign indicating Pancole and Fattoria del Monte. The walk follows this road, rising gently southeast among houses, then **vineyards and olive groves**, and quickly affords **beautiful views** of Certaldo to the northeast and (later) San Gimignano to the south.

03 After about 3km of climbing on the road, you reach the little church of **Canonica**, where a double row of cypress trees lines the road up to the **majestic Villa del Monte**. The undulating road continues for another 2.5km to the *borgo* of **La Piazzetta**.

📖🖊 Boccaccio

The great Italian author, poet and humanist, Giovanni Boccaccio, is popularly regarded as one of Tuscany's most famous literary sons. He was most likely born in Certaldo in 1313 and certainly died in the town in 1375 after an influential career capped by the publication in the early 1350s of the seminal *The Decameron*, a collection of 100 bawdy fables about love in all its incarnations. For literary scholars, *The Decameron* came to define vernacular Italian in the same way that Chaucer's *The Canterbury Tales* would ultimately define Old English. Indeed, today Boccaccio, along with Petrarch and Dante, is considered to be one of the three founding fathers of the modern Italian language.

DRIMAFILM/SHUTTERSTOCK ©

04 Veer left at a fork following the Via Francigena sign and enter the larger *borgo* of **Pancole**. The **17th-century sanctuary** on the far side of Pancole was originally built in 1670, but was destroyed by the Germans in WWII. The existing road-spanning arch was rebuilt in 1949.

05 About 1km past the sanctuary, turn right on a hill onto a dirt track signposted **Collemucioli**. The track bends to the left and leads up past a **farmhouse** and through an **olive grove and garden**.

06 At a T-junction, turn left and then right at a small Via Francigena sign. Forging uphill, you'll pass through a recently restored *borgo* with a lovely tower. Continue along this road, passing under an archway, and you'll come to a wide clearing aside the splendid **Pieve di Cellole**, a working monastery with an adjoining church and small shop run by monks.

07 Descend south on a paved road that, after 300m, meets up with provincial SP63, where you turn left. This road can be busy; there are some blind bends so proceed with caution. At a roundabout, follow signs for San Gimignano and make use of the pavement for the last couple of kilometres. Just before reaching town, veer right onto Via Niccolo Cannicci, which takes you up to the **San Matteo gate**.

Hold off your hunger pangs, if you can, until you reach San Gimignano. **Gelateria Dondoli** (☎ 0577 94 22 44; www.gelateriadipiazza.com; Piazza della Cisterna 4; gelato €2.50-5; ⏰ 9am-11pm summer, to 7.30pm winter, closed mid-Dec–mid-Feb), the town's most famous eatery, is not a trattoria or pizzeria, but a legendary ice cream shop, decorated by multiple 'best ice cream in the world' awards and so popular its queues sometimes stretch right across the main square.

23

CHIANTI CLASSICO

DURATION	DIFFICULTY	DISTANCE	START/END
5½hrs	Moderate	18km	Radda in Chianti/ Vagliagli
TERRAIN	Undulating dirt roads with some easy single-track footpaths		

A Tuscan classic during which you can practically taste the fermenting grapes. This pastoral jaunt snakes along rutted farm roads, sloping vineyards and gnarly woodland on its way past medieval *pievi* (rural churches), farms reconfigured as *agriturismi* and deluxe villas. It's vintage in more ways than one.

GETTING HERE

Radda in Chianti is connected by several daily buses to both Siena and Florence.

STARTING POINT

Head out from the eastern side of the small circular urban hub of Radda in Chianti.

01 Descend east on the busy paved road to Villa Radda, 1km east of Radda in Chianti. Cross a bridge, descend to a roundabout and take the first exit (east).

02 In 300m turn right off the main road just past **Villa Miranda**. A pleasant little country road heads south into a small, cultivated valley. You'll pass the **ancient tower of Canvalle** on the right as you head up the other side of the valley.

03 Soon after, as the paved road descends to the right at a junction, continue straight on along a stony track heading up into the forest. In a few minutes you'll join another track: follow it straight ahead along a hill-crest, ignoring any deviations. Pass a wooden cross encircled by cypresses and enjoy views over the territory of Radda to the right and the **towers of Vertine and the 16th-century Villa Vistarenni** (pictured) to the left.

04 Continue to a wide, grassy clearing with a four-way crossroads. Go straight ahead here, following the main dirt road downhill (it curves slightly to the right) until you reach a T-junction where you turn right downhill in the direction of San Giusto in Salcio.

05 The road now descends in a couple of steep curves past fields and farm buildings, veering right at a Y-junction, crossing a **little bridge over a stream**, and leading to a paved road at the valley bottom, where you turn left.

06 About 100m along the road there's a turnoff for Vagliagli–San Fedele on the right. Ignore it and continue on the paved road for another 200m before turning right (signposted Poggio Antinora) onto the cypress-lined dirt road to reach **Pieve di San Giusto in Salcio** (pictured). This 11th-century, triple-apsed church is marvellously positioned among ancient farmhouses, grassy courtyards and centuries-old trees.

07 Continue past the church and walk uphill until you meet up with a dirt road, marked by a red-and-white sign on a tree, where you turn left. After 20m you'll reach a three-pronged fork with two parallel dirt roads in front of you (480m); follow the right one for Galenda-Ama. The path follows the course of an **ancient stone wall** on your right. When the wall runs out, the path swerves left downhill before crossing a shallow stream. It then proceeds uphill to **Galenda**, a delightful rural *borgo* where you can make a pleasant rest stop among the cypresses (there's a water fountain here).

08 Leave the *borgo* through the vaulted passageway

Return Walk

If 18km of rolling Tuscan countryside have left you suitably inspired, you can skip the bus ride back to Radda in Chianti (via Siena) and walk instead. A shorter 10km route along the part-paved but refreshingly quiet SP102 links Vagliagli with Radda, passing several wineries and *agriturismi* en route. The road is mainly downhill or flat with a short uphill stretch at the end. Follow the Radda sign just off Vagliagli's main square and keep walking.

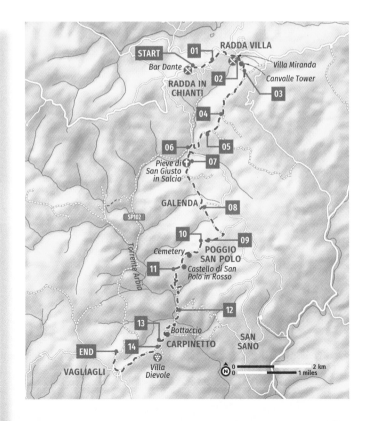

between the houses and, heading south, follow the narrow grassy path that traverses the side of a **vineyard**. Note the small **shrine** on your right. Walk downhill to the bottom of the small valley, cross the stream and dirt road and continue to follow the path uphill (southeast) with vines on your right and olive trees to your left. Go through one iron gate and then another, all the time keeping the vines on your right, until you reach a quiet paved road where you turn right.

09 Within five minutes you will be among the lovely houses of **Poggio San Polo**. Of interest is the ancient *parata* (a kind of vaulted garage for housing farm equipment), which has been transformed into an elegant country home. There's also a good restaurant here, called Il Poggio.

10 Continue your descent on the asphalt road towards Castello di San Polo in Rosso, following Club Alpino Italiano (CAI) route 66. The road becomes a pleasant cypress-lined dirt track, which passes through a forest and leads to a small **cemetery**. There is a **splendid view** of San Polo in Rosso and the Sienese Chianti. Pass an elegant *casale* (farmhouse) with a portico surmounted by a rustic, double-arched window and you'll soon reach the ancient **Castello di San Polo in Rosso**. The 'castle' was founded in AD 1000 as a *pieve* (parish church), fortified in the 13th century and later

MARCO SALLESE/SHUTTERSTOCK ©

embellished with a Renaissance loggia. Unfortunately, it's closed to visitors, although you can admire the grounds.

11 Take the dirt road that heads downhill beside the parking area, passing a house with a lovely staircase supported by a column. The dirt road veers to the left and then winds down into the forest, affording a view of the *pieve* from the south. The road continues its long descent through the forest towards Torrente Arbia. As it gets less road-like and more path-like, you'll begin to notice the rich **birdlife**. As the road-path approaches the bottom of the valley, it crosses a little grassy

bridge spanning a secondary stream next to a ruined building, and continues among the poplars, maintaining a distance from the true left of the river.

12 In a few minutes you'll come to a junction marked with a **miniature shrine**. Turn right and you'll soon come to a small clearing. Just beyond here, the trail crosses the main river, veers to the left and tracks uphill; this old road, used by vehicles until 30 years ago, is now regularly consumed by rainwater. It ascends through the forest in steep, sharp curves, ultimately coming out on a dirt road beside the beautiful restored *casale* of **Bottaccio**. From here you

Chianti Wines

Chianti's blockbuster wines are the ruby-red Chianti and Chianti Classico DOCGs, both of which have a minimum Sangiovese component (75% for Chianti and 80% for Chianti Classico).

The biggest wine-producing estates have *cantine* (cellars) where you can taste and buy wine, but few vineyards – big or small – can be visited without reservations. For a comprehensive list and map of wine estates, buy a copy of *Le strade del Gallo Nero* (€2.50) at the tourist office in Radda in Chianti.

A high-profile consortium of local producers, the Consorzio Vino Chianti Classico (www.chianticlassico.com) operates Casa Chianti Classico in Radda in Chianti, which is home to a small wine museum, *enoteca* and bistro. The *corsorzio*'s website has plenty of information on the wines and wine-related events.

can enjoy the panorama with the village of San Sano nestled among the vineyards.

13 Continue ascending on the dirt road to the southwest of the *casale* and, in 300m, after passing a wall on the left, turn sharp left up some steps and under a passageway to reach the courtyard and Renaissance chapel of the tiny borgo of Carpineto. As you continue uphill on the road, you now have a view of the remarkably beautiful **Crete Senese**, whose dry clay hills are known for their white truffles.

14 Follow the road on the ridge, ignoring the first deviation to the left, and after

a few metres you'll reach a broad semicircle of cypresses. Here you can take the dirt road to the left, descending to the noble manor house of **Villa Dievole**, today an elegant wine resort that's been around in one form or other since the 10th century. To continue to Vagliagli, follow the main cypress-lined road uphill to the asphalt road and turn right. **Vagliagli** is 2km from the entrance to Villa Dievole. Sporadic buses depart the village to Siena, where you can change for Radda.

TAKE A BREAK

No fuss, no pretension, family-run **Bar Dante** (☎ 0577 73 88 15; www.bardantechianti.com; Piazza Dante Alighieri 1; meals €20; ⏰7am-10.30pm; 🚻) is a fine place to plonk down after a long day on your feet, especially if you're in the mood for bruschetta, coffee, cake or simple pastas (best enjoyed on the florid deck out front).

24

TUSCAN HILL CRESTS

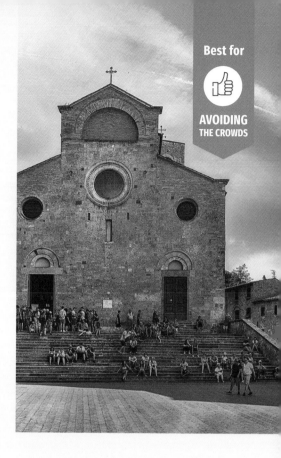

DURATION	DIFFICULTY	DISTANCE	START/END
6hrs	Moderate	20km	San Gimignano

TERRAIN	Mostly dirt roads, several paved sections, grassy paths through olive groves

Starting one small step outside the walls of San Gimignano, but one giant leap from the gelato-consuming tour groups for which the town is famous, this elongated pastoral circuit traverses the little-frequented hill crests of the province's bucolic hinterland.

Journeying mainly through farmland, it syncs briefly with the Via Francigena, the ancient pilgrim's route that links Canterbury with Rome.

GETTING HERE

San Gimignano is connected by regular buses (every 30 minutes) to the town of Poggibonsi and its train station.

STARTING POINT

Starting at San Gimignano's Porta San Giovanni, head south around the Piazzale dei Martiri di Montemaggio to where a flight of steps cuts down to the road below (signposted 'Checkpoint Bus Turistici').

01 Turn right into Via Baccanella following the Via Francigena sign. At the roundabout, take the Volterra exit (straight ahead) and, within 50m, turn left onto a road signposted 'Santa Lucia 2.3 km'. This pleasant lane has a pedestrian pavement for the first kilometre or so and takes you past the **Agriturismo Monte Oliveto**, followed by the **imposing Monte Oliveto Convent** on the right. The convent was founded in 1340 and guards a fresco of the Crucifixion by Renaissance painter Benozzo Gozzoli from the 1460s.

02 Fork right on the edge of Santa Lucia, bypassing the main part of the village. Where the paved road bends right on the other side, stay straight, entering an **olive grove**. The narrow lane leads sharply downhill, passes some handsome country abodes, and veers left at a junction by a **fountain**. Continue downhill and turn right at a T-junction with a dirt road at the bottom of the slope, following signs to Molino di Foci.

03 At the **Molino di Foci B&B**, veer right and push uphill through several switchbacks to a junction on the crest where you fork left (signposted

'Torraccia di Chiusi.') You're now on a magnificent hill crest with **quintessential Tuscan views** towards San Gimignano and its towers to the north. The town looks deliciously tranquil from this vantage, the gelaterie, tour groups and selfie sticks a distant memory.

04 At the **Torraccia di Chiusi** – a tempting *agriturismo* – ignore the Via Francigena sign to the left and continue straight, looping around the building. Veer left behind the house by a pylon and take a grassy track through an olive grove. Enter a wood briefly and then skirt alongside another olive grove to

reach a dirt track leading to the **Fattoria Il Piano** (a farm). Cross this track and the next one and merge with another dirt track leading to the small semi-abandoned *borgo* of **Ciuciano** with its engaging chapel.

05 At a T-junction of dirt roads at the bottom of a short downhill section, go right and head towards **Ranza**, visible in the distance. Ostensibly a typically quaint Tuscan *borgo,* Ranza is also the site of San Gimignano's main prison, the **Casa di Reclusione**, a modern facility located just south of the settlement.

Collegiata

Take time to admire San Gimignano's Romanesque **cathedral** (pictured; Basilica di Santa Maria Assunta; www.duomosangimignano.it; Piazza del Duomo; adult/reduced €4/2; ☺10am-7pm Mon-Sat, 12.30-7pm Sun Apr-Oct, 10am-4.30pm Mon-Sat, 12.30-4.30pm Sun Nov-Mar, closed 2nd half Jan & 2nd half Nov) **before** or after this walk. Parts of it were built in the second half of the 11th century, but its remarkably vivid frescoes, depicting episodes from the Old and New Testaments, date from the 14th century. Look out, too, for the Cappella di Santa Fina near the main altar – a Renaissance chapel adorned with naive and touching frescoes by Domenico Ghirlandaio depicting the life of one of the town's patron saints.

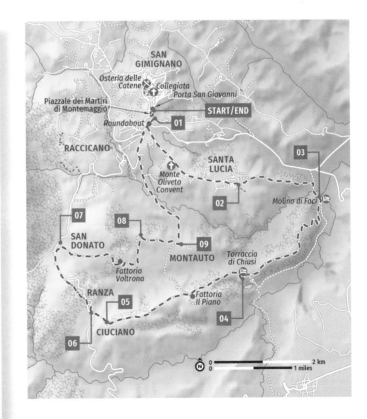

06 Veer right at a fork and pass through the hamlet to arrive at the main road to San Gimignano. Turn right and follow the road for around 100m before ascending on a narrow overgrown path that branches off on the opposite side. This path crests a rise and soon descends to rejoin the main road. Veer left and within a few minutes you'll reach the turnoff for the village of **San Donato** on the right. This is a great place for an elongated rest. The settlement sports a small **chapel-sized church** and a farm-winery called the **Fattoria San Donato** that offers daily tastings. It is also one of several farms in the area that produces saffron. San Gimignano's saffron is famous for its high quality. The violet crocuses have been grown in the area since the 12th century and fortunes were once made in its trade. Changing circumstances meant cultivation died out in the mid-17th century, but the product was enthusiastically reintroduced in the 1990s and has since been designated a PDO (protected designation of origin).

07 From San Donato, turn right at the far end of the village on a dirt road signposted 'Voltrona'. The road with **fine views of San Gimignano** bends left and right before passing the **Fattoria Voltrona**, near a small lake, and ending by a lone house and a wooden 'San Gimignano' sign. Follow the sign along a dried-up riverbed before emerging on the edge of a vineyard. Pitch straight up the vine-striped slope on a tractor track towards a cluster of houses visible on the crest.

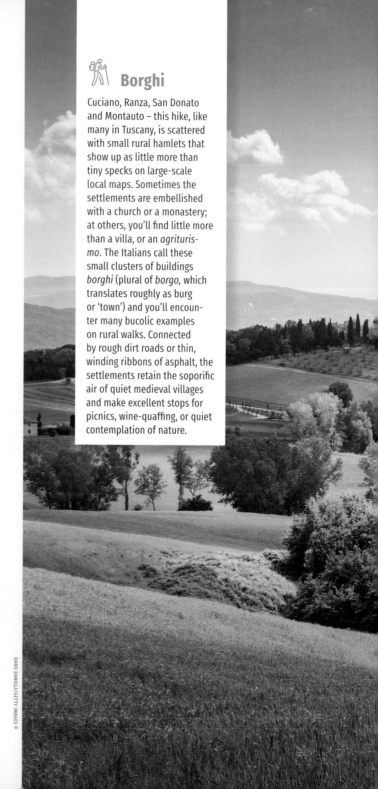

Borghi

Cuciano, Ranza, San Donato and Montauto – this hike, like many in Tuscany, is scattered with small rural hamlets that show up as little more than tiny specks on large-scale local maps. Sometimes the settlements are embellished with a church or a monastery; at others, you'll find little more than a villa, or an *agriturismo*. The Italians call these small clusters of buildings *borghi* (plural of *borgo*, which translates roughly as burg or 'town') and you'll encounter many bucolic examples on rural walks. Connected by rough dirt roads or thin, winding ribbons of asphalt, the settlements retain the soporific air of quiet medieval villages and make excellent stops for picnics, wine-quaffing, or quiet contemplation of nature.

08 Veer right on a dirt road here and you will soon arrive on the edge of the *borgo* of **Montauto**, where the road becomes paved.

09 Turn left before entering the *borgo* onto another paved lane that weaves pleasantly back towards San Gimignano, visible in the distance. After approximately 2km it joins the main Volterra road. Turn right and within 1km you will be delivered back to the main roundabout, from where you can retrace your steps back to the Porta San Giovanni. This **Siennese-style gate** is the most important of the three main entrances to the town and was built, along with the famous 2176m-long walls, in the 1260s. The Via Francigena pilgrim's route passes through the gate and bisects the town before passing under the San Matteo gate and pitching north towards Lucca. From the Porta San Giovanni, the Via Francigena heads south to Siena and Rome.

TAKE A BREAK

Osteria delle Catene (0577 94 19 66; www.osteriadellecatene.it; Via Mainardi 18; mains €30; noon-2pm & 7-9pm Thu-Tue, closed Sun dinner Nov-Mar), 'The Prison', is as popular with San Gimignano locals as it is with visitors, something that can't be said of many places in this tourist-driven town. The menu is full of delightful surprises – dishes are seasonally focussed and many utilise local saffron and Vernaccia wine.

25

MEDIEVAL TOWNS & VILLAGES

Best for

HISTORY & CULTURE

DURATION	DIFFICULTY	DISTANCE	START/END
7hrs	Moderate	26km	San Gimignano/ Volterra

TERRAIN	Mostly dirt roads, some paved sections, a short stony path in the middle

Taking in the full sweep of Tuscan history, this long but easy to negotiate walk links the two walled towns of San Gimignano and Volterra (pictured) and visits the ruins of an early medieval citadel en route. Landscapes sway between gnarly woodland to graceful cypress-lined lanes. Villas, farm stays and bucolic *borghi* dot the countryside.

GETTING HERE

San Gimignano is connected by regular buses (every 30 minutes) to the town of Poggibonsi, from where trains runs to Florence and Siena.

STARTING POINT

Sally forth from the southern San Giovanni gate of San Gimignano.

01 Turn right outside San Gimignano's Porta San Giovanni and take the lane to the left of the car park just off the main plaza, signposted 'Santa Margherita'. After about 600m, pass under a **low bridge** and follow a gravel track on the left. The track loops around the back of a farmhouse, heads uphill and joins a paved road lined with houses.

02 At a T-junction at the top of a rise, turn left and enjoy some **magnificent views** back over San Gimignano. Keep left at a fork and pass through the tiny *borgo* of **Raccicano**. The minor road joins the main road (SP47) on a bend. Turn right and follow the SP47 – which has some wide verges – for 1.5km before turning left into the village of **San Donato**, a tiny, medieval *borgo* with its own *fattoria* (farm) producing wine, olives and saffron. The farm shop offers **wine tasting**.

03 From San Donato's **Romanesque church**, head southwest to rejoin SP47. Turn right onto the road and, after about 30m, turn left and ascend a steep dirt road signposted 'Riserva Naturale di Castelvecchio'. A few steps down the road an informative map-board marks out the details of this **nature reserve**.

04 As the dirt road emerges onto a rocky crest, you'll be able to see the ruins of Castelvecchio dotting the narrow, wooded valley below. Shortly after, the dirt road descends steeply and then goes uphill to a clearing in the woods in front of **La Tenuta di Castelvecchio**, an *agriturismo*.

05 From here descend southeast on a steep and sharply curving trail to reach a ford over the **Botro di Castelvecchio stream**. Once on the other side, continue west along the trail.

06 After a fairly brief climb, you come to a clearing where there is a dirt road closed with a chain. If you want to visit the interesting **ruins of Castelvecchio**, turn left (east) and hop over the chain. You'll probably need about 30 minutes for a decent exploration. If you don't want to visit the ruins, turn right at the clearing and ascend on the dirt road. Cross through woods, ignoring all turnoffs,

until you reach an open plain. The road then passes under some high-tension wires, veers left and gradually descends until it reaches the intersection for the **Casa Campore farm** on your right. Follow the main dirt road to the left (west) and after a little more than 1.5km, you'll reach SP53, locally known as di Poggio Cornocchio.

07 Turn left (south) and walk along the road (which has some light traffic) on a panoramic crest for just over 1km. Here you'll find a dirt road on the right (west), marked with two **stone wayside posts**. Descend among the trees for 300m to

Volterra's Etruscan Museum

The vast collection of artefacts exhibited at Volterra's **Museo Etrusco Guarnacci** (☎ 0588 8 63 47; www.volterratur.it/en/come/arts-culture/the-museum/guarnacci-etruscan-museum; Via Don Minzoni 15; adult/reduced €8/6; ⏲ 9am–7pm mid-Mar–Oct, 10am–4.30pm Nov–mid-Mar) makes this one of Italy's most impressive Etruscan collections. Found locally, they include some 600 funerary urns carved mainly from alabaster and tufa – the *Urna degli sposi* (Urn of the Spouses) is a strikingly realistic terracotta rendering of an elderly couple. The finds are displayed according to subject and era; the best examples (those dating from later periods) are on the 2nd and 3rd floors.

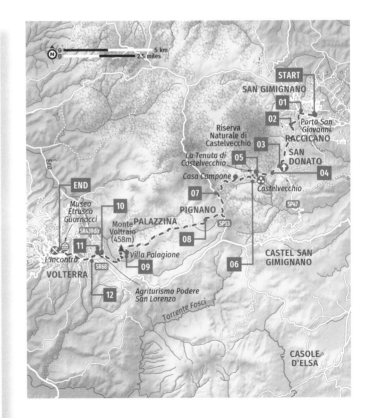

a T-junction with another dirt road, where you head right again. Follow this cypress-lined walk up to the *borgo* of **Pignano**, a rambling country estate reborn as a luxury eco-resort.

08 From Pignano, follow the main dirt road, which descends sharply southwest, to a small **bridge**, offering a panorama over the wooded territory south of Volterra. The route continues ascending west and then descends slightly along the ridge to the buildings of Grignano. Continuing southwest, in 1.3km you arrive at **Palazzina** with its abandoned **12th-century San Lorenzo chapel**. A little more than 2km further on you reach **Villa Palagione**. Built in 1598 under the rocky hump of **Monte Voltraio** (458m), it functions today as a cultural and study centre. If you have the energy, climb the termite mound–shaped *monte*. There is a path just across the road from the entrance Villa Palagione (50 minutes return).

09 From Villa Palagione, continue on the dirt road, which descends in steep, sharp curves southward. Cross a bridge over the **Fiume Era Morta**, continuing northwest until you reach SR439dir, a paved road with signs for Pontedera to the right and Saline di Volterra to the left.

10 Turn left onto the winding state road and, after just 20m, look for trail markers on the guard rail and on a tree, indicating trail 21 to the right. Ascend on a cobbled mossy trail for about 400m until you see the terraced gardens and sandy facade of **Agriturismo Podere San Lorenzo**.

Castelvecchio Nature Reserve

The section of this walk between San Donato and Pignano is protected in a small nature reserve that harbours beech forest, a wintertime population of peregrine falcons and the medieval ruins of the fortified settlement of Castelvecchio.

A citadel first grew up here in the 7th century and, by the 1200s, it had became a fortified garrison in the century-long conflict between San Gimignano and Volterra. Its demise came with the arrival of the plague in the late 1400s, after which it was largely abandoned.

The site was restored by a local historical group in the late 1970s. Today the evocative ruins, including a tower, a chapel and cistern, huddle enigmatically in the fecund forest.

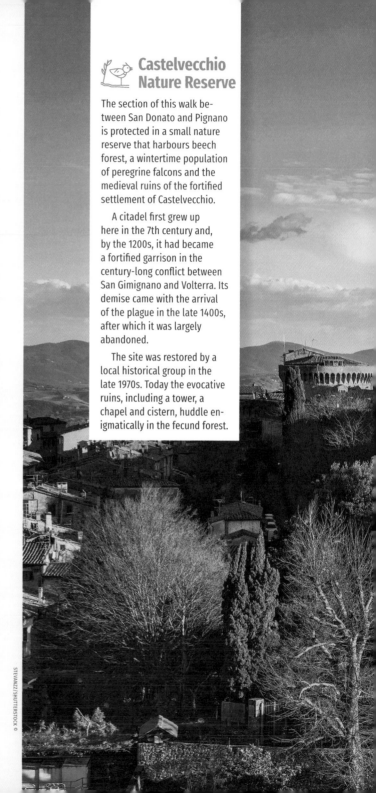

STEVANZZI/SHUTTERSTOCK ©

11 To continue to Volterra, go straight up the San Lorenzo's approach road, ascending among the fields until you reach an **intersection** with another narrow, paved road. Turn left and, in a few metres, you'll be on the SR68 at Strada.

12 Turn right on the state road and continue along the moderately busy road. In about 2km you'll reach **Volterra.** Turn right onto a path just past an Esso garage, ascend the steps and emerge beside an arch that takes you underneath the old **Medici fortress** (pictured) and into the historic town. It was founded by the Etruscans, probably in the 8th century BC, and parts of its walls date from the 3rd century BC. A wander through the winding cobbled streets dotted with **Roman, Etruscan and medieval structures** is a rare pleasure. Look out for **alabaster carving**, part of the town's wealthy artisanal heritage. Volterra's bus station is in Piazza Martiri della Libertà, atop a bluff in the centre of town. Regular buses go to Colle di Val d'Elsa, where you can catch a connecting service back to San Gimignano.

☕ TAKE A BREAK

The rear *salone* of Volterra cafe **L'Incontro** (📞 0588 8 05 00; Via Matteotti 18; panini €2-4, biscuits €1.50-2.50; 🕐 6am-midnight, to 2am summer, closed Wed winter; 📶) is a top spot to grab a quick antipasto plate or *panino* for lunch, and its front bar area is always crowded with locals enjoying coffee or *aperitivi*. The house-baked biscuits are noteworthy – try the chewy and nutty *brutti mai buoni*.

Also Try...

CLAUDIOBEDUSCHI/GETTY IMAGES ©

PROCINTO, FORATO & PANIA DELLA CROCE

Despite the three peaks in the title, this hike is more of a ridge walk than a summit strike. The saw-toothed crest between Procinto and Pania della Croce in the Apuan Alps is a stunner that requires some steep ascents and rocky scrambles.

A highlight is the 'Mountain with a Hole', the local name given to surreally shaped Monte Forato (pictured). The high point is 1858m Pania della Croce, whose summit is reached via a short side trip.

Although the first few kilometres are relatively gentle, the hike has its arduous moments – hand chains over exposed sections – while the wildness of the terrain enables you to feel a degree of poetic isolation. But, surrounded on all sides by marble quarries, clustered Apuan villages and cosy *rifugi*, civilisation is never far away.

DURATION 2 days
DIFFICULTY Hard
DISTANCE 26km

SAN FABIANO TO GREVE IN CHIANTI

On the northern (Florence) side of Chianti, this largely rural walk incorporates mainly paved roads and passes a number of Tuscan *pievi* (rural churches) and abbeys. It starts in San Fabiano, a tiny *borgo* featuring a Romanesque facade that's an hour by bus from Florence.

Follow the Via Fornace Casavecchia past the Castello il Palagio, a small, medieval castle, to the Romanesque Pieve di Santo Stefano a Campo. The grassy churchyard, surrounded by stands of cypresses, provides a pleasant setting to kick back and contemplate this ancient country church, built in the 10th century.

From here, Vias Campoli and Vigondoli wind south past several *agriturismi* as far as the majestic abbey of Badia a Passignano, before pitching east to the important wine-producing town and regional hub of Greve in Chianti.

DURATION 5hrs
DIFFICULTY Easy
DISTANCE 16km

ARIADNA DE RAADT/SHUTTERSTOCK ©

VIA FRANCIGENA

The Via Francigena is an old pilgrims' route that has recently been gaining in popularity thanks, in part, to the renaissance of Spain's Camino de Santiago.

Several sections pass through central Tuscany. The easiest chunk for a day walk is stage 31 between the spa town of Gambassi Terme and San Gimignano, which shares part of its route with our Certaldo to San Gimignano walk. The path is marked with brown signposts and/or red-and-white-backed pilgrim symbols . See www.viefran cigene.org for more information and downloadable maps.

DURATION 4hrs
DIFFICULTY Moderate
DISTANCE 13.5km

CASTELPOGGIO TO CAMPOCECINA

For a mild introduction to Tuscany's Apuan Alps, take this wooded jaunt from the village of Castelpoggio up to the Rifugio Carrara in Campocecina.

This is the first part of the eight-stage 'Alta Via delle Alpi Apuane' and follows track 185 on a gently ascending path to the Gabellaccia Pass at 895m, where it crosses a paved road. The path continues in a mainly easterly direction, passing rock walls, caves and an unusual natural arch before it hits the road again at the former shepherd's settlement of Acquasparta.

DURATION 2½hrs
DIFFICULTY Moderate
DISTANCE 5km

LUCCA'S CITY WALLS

Lucca's *mura* (wall; pictured) was built in the 16th and 17th centuries and is still in fantastic condition.

Twelve metres high and approximately 4km long, today's ramparts are crowned with a footpath looking down on the historic centre and – by the Baluardo San Regolo (San Regolo Bastion) – the city's vintage Orto Botanico with its magnificent centurion cedar trees.

The wall-top path is a favourite location for the locals' *passeggiata* (evening stroll). Children's climbing frames, swings and picnic tables beneath plane trees add a buzz of weekend activity.

DURATION 1hr
DIFFICULTY Easy
DISTANCE 4km

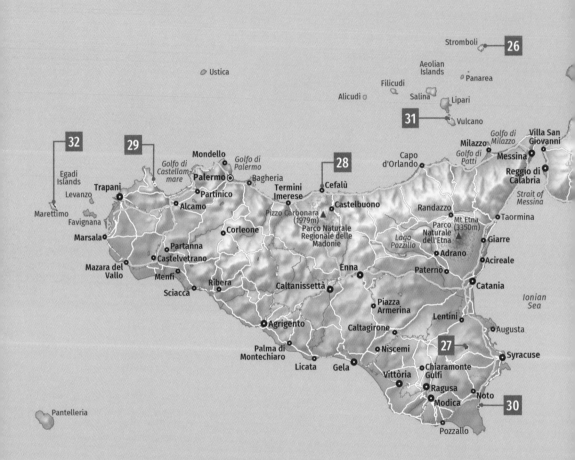

Tyrrhenian
Sea

26

Stromboli

Aeolian
Islands

Panarea

Filicudi

Ustica

Alicudi

Salina

Lipari

31

Vulcano

Golfo di
Milazzo

Villa San
Giovanni

Milazzo

32

29

Mondello

Golfo di
Palermo

Capo
d'Orlando

Golfo di
Patti

Messina

Reggio di
Calabria

Egadi
Islands

Golfo di
Castellam-
mare

Palermo

Bagheria

28

Cefalù

Randazzo

Strait of
Messina

Levanzo

Trapani

Partinico

Termini
Imerese

Castelbuono

Taormina

Marettimo

Favignana

Alcamo

Pizzo Carbonara
(1979m)

Mt Etna
(3350m)

Giarre

Marsala

Corleone

Parco Naturale
Regionale delle
Madonie

Lago
Pozzillo

Parco
Naturale
dell'Etna

Acireale

Partanna

Castelvetrano

Adrano

Mazara del
Vallo

Menfi

Ribera

Enna

Paternò

Catania

Sciacca

Caltanissetta

Ionian
Sea

Agrigento

Piazza
Armerina

Lentini

Augusta

Caltagirone

Palma di
Montechiaro

Niscemi

27

Syracuse

Licata

Gela

Vittòria

Chiaramonte
Gulfi

Pantelleria

Ragusa

Noto

30

Modica

Pozzallo

Mediterranean
Sea

MALTA

★VALLETTA

Linosa

SICILY

26 **Stromboli** Watch eruptions illuminate the sky from atop this island volcano. **p120**

27 **Necropoli di Pantalica** Follow the Anapo River between limestone walls riddled with ancient tombs. **p122**

28 **La Rocca di Cefalù** Climb to a ruined castle overlooking Cefalù's stunning Arab-Norman cathedral. **p124**

29 **Riserva Naturale dello Zingaro** Zigzag among coves in Sicily's oldest nature reserve. **p126**

30 **Oasi Faunistica di Vendicari** Wander past flamingo-dotted lagoons and photogenic ruins to a pretty beach. **p130**

31 **Fossa di Vulcano** Hold your nose and conquer the rim of this sulphur-belching volcanic crater. **p132**

32 **Punta Troia** Walk to the far tip of an idyllic offshore island. **p134**

Explore
SICILY

For lovers of volcanoes, islands and rugged coastlines, few walking destinations compare with Sicily. The arc of fire that starts at Naples' Mt Vesuvius resurfaces in Sicily's seven volcanic sisters – the Aeolian Islands – and reaches its pinnacle at Mt Etna, Europe's loftiest active volcano. Sicily's Mediterranean, Tyrrhenian and Ionian shorelines abound in idyllic coastal strolls. Offshore, another half-dozen islands offer scenic ambles on traffic-free roads and trails, while inland the Madonie and Nebrodi mountains are home to some superb off-the-beaten-track walking. Adding icing to the cake are Sicily's exceptional home-grown cuisine and seemingly countless layers of history.

CATANIA

Perfectly placed for climbs up Mt Etna, vibrant Catania (Sicily's second-largest city) sits smack at the foot of the volcano, many of its grey-hued buildings built directly from the debris hurled down during the disastrous eruption of 1669. For all its noise, chaos and scruffiness, Catania compensates with cool and gritty bars, an earthy spirit and a Unesco-listed historic core where *palazzi* tower over sweeping baroque piazzas. Food is another local forte. This is the home of Sicily's iconic *pasta alla Norma* and the extraordinary La Pescheria fish market.

NOTO

A lovely base for hikers planning excursions to nearby Vendicari and Pantalica, the honey-coloured hill town of Noto is home to one of Sicily's most beautiful historic centres, rebuilt in the early 18th century after a devastating 1693 earthquake. Claiming centre stage is Corso Vittorio Emanuele, an elegant walkway flanked by baroque *palazzi* and churches. Dashing at any time of the day, it's especially hypnotic in the early evening, when the red-gold buildings seem to glow with a soft inner light.

LIPARI

The Aeolian Islands' main transport hub, Lipari retains a charming, laid-back island vibe while offering a full range of tourist services. The clifftop citadel and archaeological museum make a nice half-day diversion, and there are excellent day hikes along the island's north and west coasts – but it's also lovely to simply stroll Lipari's labyrinthine alleyways or sip drinks at sunset down by the Marina Corta docks. Lipari's many boat operators offer daily hiking excursions to Stromboli, while hydrofoils make frequent connections to Vulcano and other islands in the archipelago.

CEFALÙ

Huddled beneath the imposing cliffs of La Rocca, Cefalù is one

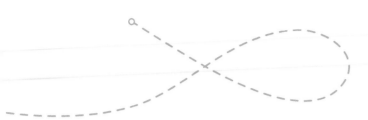

of Sicily's most photogenic seaside towns. The big draws here are Cefalù's gorgeous beaches, side-by-side with one of Sicily's greatest Arab-Norman cathedrals – and a compact medieval centre packed with squares and alleys perfect for slow, pedestrianised meandering. Cefalù makes a convenient base for hiking in the nearby Monti Madonie, and its location on Sicily's main north-coast train line makes it an easy stopover between Palermo and the Aeolian Islands ferry docks at Milazzo.

SCOPELLO

The seaside hamlet of Scopello couldn't be more charming if it tried. Built around an 18th-century *baglio* (fortified manor house), the village centre is graced by white houses and smooth-stone streets, with a historic *tonnara* (tuna fishery) on the shoreline below. Scopello's handful of hotels, *pensioni* and restaurants make it a tranquil base for exploring the adjacent Zingaro nature reserve and nearby treasures such as Segesta and Erice. When it's time to move on, you're only a 45-minute drive from Palermo airport or the docks at Trapani, where hydrofoils sail for the Egadi Islands.

 WHEN TO GO

Spring and autumn are delightful seasons for hiking along the coast, especially May, September and October when prices are lower, beach crowds thinner and temperatures pleasant. March and October are good for flamingo sightings in Vendicari. High-altitude destinations such as Mt Etna and the Monti Madonie and Nebrodi are suitable any time between May and October.

 TRANSPORT

There's frequent hydrofoil service to the Aeolian and Egadi Islands from Milazzo and Trapani, respectively. Reliable train service in Sicily is largely limited to the Tyrrhenian and Ionian coasts, from Palermo to Messina and from Messina to Syracuse. Buses serve many interior towns, but you'll generally need your own wheels to reach the more remote trailheads.

 WHERE TO STAY

Accommodation in Sicily runs the gamut from resort hotels to reasonably priced B&Bs. Some

Resources

Arbatus (www.arbatus.com) Publishes excellent multilingual trekking maps and guides for each of the seven Aeolian islands.

Assessorato Turismo Sport e Spettacolo (www.visitsicily. info) Sicily's official regional tourist authority.

Stella Alpina (www.stella -alpina.com) Sells Selca's 1:25,000 *Mt Etna – Carta Escursionistica Altomontana* for walks around Mt Etna.

of the most attractive options for walkers are the *pensioni* (smaller family-run hotels) and *agriturismi* (farm stays, often serving food grown onsite) that abound in smaller towns and rural areas.

 **WHAT'S ON**

Pasqua (Easter) Solemn processions and passion plays mark Holy Week in March or April.

Festival del Teatro Greco (www.indafondazione.org) World-class actors celebrating Greek theatre stage dramas in Syracuse's 5th-century-BC amphitheatre in May and June.

Cous Cous Fest (www.couscous fest.it) International musicians and chefs gather for 10 days in the last week of September to celebrate western Sicily's famous fish couscous.

26

STROMBOLI

DURATION	DIFFICULTY	DISTANCE	START/END
5hrs	Moderate	14km	Piazza San Vincenzo

TERRAIN	Steep volcanic slopes

No destination in Italy tantalises like Stromboli. This charismatic little island at the Aeolian archipelago's eastern edge has been spewing red-hot rock since the age of Odysseus. Gazing down from its summit at sunset, with daylight's last glow shimmering on the Tyrrhenian Sea and the crater's fireworks exploding into a darkening sky overhead, is a volcano-lover's dream come true.

GETTING HERE

Ferries and hydrofoils serve Stromboli from Milazzo and Naples. Piazza San Vincenzo, where most tours start, is a 10-minute walk from the docks.

STARTING POINT

Surrounded by restaurants, bars and shops, Piazza San Vincenzo is the hub of Stromboli village.

01 Hikers begin assembling every afternoon about three hours before sunset in **Piazza San Vincenzo**. From here, the walk's first stage leads gently uphill along a glorified sidewalk at the edge of town, but you soon veer right and begin climbing a well-trodden trail through a landscape of yellow broom and wild capers. As you climb, the village of Stromboli assumes dollhouse-like proportions below, with the town's **walled cemetery** and the **San Vincenzo church tower** providing convenient landmarks.

02 An hour or so of climbing brings you to the tree line, where the trail opens onto bare slopes of black volcanic rock, revealing distant vistas of Stromboli town, the sparkling sea and the tiny volcanic islet of **Strombolicchio**. Silhouetted against the late afternoon sky, a zigzag line of fellow hikers slogs steadily across the slopes above towards the summit.

Stromboli Climbing Tips

- You're required to hire a guide if climbing above 400m.
- Many agencies lead tours, but it's still best to reserve ahead. Group size is limited to 20, and kids under seven aren't allowed to climb.
- The standard fee for all guided group tours is €28 per person.
- You'll need hiking boots, a torch (flashlight) and a pack large enough to hold warm clothes for the summit. All these items can be rented from Totem Trekking in Piazza San Vincenzo.

HEMIS/ALAMY STOCK PHOTO ©

03 Crest the summit after what may seem like an eternity (it's actually closer to two or 2½ hours), and emerge into a surreal landscape of **smouldering craters** framed by the setting sun. The weather up top is often quite a bit colder than at the base, and guides generally give their groups time to rest and add layers under a pair of concrete mountaintop shelters. For the next 45 minutes you're treated to full-on **views of Stromboli's pyrotechnics from a perfect vantage point** above the craters. The periodic eruptions grow ever brighter against the darkening sky, changing with the waning light from awe-inspiring

puffs of grey smoke to fountains of brilliant orange-red, evoking oohs and aahs that mix with the sound of sizzling hot rocks rolling down the mountainside.

04 Ready for one last moment of magic? Don your headlamp for the descent, and join the single-file line of hikers plunging across the talus-strewn wasteland of **Stromboli's precipitous eastern slope**, with the moonlit sea at your feet stretching clear to the twinkling lights of Italy's mainland. The trail down is steeper and dustier that the path you came up on, so you'll need high-top hiking boots and a bandana to keep the

fine volcanic sand out of your socks and lungs. About halfway down, groups enjoy a rest stop to shed layers and shake out shoes before continuing back to Stromboli town.

TAKE A BREAK

Before heading up the mountain, get your sugar fix at **Lapillo Gelato**, an amazing gelateria on Via Roma. Afterwards, unwind with pizzas and beer on the panoramic terrace at **Ritrovo Ingrid**, a Stromboli institution on the main church square.

27

NECROPOLI DI PANTALICA

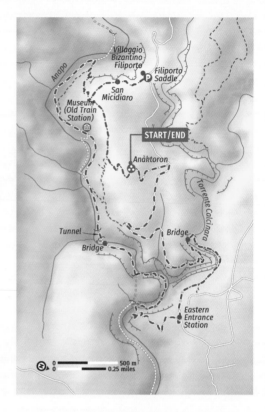

DURATION	DIFFICULTY	DISTANCE	START/END
4hrs	Moderate	12km	Anàktoron parking area

TERRAIN	Rocky trails, converted railway bed

With its thousands of ancient tombs honeycombed into the limestone cliffs west of Syracuse, Pantalica (pictured) is Sicily's most important Iron and Bronze Age necropolis. This engaging loop weaves past stone-carved burial chambers and into the lush Anapo and Calcincara river gorges.

Begin at a dirt parking area 11km east of Ferla, next to the scant foundations of the **Anàktoron**, a ruined prince's palace. Follow signs initially for Valle dell'Anapo, then Villaggio Bizantino Filiporto. The latter (reached after 1.5km) is one of Pantalica's best-preserved **necropolises**, with an eerie series of stone openings peering like eyes from the cliff face.

Enjoy **stunning views** of the cliff-framed Anapo valley as the trail descends to meet an old riverside railway bed. An abandoned train station here serves as a **cultural museum** filled with artefacts of Sicilian rural life. Follow the tree-shaded valley floor past citrus orchards and colourful cliff faces, through a tunnel and over a couple of bridges.

After an hour in the valley, cross the Anapo on stepping stones, following signs for Saramenzana. Climb a dirt road to Pantalica's eastern entrance station and turn left, passing through a gate onto a narrower path marked 'Fiume Calcinara/Necropoli Nord'. You'll soon pass a rock face on your right pockmarked with more **stone-cut tombs**.

Ignore a left-hand turnoff pointing straight down to the Grotta dei Pipistrelli (Bat Cave), opting instead for the slightly more gradual descent to pools along the **Fiume Calcinara**. Cross the river and climb to a signposted dirt road that leads back to the Anàktoron (total walking time from the Saramenzana entrance about 1½ hours).

28

LA ROCCA DI CEFALÙ

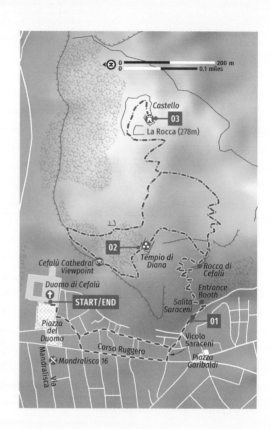

DURATION	DIFFICULTY	DISTANCE	START/END
1½hrs	Moderate	3km	Piazza del Duomo, Cefalù

TERRAIN	Staircases and rocky trails

Towering high above Cefalù's sandy beach and Arab-Norman cathedral, the craggy outcrop of La Rocca makes an exhilarating half-day adventure. The 45-minute ascent traverses pine-dotted slopes and old town walls to reach the vertiginous 270m summit. Along the way, enjoy pretty views of the cathedral's honey-coloured towers juxtaposed against the deep blue sea. Crowning the hilltop are a ruined 12th-century Norman castle super-imposed on a 9th-century Arab citadel, surrounded by sweeping 360-degree panoramic views.

GETTING HERE

Cefalù (pictured p13, p117) is on the main Palermo to Messina train line, served by dozens of trains daily. The Duomo is a 10-minute walk northeast of the station.

STARTING POINT

The Duomo is the focal point of Cefalù's pedestrianised centre, surrounded by restaurants, bar-cafes and other facilities. Parking in downtown Cefalù is nearly impossible.

01 Head south from the cathedral square into Cefalù's narrow streets, walking 300m down bustling Corso Ruggero and turning left onto narrow Vicolo Saraceni. From here, the ancient stone staircase known as **Salita Saraceni** begins winding up the hillside. Pay admission (€4) at the La Rocca entrance booth on your left and continue climbing. Within 10 minutes, cross through the first tier of Cefalù's crenellated town walls, enjoying splendid views over the Tyrrhenian, with a steep rock face in the foreground framing the long sweep of shoreline to your left.

Cefalù's Magnificent Cathedral

One of the jewels in Sicily's Arab-Norman crown, Cefalù's magnificent palm-fringed 12th-century Duomo (pictured) earned Unesco World Heritage status in 2015, along with Palermo's Cappella Palatina and the Cattedrale di Monreale. Filling the central apse, a towering figure of Cristo Pantocratore (Christ All Powerful) is the focal point of the elaborate Byzantine mosaics – Sicily's oldest and best preserved.

Best for

QUAINT VILLAGES

GREGOR CLARK/LONELY PLANET ©

02 Turn left at a junction just up the hill, following signs for Tempio di Diana. Here the trail opens onto a high plateau. Continue straight to the cliff's edge, where guardrails allow you to peer straight down over the imposing fortress-like cathedral and the red tile rooftops of Cefalù's medieval centre, which contrast with the deep blue sea far below. Circle back from the **cathedral viewpoint** and stop in at the **Tempio di Diana**, a megalithic structure dating to the 4th or 5th century BC, built of limestone blocks quarried directly from the mountainside. On the same site are a sacred dolmen-type cistern dating to the 8th or 9th century BC, and the remains of a Byzantine church dedicated to St Venera.

03 A wooden signpost directs you uphill towards the **Castello**, which you'll reach after a steady 15- to 20-minute climb. A longtime stronghold for both the Arabs and the Normans, the remains of the castle feature a few decaying battlements commanding exceptional views east and west along the Tyrrhenian coast. A straightforward if sometimes steep trail descends from the castle through open fields bordered by eucalyptus trees to rejoin the trail you came up on. From here, simply retrace your steps to the Duomo.

TAKE A BREAK

Picturesque setting combines with scrumptious Sicilian cuisine at **Mandralisca 16** (0921 99 22 45; www.facebook.com/mandralisca16; Via Mandralisca 16; meals €25-35; noon-3pm & 7-11pm Tue-Sun), a bistro with sidewalk seating in an alley gazing up at Cefalù's cathedral towers. Start with a perfect *caponata* (eggplant, olives, capers, onions and celery in a sweet-and-sour tomato sauce), then move on to chickpea, chard and sage soup or *involtini* (roulades) of fish with citrus, bay leaves and breadcrumbs.

29

RISERVA NATURALE DELLO ZINGARO

Best for

COASTAL SCENERY

DURATION	DIFFICULTY	DISTANCE	START/END
4–5hrs	Moderate	14km	Scopello entrance

TERRAIN	Undulating coastal hike on dirt paths

Riserva Naturale dello Zingaro (pictured) shelters one of Sicily's most gorgeous and readily accessible stretches of wild coastline. A network of well-maintained and signposted trails weaves through the park – but the indisputable highlight is the 7km walk hugging the shoreline between the park's Scopello and San Vito Lo Capo entrances. From the main coastal path, side trails fan out to a series of beaches and small museums focusing on the Zingaro's cultural and natural history.

GETTING HERE

From the town of Scopello, take the SP63 north 2km; the road dead ends at a parking area adjacent to the park's southern entrance.

STARTING POINT

The walk starts and ends at the park ticket office, where you'll find trail maps and an occasional food truck selling drinks and snacks.

01 Within paces of the park entrance, you'll pass through a **two-lane tunnel** blasted into the rock. This marks the beginning of the would-be highway through the Zingaro that was cancelled in the early 1980s due to local opposition. As you enter the tunnel, look along the side of the trail for **wooden cutouts** commemorating the 3000 people who staged a pivotal protest march along this stretch of coast in May 1980, eventually leading to the establishment of the Zingaro nature reserve.

02 After a brief initial downhill, the trail climbs gently to a right-hand turnoff for the **Museo Naturalistico**, worth a quick visit for its exhibits on the Zingaro's flora, fauna and geology. Lovingly rendered dioramas and drawings introduce you to key park inhabitants, from kestrels, owls and Bonelli's eagles to foxes, dormice and hedgehogs. Additional exhibits feature the Zingaro's wild orchids, geophytes, ferns, lichens and mushrooms, along with medicinal herbs and endemic plants such as the Sicilian snapdragon and yellow star thistle.

03 **The beautiful crescent-shaped cove of Cala Capreria** comes into view a few

hundred metres north of the museum. A side path descends here to meet the pebbly beach and turquoise waters below.

04 Rejoin the main trail, climbing steadily uphill for about 1km to the **spectacular viewpoint overlooking Punta Leone**. Here you enjoy your first long views north along the rugged coast, stretching all the way to the park's northern entrance 5km ahead.

05 A few paces downhill, the **Museo della Manna** appears on the left-hand side of the trail. This converted one-room cottage traces Sicily's

long history of producing manna, the natural sweetener celebrated in the Bible and derived from the sap of the manna ash tree *(Fraxinus ornus)*. Manna production was once common throughout Sicily, including the Zingaro area, but is now limited to the towns of Castelbuono and Pollina in the Monti Madonie.

06 Enjoy more fine views north along the coast as you descend along a wooden fence to a right-hand turnoff for two small beaches tucked into rocky coves. **Cala della Disa**, popular with families, is a shady fine-shingle beach with shallow

Sicily's Original Nature Reserve

The idyllic coastal trail featured in this walk was supposed to be a highway – that is, until concerned local citizens intervened to conserve the Zingaro as Sicily's very first Riserva Naturale. In the late 1970s, planners had begun work to extend the SP63 north from Scopello to San Vito Lo Capo, which would have forever changed this pristine stretch of coast. In spring 1980, a multi-generational mix of residents and environmentalists joined to protest the proposed road, organising a march through the Zingaro that drew 3000 people and turned the tide in favour of creating the new park.

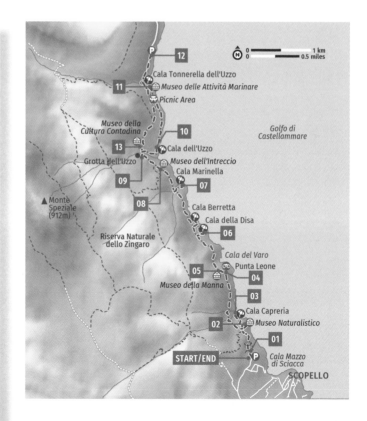

water, while **Cala Berretta**, just to the north, has big rocks perfect for sunbathing. Along the way, you'll pass a sign on the right for *frutta fresca* – fresh fruit sold by the Zingaro's lone remaining resident, Massimo Amodeo; it's worth popping in to see if he's home!

07 You're now roughly at the trail's midpoint, where a relatively flat stretch leads past a pair of pretty houses on the left painted yellow and salmon pink, shaded by trees and backed by the Zingaro's steep slopes. Nearby, you'll pass another turnoff on the right for **Cala Marinella**. There's no beach as such, but snorkellers love the piercing emerald green waters here, accessed directly from the rocks.

08 A few hundred metres further on, watch for a right-hand turnoff for the wonderful **Museo dell'Intreccio** (Weaving Museum). Housed in an attractive two-room stone building with a red tile roof, the museum is flanked by a few fine examples of the *Palma nana* (European fan palm tree), whose fronds were traditionally woven by Zingaro residents to create functional and aesthetically pleasing household objects. Inside the main room you'll find a full spectrum of locally woven pieces, including baskets, mats, hats, chair seats and an impressive cylindrical grain storage silo. Upstairs, a second room houses more contemporary woven pieces designed by students from the University of Palermo; the sur-

GANDOLFO CANNATELLA/SHUTTERSTOCK ©

rounding walls are decorated with hand-painted frescoes left behind by a German hermit named Hans, who lived here with his dogs in the 1970s.

09 Next stop is the **Grotta dell'Uzzo**, a massive cave reached by a short descent about 15 minutes north of the Museo dell'Intreccio. (En route, ignore a sign on the left for the spur trail to Sughero and Borgo Cosenza, and continue straight on the main trail.) During the Mesolithic period, the cave offered shelter to hunter-gatherers who left behind one of the Mediterranean's most impressive necropolises. These days its most striking feature is its size, with sheer walls of orange and grey rock towering dozens of metres overhead.

10 Turn right towards the coast, following signs to **Cala dell'Uzzo**, the Zingaro's largest and most popular beach. A five-minute walk brings you to this attractive stretch of pebble-strewn sand backed by cacti and fan palms, where swimmers and sunbathers congregate in good weather.

11 Beyond the beach, the trail continues north along the shoreline, passing a **terraced picnic area** with tables and benches where you can break for a snack. Two minutes north of the picnic area you'll come to the Zingaro's former tuna-processing plant, Tonnarella dell'Uzzo, now converted into a museum, the **Museo delle Attività Marinare**. The collection here includes

An easy 35-minute drive south of Scopello, the ancient temple and amphitheatre at Segesta constitutes one of Sicily's most evocative and enduring archaeological highlights. Set on the edge of a deep canyon amid desolate mountains, these 5th-century BC ruins are all that remains of the principal city of the Elymians, an ancient civilisation claiming descent from the Trojans that settled in Sicily in the Bronze Age. Segesta's centrepiece is its remarkably well preserved temple, with a full set of Doric columns topped by a perfectly intact entablature and pediment, standing in splendid isolation amid fields of wildflowers and grasses. Occasional music concerts held beneath the stars in the amphitheatre just up the hill are nothing short of magical.

framed portraits of local fish and fishermen and a map of Sicily's tuna fisheries – but perhaps most interesting is the series of newspaper articles and photos documenting the protest marches that helped create the Zingaro nature reserve back in 1980.

12 Just below the museum, a side path descends to **Cala Tonnarella dell'Uzzo** (pictured above and on p12), a semicircular beach picturesquely framed by low cliffs and Mediterranean *macchia*. From here, a 10-minute uphill walk brings you to the park's **northern (San Vito Lo Capo) entrance**, where you'll begin the two-hour hike back south to Scopello.

13 About 15 minutes into your return journey, detour briefly inland to visit the last of the park's five museums, the **Museo della Cultura Contadina**. The collection here showcases the Zingaro's rural traditions, with displays of traditional farm equipment and cooking utensils, and bilingual photo exhibits documenting the Zingaro's annual agricultural cycle of ploughing, sowing, reaping, threshing and storage. Retrace your steps back to the Scopello entrance, another 1¾ hours south along the main coastal trail.

TAKE A BREAK

It's worth lingering overnight in Scopello, just to enjoy a multi-course dinner at **Pensione Tranchina** (☎0924 54 10 99; www.pensione tranchina.com; Via Armando Diaz 7; B&B per person €35-50, half-board per person €60-75; ❄ 🛜) in the heart of the village. This long-standing family-run *pensione*, 2km south of the nature reserve, serves stellar meals featuring home-grown olive oil and abundant local seafood and produce. To be sure of a spot for dinner, book a room with half-board; alternatively, day-trippers can inquire to see if it has a table free.

30

OASI FAUNISTICA DI VENDICARI

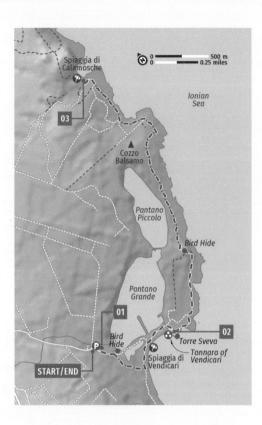

DURATION	DIFFICULTY	DISTANCE	START/END
2hrs	Easy	8km	Vendicari parking area

TERRAIN	Flat dirt roads and sandy paths

One of Sicily's easiest and most rewarding coastal walks runs through this birdwatcher's paradise just south of Syracuse, where marshes rich in migratory waterfowl share the stage with pretty beaches and the photogenic remains of a historic tuna-processing plant.

GETTING HERE

You'll need your own wheels. The reserve entrance is down a signposted dirt road off the SP19 between Noto and Pachino.

STARTING POINT

A dusty car park (€3.50 daily) and a restaurant sit just outside the reserve. Staff at the nearby entrance kiosk hand out free maps.

01 From the car park, follow a stone wall bordered by olive trees to the **park entrance station** (no fee required). The broad, flat dirt path soon comes to a left-hand turnoff for a bird hide overlooking **Pantano Grande**, Vendicari's largest lagoon. Bear right towards the coast, following a stone-paved walkway onto a wooden boardwalk. You'll soon reach the junction of three broad sand-strewn paths. Straight ahead lies a long beach, right is a bird hide overlooking the Pantano Roveto. Take the left fork, following signs for Tonnara and Calmosche. Within minutes, another left-hand detour leads to the edge of Pantano Grande, where flamingoes often throng the shoreline, while the main trail curves right to Vendicari's abandoned *tonnara* (tuna factory).

02 The impressive ruins ahead of you testify to Vendicari's multi-layered history. The ancient Romans processed garum here – a highly

Sicilian Cuisine

Sicily boasts one of Italy's finest and most unique cuisines. Feed your post-hike cravings with these specialities:

Arancine Savoury, fried rice balls.

Caponata Sweet-and-sour mix of eggplants, capers and olives.

Pasta alla Norma Pasta with tomatoes, aubergines and salted ricotta.

Pasta con le sarde Pasta with sardines, pine nuts, raisins and wild fennel.

Couscous alla trapanese Fish couscous, typical of Western Sicily.

Cannoli (pictured) Pastry tubes filled with sweetened ricotta, often finished off with crumbled hazelnuts or pistachios.

OLGAMIEROLLA/SHUTTERSTOCK ©

prized condiment of salty fermented fish; tuna production also thrived under the Greeks and Arabs, and remained a mainstay of the local economy until WWII. The **tonnara** – now reduced to a maze of processing pools, stone columns and a tall brick chimney – stands lonely sentinel over the waterfront, side by side with the **Torre Sveva**, an imposing stone defensive tower commissioned by the Duke of Noto in 1424 and modified by 16th-century Spanish military engineers.

03 Dwarf palms, wild thyme and prickly pear cactus border the broad path, which

soon becomes rockier, threading its way north between the Pantano Piccolo and the Ionian Sea. Lizards scurry underfoot as you curve left around a crumbling stucco building and come to another bird hide on the shores of **Pantano Piccolo**. Just beyond a sign for Cozzo Balsamo, the trail splits, with the right fork contouring the shoreline and the left fork charting a more direct course inland. Within 45 minutes of leaving the tuna factory, a flight of steps on your right drops down to lovely **Calamosche beach**, wedged between low headlands. Linger as long as you like, then retrace your steps to the parking lot.

TAKE A BREAK

The baroque hill town of Noto, 13km north of Vendicari, claims two of Italy's finest gelaterie: **Dolceria Corrado Costanzo** (Via Silvio Spaventa 9) wins the prize for best ice cream – try a lick of pistachio or *amaro* (dark liqueur) – but **Caffè Sicilia** (Corso Vittorio Emanuele 125) steals the show when it comes to *granite* (flavoured crushed ice); try classic flavours such as *caffè* (coffee) and *mandorla* (almond), or indulge in seasonal specials like *fragolini* (tiny wild strawberries) and *gelsi* (mulberries). Don't know which to choose? Try them both. (Your secret is safe with us.)

31

FOSSA DI VULCANO

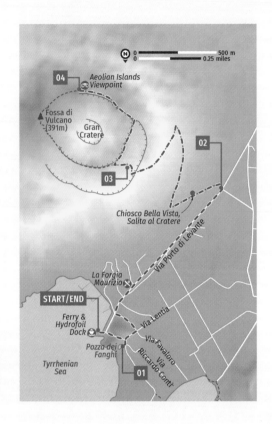

DURATION	DIFFICULTY	DISTANCE	START/END
2hrs	Moderate	7km	Vulcano hydrofoil dock
TERRAIN	Paved road and broad dirt track		

Smoky gateway to Sicily's Aeolian archipelago, the island of Vulcano was celebrated in Roman times as the site of Vulcan's forge. Today it's the first stop on the hydrofoil north from Milazzo. For walkers, Vulcano's star attraction is the straightforward trek up to Fossa di Vulcano (391m; pictured), a massive crater whose sulphurous plumes are visible (and sniffable) long before you reach the dock.

GETTING HERE

Liberty Lines (www.libertylines.it) runs hydrofoils to Vulcano several times daily from neighbouring Lipari (10 minutes) and from Milazzo on the Sicilian 'mainland' (45 minutes).

STARTING POINT

The hydrofoil dock sits just north of the crater in Vulcano Porto, the island's commercial hub, where you'll find restaurants, cafes, shops and other tourist amenities.

01 Brace yourself for the stench of rotten eggs as you walk 150m west from Vulcano's main dock to the **Pozza dei Fanghi**. Long the island's favourite beauty spot, this pool of thick, coffee-coloured mud is usually filled with curious swimsuit-clad tourists dousing their bodies with sulphurous gloop, then running out to the adjacent seawater pool to rinse off and dip their toes in the natural hot springs bubbling up from under the sea.

02 Return towards the hydrofoil dock and turn right (south) along Vulcano's eastern waterfront. Continue 15 minutes down Vulcano's

main street, passing the port and a mix of ferry ticket offices, hotels, restaurants and rental agencies to reach the trailhead, on the left side of the road at the base of the volcano. Along the way you'll enjoy insanely cool perspectives of the **mineral-rich slopes** – streaked grey, yellow and pink – above you.

03 **Splendid views of the island** unfold as you begin climbing the wide zigzag path gently up the volcano's ruddy, sulphur-streaked flanks. A climb of less than 300m brings you to the **rim**, where you can peer down into the crater, a spot long mythologised by the Romans as

Vulcan's forge. There's no lava here, just hot steam and hissing smoke emanating from the crater's otherworldly depths.

04 For truly **all-encompassing views**, continue climbing anti-clockwise around the crater. From the heights along the southern rim, the panorama is breathtaking, with the other six Aeolian islands lined up on the northern horizon and the gaping crater smoking in the foreground. To return to Vulcano's port, simply retrace your steps.

For a post-volcano feast, stop in at **La Forgia Maurizio** (☏ 334 7660069; www.laforgiamaurizio.it; Strada Provinciale 45, Porto di Levante; meals €30-45; ⏱ 12.30-3pm & 7-11pm; 🖉), smack on the path from the volcano to the hydrofoil dock. Maurizio, owner of this devilishly good restaurant, spent 20 winters in Goa, India. Eastern influences sneak into his menu of Sicilian specialities, and several items are vegan- or vegetarian-friendly. Check out the multicourse tasting menu, finished off with homemade kumquat-cardamom liqueur.

32

PUNTA TROIA

DURATION	DIFFICULTY	DISTANCE	START/END
3hrs	Moderate	8km	Marettimo hydrofoil dock
TERRAIN	Packed dirt trails		

The wildest, westernmost and least developed of the Egadi Islands off Sicily's west coast, Marettimo is a collection of green mountain peaks and white-washed houses surrounding a harbour lapped by iridescent turquoise waters. Fanning out from the port, a beautifully maintained, well-marked trail network leads quickly into the unspoilt nature of Marettimo's hinterland: fragrant pine forests, dramatic coastal lookouts and remote beaches.

GETTING HERE

Liberty Lines (www.libertylines.it) runs hydrofoils to Marettimo several times daily from Trapani on Sicily's west coast. Travel time is 1¼ to 1½ hours.

STARTING POINT

The hydrofoil dock sits at the centre of Marettimo village, with restaurants, bar-cafes and other services all within easy walking distance.

01 Follow the shoreline north from Marettimo's **hydrofoil dock**, passing Il Veliero restaurant on your left and continuing onto a dirt trail that transitions into a broad flagstoned path. A signboard announces your entry into the **Area Marina Protetta degli Egadi**, a conservation zone protecting the three Egadi islands.

02 Ten minutes from the dock, turn left onto a narrower trail, following signs for Punta Troia. Stone steps help navigate the steeper sections as you climb steadily up the hillside. Soon you're enjoying **unimpeded views of the shoreline**, with the craggy headland of Punta Troia looming in the distance. Continue

The Prehistoric Cave Art of Levanzo

En route to Marettimo, jump ship on the tiny island of Levanzo (pictured) to see the prehistoric cave art at **Grotta del Genovese**. Between 6000 and 10,000 years old, the Upper Palaeolithic wall paintings and Neolithic incised drawings at this seaside cave feature bulls, horses, men and tuna. Visits are by guided tour only, and reservations are required (www.grottadelgenovese.it). The all-inclusive tour takes two hours; transport is by boat if weather conditions are favourable – otherwise, it's a 10-minute drive by 4WD, then a steep but scenic 700m descent on foot from the end of the rough gravel road to the cave.

Best for

👍

AVOIDING
THE CROWDS

ELESI/SHUTTERSTOCK ©

contouring Marettimo's eastern bluffs for the next 45 minutes on a narrow trail high above the deep blue sea. Clusters of flowering **wild rosemary** appear along the trailside, as **amazing views** unfurl back to the whitewashed village of Marettimo splashed upon the rocks far to the south.

03 Signs warn you to watch your step and stay close to the rock wall on the left as you round the edge of a **picturesque gorge** cutting inland from the sea. Within minutes, you're enjoying tantalising full-on **views of Punta Troia** juxtaposed against the vast, deep-blue sweep of the Mediterranean. Concrete walls

and steps facilitate your descent along a steep stretch of trail, as a long downhill leads to the flat isthmus that separates Punta Troia from the rest of the island.

04 It's now just a short climb to the **old fortress** up top, built on the ruins of an earlier Saracen watchtower, on this strategically important pinnacle of land at Marettimo's northeastern tip. Not far from here, in 241 BC, the Romans and Carthaginians once fought the decisive battle of the First Punic War; these days it's about as peaceful a spot as you could wish for. When you're ready to retrace your steps, the walk back

to Marettimo's port takes about 1½ hours.

TAKE A BREAK

On the waterfront just north of Marettimo's hydrofoil dock, family-run **Trattoria Il Veliero** (📞 0923 92 32 74; Via Umberto 22; meals €30; ⏰ noon-2pm & 7-10pm Mar-Oct) is a seafood-lover's fantasy. Chef-owner Peppe Bevilacqua goes to the market daily, picking out the freshest catches. Superbly prepared Sicilian classics like *pasta con le sarde* (pasta with sardines) and *fritto misto* (fried shrimp and calamari) share the menu with octopus salad, tuna carpaccio, perfectly grilled fish and countless other delights.

Also Try...

OLLIRG/SHUTTERSTOCK ©

ALICUDI

Ever dream of getting away from it all? The remote island of Alicudi off Sicily's north coast is as isolated a place as you'll find in the entire Mediterranean. Last stop on the Aeolian Islands' hydrofoil line, Alicudi has less than 100 residents and no roads, with boats, mules and hiking providing the only transport.

To reach Alicudi's central peak (675m), simply follow the blue arrows up from the port. The two-hour trek scales a relentlessly steep series of stone staircases (nearly 1400 steps in all) past pastel-coloured houses, citrus trees, cactus and wildflowers, with the church of San Bartolo marking the hike's midpoint. At the T-intersection up top, turn left along a stone wall to circle the extinct volcanic crater, or right across a grassy plateau to the vertigo-inducing cliffs at Alicudi's western edge. The end-of-the-world feeling here is downright intoxicating.

DURATION 3½hrs
DIFFICULTY Hard
DISTANCE 5km

LAGO DI BIVIERE

Central Sicily's sun-dappled beech forests are the setting for this walk through the wilds of the Nebrodi Mountains.

From Portella Calacudera, 1.5km off the SS289, follow signs for Lago di Biviere (pictured) downhill along a broad unpaved track. You're walking along the Dorsale dei Nebrodi, a 70km segment of the Sentiero Italia, Italy's classic long-distance hiking trail. Passing the Lago Maulazzo reservoir after 2.5km, the road descends another 5.3km, opening onto distant views of the Aeolian Islands framed by the craggy Rocche di Crasto as you approach tranquil Lago di Biviere. On a clear day, Mt Etna is reflected in the lake's waters, while wild horses and pigs scurry about the surrounding fields and forest. Afterwards, stop in at nearby **Relais Villa Miraglia** (www.relaisvillamiraglia.it/ristorante; SS289; meals €27-35), a converted hunting lodge serving Nebrodi specialities such as roast lamb, pork and wild mushrooms.

DURATION 5hrs
DIFFICULTY Moderate
DISTANCE 16km

RSFOTOGRAPHY/GETTY IMAGES ©

MT ETNA

Europe's largest active volcano, Mt Etna (3350m) is an irresistible magnet for walkers.

From Rifugio Sapienza (1920m) on Etna's southern slopes, the **Funivia dell'Etna** (www.funiviaetna. com; return adult/child €30/23, incl bus & guide adult/child €65/48; ⏲9am-4pm) whisks you up to 2500m, where a wide gravel road ascends through an otherworldly landscape of grey ash to the Torre del Filosofo (2920m), a favourite vantage point over Etna's craters (pictured). How close you can get depends on the level of volcanic activity. Return downhill in time to catch the last cable car.

DURATION 1½hrs
DIFFICULTY Moderate
DISTANCE 5km

CAPO DI MILAZZO

On Sicily's north coast, the one-hour loop around sickle-shaped Capo di Milazzo makes for an easy, scenic day hike.

Park near the lighthouse at the end of the isthmus and walk through a landscape of olive groves, cactus and stone walls to reach the Piscina di Venere, an idyllic natural pool at the cape's western tip. Next, follow the shoreline south past the atmospheric ruins of the 13th-century Santuario Rupestre di San Antonio, where St Anthony of Padua famously sought refuge after a shipwreck. From here, the trail climbs back to the parking lot.

DURATION 1hr
DIFFICULTY Easy
DISTANCE 2km

PIZZO CARBONARA

For a classic climb in the Parco Naturale delle Monti Madonie, set your sights on Pizzo Carbonara (1979m) – Sicily's second-highest peak.

Leave the main road at Piano Battaglia, a windswept plateau 44km south of Cefalù, and set off on a dirt track near the 'Sentiero Battaglietta' informational display. Climb steadily through the rocky terrain, enlivened with magnificent wildflowers in springtime. Views up top are truly awe-inspiring, stretching north to the Tyrrhenian Sea, east to the Nebrodi Mountains, and southeast to Mt Etna.

DURATION 3hrs
DIFFICULTY Moderate
DISTANCE 6km

DOLOMITES & STELVIO

33 **Hans & Paula Steger Weg** Wander the wide-open expanses of Europe's largest alpine meadow. **p142**

34 **Passo Gardena to Vallunga** Descend from sublime rocky high country to a steep-walled green valley. **p144**

35 **Sassolungo Circuit** Watch hang-gliders soaring between above Val Gardena. **p148**

36 **Tre Cime di Lavaredo** Circumnavigate this iconic three-toothed massif near Cortina d'Ampezzo. **p150**

37 **Alpe di Fanes** Follow the legendary Alta Via 1 to an alpine hut and over a steep pass. **p152**

38 **Pragser Wildsee** Enjoy a family-friendly stroll around this mountain-fringed lake. **p156**

39 **Percorso delle Segherie** Tour historic water-driven mills in a verdant valley at Stelvio National Park. **p158**

40 **Adolf Munkel Weg** Gaze up at the soul-stirring spires of the Odle (Geisler) group. **p160**

Explore
DOLOMITES & STELVIO

Among the planet's most bewitching mountains, the Dolomites thrust their jagged spires up from the emerald pastures of northeastern Italy. Until WWI, much of this region belonged to Austria, a fact reflected in the continued prevalence of German and in the ubiquitous apple strudel and dumplings served at the region's trailside huts. The walking tradition here goes back centuries, and the wealth of trails – impeccably signposted and easily accessible by summer gondolas and chairlifts – is astounding. To the west, the alpine heights of Parco Nazionale dello Stelvio offer similar enticement for hikers, with a comparable network of trails and mountain *rifugi*.

BOLZANO

Straddling the confluence of the Adige and Isarco rivers and well-placed on the busy train line between Verona, Innsbruck and Munich, South Tyrol's capital makes a delightful gateway to the Dolomites. A long-time conduit between Italy and the Alps, Bolzano (Bozen in German) buzzes with multicultural energy and a high quality of life. The city's backdrop of verdant foothills and rocky pinnacles sets off rows of pastel-painted townhouses, while bicycles ply riverside paths and wooden market stalls heave with alpine cheeses, *speck* (cured ham) and dark, seeded loaves.

SELVA DI VAL GARDENA

Cradled between the mountain walls of Sassolungo, the Sella massif, and Parco Naturale Puez-Odle, tiny Selva sits at the far end of Ladin-speaking Val Gardena, equipped with gondolas that can whisk you in minutes to the surrounding high-country trails.

CORVARA IN BADIA

Val Badia's tourist hub, chic Corvara bustles with skiers in winter and hikers in summer. Its prime position at the foot of Passo Gardena makes it a good jumping-off point for hikes in the high country of Parco Naturale Puez-Odle, but it's also a convenient base for exploring Parco Naturale Fanes-Sennes-Braies to the east.

CORTINA D'AMPEZZO

The Italian supermodel of ski resorts, Cortina d'Ampezzo is pricey and undeniably beautiful. The town's stone church steeples and pleasant cascading piazzas are framed by magnificent mountains, making Cortina a sought-after summertime base for hiking, biking and rock climbing.

 WHEN TO GO

Summer and early autumn are prime time for exploring the

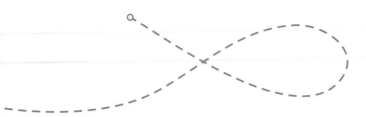

South Tyrol Tourism (www.suedtirol.info) Excellent website with abundant info about hiking trails and other tourist attractions.

Parco Nazionale dello Stelvio (www.stelviopark.it) Comprehsnsive info on this national park just west of the Dolomites.

Sportler (www.sportler.com) Superb source for outdoor gear and trekking maps, with shops in Bolzano, Selva di Val Gardena and several other locations around Trentino and South Tyrol.

SAD (www.sad.it/it/siitime tablesquery) Helpful resource for bus timetables throughout South Tyrol.

Salewa (www.salewa.com) South Tyrolean manufacturer of alpine footwear, with a huge showroom and climbing wall in Bolzano.

La Sportiva (www.lasportiva.com) Trentino-based manufacturer of hiking boots and outdoor gear, with headquarters and a retail outlet in Ziano di Fiemme.

Dolomites' *alte vie* (high-altitude walking trails). Note that many *rifugi*, hotels, chairlifts and gondolas wait till late May or early June to open for the summer season, and close up shop in late September or early October.

TRANSPORT

The closest airports are at Verona, Venice and Innsbruck (Austria). From Verona, Trenitalia's north–south railway line parallels the A22 motorway up through the Adige valley to Trento and Bolzano, then over Brenner Pass to Innsbruck. An admirably efficient network of smaller train and bus lines, operated by SAD (www.sad.it), fans out from Bolzano to side valleys such as Val Gardena, Val Badia, Val Venosta and Val Pusteria. Many local hotels offer a free public transport pass.

In neighbouring Trentino, **Ferrovia Trento–Malè** (☎ 0461 23 83 50; www.trentinotrasporti.it/en/travel-with-us/train) runs trains through the Val di Sole at the edge of Parco Nazionale dello Stelvio, while **Dolomiti Bus** (☎ 0437 21 71 11; www.dolomitibus.it) serves Cortina d'Ampezzo to the east. If you're short on time, hiring a car may still be the most efficient way to get around; roads are notoriously squiggly but well signposted and maintained.

WHERE TO STAY

The Dolomites boast some of the world's most stylish alpine resorts, small hotels and campgrounds, along with numerous comfy farm stays (see www.redrooster.it). Higher up the mountainside, a host of well-placed and impeccably maintained *rifugi* (mountain huts) offer cosy dorm-style accommodation with down duvets, hot showers and hearty home-cooked meals.

WHAT'S ON

Soirées at Tyrol Castle In June and July, enjoy live concerts by international ensembles in the Great Hall of South Tyrol's ancestral 12th-century castle.

South Tyrol Knights' Games The Alps' largest festival of medieval-style jousting is held against the atmospheric backdrop of castles and abbeys in Schluderns in August.

Kalterer Weinfest The wine-growing village of Kaltern celebrates the Adige Valley's viticultural traditions in August, with free-flowing wine, traditional culinary specialties and music in the streets.

Vipiteno/Sterzing Dumpling Festival Savoury and sweet dumplings, a mainstay of every Dolomites hiker's diet, take centre stage at this annual culinary festival in September near Brixen.

33

HANS & PAULA STEGER WEG

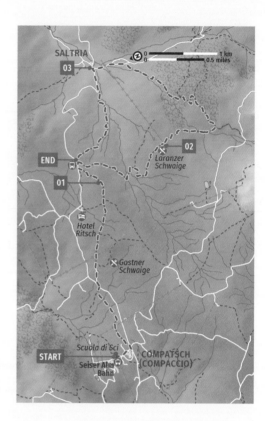

DURATION	DIFFICULTY	DISTANCE	START/END
3hrs	Moderate	9km	Seiser Alm Bahn/Ritsch bus stop

TERRAIN	Undulating dirt roads and trails

Spreading like a soft green blanket at the foot of the Dolomites, the Seiser Alm (Alpe di Siusi; pictured) is Europe's vastest alpine meadow, threaded with some of Italy's most enchanting footpaths. This walk between the ski villages of Compatsch (Compaccio) and Saltria undulates through forests and green pastures.

GETTING HERE

Take the Seiser Alm cable car (www.seiseralm.it) from Seis (Siusi) to Compatsch. There's paid parking at Compatsch, but the road from Seis closes between 9am and 5pm to discourage driving.

STARTING POINT

Compatsch has abundant shops, restaurants and free restrooms at the Seiser Alm cable car station.

01 From the cable-car station, head 250m downhill to the paved Compatsch–Saltria road. Turn left, passing the tourist office on your right, then left again at the Bergrettung Südtirol first aid station. Trail 30 (also labelled 'Hans and Paula Steger Weg') starts as a broad dirt road heading east across the ski slopes. Within 10 minutes, cross the paved road at a bus stop and continue gently uphill. Past a junction with trail 6B for Gostner Schwaige, the unpaved track soon emerges into grassy pastures extending to the mountainous horizon on all sides. Just beyond a new junction with trail 6, you'll come to the edge of a meadow swooping east towards Sassolungo. **Tree-shaded benches** invite you to sit and contemplate this majestic landscape. Your path ahead is visible on the hillside far below, dotted with cows and hikers. About 45 minutes from Compatsch, trail 30 again meets the paved road. Turn right (south) here, following signs for trail 12A (still marked 'Hans and Paula Steger Weg').

02 Grazing cows and wooden huts with enormous piles of stacked firewood spread across green waves of pastureland as far as the eye can see. Starting as a broad unpaved farm track, trail 12A meanders between fields and forest, reaching **Laranzer Schwaige hut** – a pleasant spot for a snack break – in about half an hour. Trail 12A branches left here onto a narrower path (signs for Almrosen Hütte), soon crossing a creek and passing through a gate. The forest encroaches as you continue along the creek valley. After crossing another bridge, climb away from the creek, soon reaching another signpost.

03 Briefly jog right, then left on trail 12 towards **Saltria**, following the fence line at the meadow's edge. Cross a boardwalk and drop into the forest, where the trail widens into a dirt road. Within 15 minutes, turn left again, descending a narrow woodsy path (signs for Saltria). Turn right at the bottom, then left onto a paved road on Saltria's outskirts. Beyond the Sporthotel Floralpina, come to a T-intersection near a bus stop. Turn left on trail 30 towards Compatsch, briefly following the pavement, then forking left onto a footpath through a mix of forest and meadows. After crossing a wooden bridge, the trail climbs high grassy slopes with delirious **views** east to Sassolungo. About 25 minutes from Saltria, reach the Ritsch bus stop on the main road, where you can catch bus 11 or 14 back to Compatsch.

 **TAKE A BREAK**

'Locally sourced' says it all at **Gostner Schwaige** (www.gostner schwaige.com). Dairy products come from the barn next door, while salads come decorated with a rainbow of wildflowers from the adjacent garden and pastures. Other specialities include hay soup, home-cured meats and refreshing herb-infused soft drinks bottled on-site.

34

PASSO GARDENA TO VALLUNGA

DURATION	DIFFICULTY	DISTANCE	START/END
6hrs	Hard	17km	Passo Gardena/ Dantercepies cable car base station

TERRAIN	Steep rocky trails, flat dirt roads

It's hard to imagine a more satisfying or varied introduction to the Dolomites than this classic loop through the heart of Parco Naturale Puez Odle, from the windswept mountain ridges above Passo Gardena (pictured) to the lush cliff-fringed cow pastures of Vallunga. Yes, it's a long walk, with its fair share of climbing at the start – but the hike's overall profile is still mostly downhill, thanks to a cable car that zips you into the high country to start the day. Meanwhile, the opportunity to break for lunch at Rifugio Puez – one of the Dolomites' iconic mountain huts – makes the journey all the more enticing.

GETTING HERE

Reach Passo Gardena by taking the Dantercepies cable car (www.dantercepies.it) from its base station in Selva to its upper station near the pass; alternatively, drive up to Passo Gardena and park in one of the paid car parks along the SS243.

STARTING POINT

Paid parking, food, drinks and restrooms are all available at Passo Gardena.

01 A quick and easy ride on the Dantercepies gondola whisks you from Selva di Val Gardena up into the glorious high country where this walk begins. Alight into the dizzying mountainscape above **Passo Gardena**, one of the Dolomites' most magnificent passes – known in German as **Grödnerjoch** and in Ladin as **Jëuf de Frea** or **Ju de Frara**. From the upper cable car station follow trail 12A towards

Jimmi Hütte and Forcella Cir. Alternatively, if you've driven up to Passo Gardena, follow signs for trail 2 uphill (northeast) from the parking lot towards Passo Crëspeina and Jimmi Hütte.

02 From **Jimmi Hütte** (Rifugio Jimmy; 2222m), begin a steady 45-minute climb along the legendary Alta Via 2 towards the impressive sawtooth ridge to your north, enjoying **increasingly expansive views** south back over the Sella group as you go. Here you're in the northern reaches of one of Europe's most iconic long-distance hikes, stretching 185km from Brixen (Bressanone) near the Austrian border all the way to Feltre, in the Piave valley above Venice. Trekking enthusiasts devote two weeks to hiking the Alta Via 2 in its entirety; you'll be getting a taste of one of its most spectacular sections over the next two hours. As you near Forcella Cir, the trail weaves through a landscape of massive rocky spires thrusting skyward.

03 From atop **Forcella Cir** (2462m), enjoy sweeping new perspectives into the **Val de Chedul** (pictured p146), a long narrow valley to your north. Trail 2 drops abruptly over the edge, wasting no time in pointing you east towards your next goal, the 2528m Forcella de Crespeina. Climb east up the broad valley at the base of rock-strewn slopes, ignoring signs for trail 12 to Vallunga and Val de Chedul.

04 A spiky two-pronged stick marks the summit of **Forcella de Crespeina**, where glances west back down the long, distinctively U-shaped glacial Chedul valley compete for your attention with views over the rocky wasteland that lies ahead. After catching your breath, descend into the barren bowl to your northeast, following signs for Rifugio Puez en route to another saddle 30 minutes away; around the halfway point you'll pass **Lech de**

🍴 Trailside Gastronomy

Perhaps the greatest joy of hiking in the Dolomites is the food. Wherever you walk you'll find mountain huts serving home-cooked alpine treats that reflect the region's multicultural roots. Austrian-style *knödel* (dumplings) share the menu with Italian and Ladin pasta specialties such as *mezzelune* (spinach-ricotta ravioli) and *casunziei* (beet-filled pasta with poppy seeds), accompanied by excellent draft beer, refreshing *Radler* (beer mixed with lemonade) and regional wines such as sparkling Trentino DOC or ruby-red Lagrein. Afterwards, save room for the ever-tempting *Apfelstrudel* (apple strudel) and *Kaiserschmarren* (fluffy pancakes with lingonberries)!

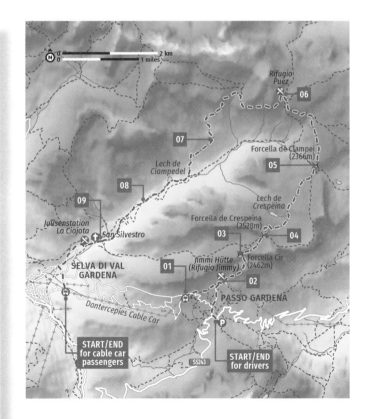

Crespëina, a lonely alpine lake to the left of the trail.

05 Your next major landmark is the **Forcella de Ciampei** (2366m), a low pass with **astounding views** east down a steep-walled valley towards Val Badia and west over the deep verdant Vallunga (which will be your return route to Selva at the end of this walk). For now, the Alta Via lives up to its name, staying high above both valleys as it forges on towards Rifugio Puez.

06 Alta Via 2 continues along the high ridgeline, yielding ever more impressive views down over Vallunga, with an occasional flock of sheep posing picturesquely beside the trail. Within 40 minutes, a set of tattered flags (representing Italy, South Tyrol and the European Union) flapping in the wind announces your arrival at **Rifugio Puez** (2475m), a perfect spot to break for lunch.

07 Leave Rifugio Puez via trail 2, peering steeply down into the deep green pastures of Vallunga 700m below. Within about 20 minutes, trail 16 branches left at a signposted junction for Vallunga (Langental), and almost immediately begins steeply descending across a meadow towards a sheer rock wall to the south. The route soon bears left, charting a zigzag course at the foot of the wall, then dropping down a series of log steps as it continues descending through rocky meadows with **fantastic views** of Vallunga ahead, slowly getting closer.

🚠 Circling the Sella Massif

The Sella Ronda, a 40km circumnavigation of the Gruppo di Sella range – linked by various cable cars and chairlifts – is one of the Alps' iconic ski routes. The tour takes in four passes and the four surrounding valleys – Val Gardena, Val Badia, Arabba and Val di Fassa – all deeply steeped in the region's unique Ladin heritage. In summer, the same trails are utilised by mountain bikers and there's a hop-on, hop-off bus for walkers. The paved roads surrounding the Sella massif also figure prominently in the annual Giro d'Italia bike race, and for one day each June, the whole driving loop around the mountain is closed to motorised traffic during Sella Ronda Bike Day (www.sellarondabikeday.com).

08 As it nears the valley floor, trail 16 re-enters the forest, then makes a final rocky descent along a river gorge as the full verdant sweep of **Vallunga** comes into view. Upon reaching the valley, turn right onto a wide, unpaved track, descending gradually for the next 40 minutes through broad grassy meadows filled with cows, dotted with occasional patches of evergreen forest and backed by sheer rock walls. About 25 minutes into the descent, you can refill your water bottles at a **freshwater spring** pouring into a hollow log on the right.

09 Standing astride a grassy field on the right, the sweet little chapel of **San Silvestro (Silvesterkapelle Wolkenstein)** marks the far end of the valley, on the outskirts of Selva. Soon thereafter, you'll pass the Jausenstation La Ciajota, a great place to break for a beer and a bite before walking the remaining 20 minutes back to the Dantercepies cable car in the heart of the village.

TAKE A BREAK

On a high craggy ridgeline with bird's-eye views down to Vallunga's green meadows, **Rifugio Puez** (📞 0471 79 53 65; www.rifugiopuez. it; mains €5-10; 🕐 noon-3pm) is the kind of mountain oasis that old-school hikers dream of: totally no frills, with a menu that's all about loading you up with calories and sending you back out on the trail. Grab a bowl of dumplings in broth or a plate of eggs, *speck* and potatoes, finish it off with a quick apple strudel, and you're good to go!

35

SASSOLUNGO CIRCUIT

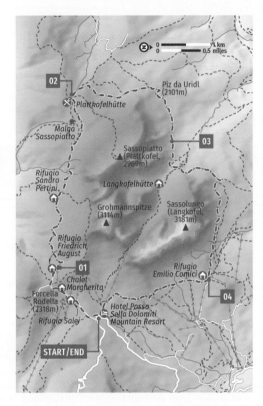

DURATION	DIFFICULTY	DISTANCE	START/END
5hrs	Moderate	14km	Passo Sella Resort

TERRAIN	Dirt roads and trails

There's no Dolomites landmark more captivating than Sassolungo (Langkofel; 3181m) or its kid brother Sassopiatto (Plattkofel; 2969m). Beloved by hikers, climbers and hang-gliders, these twin monoliths dominate the landscape south of Val Gardena. This long but leisurely high-country loop takes you around the base of both peaks.

GETTING HERE
From Selva, take SAD bus 471 to Rifugio Passo Sella (30 minutes), or drive 12km up the tortuous SS242.

STARTING POINT
At the trailhead, Passo Sella Resort has a restaurant, with ample parking nearby. Food, drinks and restrooms are available at several *rifugi* along the trail.

01 Set off southwest on trail 557 towards Col Rodela. The broad and undulating unpaved track passes **Rifugio Salei** and **Chalet Margherita** on its half-hour climb to **Forcella Rodella** (2318m), where a signboard marks the start of the Friedrich August Weg. You're now on one of the Dolomites' oldest hiking trails, named for the mountain-loving Saxon King Frederick Augustus (1750–1827) and inaugurated in 1911. **Sassopiatto** rears above grassy meadows on the northern horizon, complemented by long views south towards Canazei. A five-minute stroll brings you to **Rifugio Friedrich August** with its woodsy yak-themed decor and **killer views**.

02 For the next 90 minutes the narrow Friedrich August Weg meanders through meadows beneath Sassopiatto's rocky spires. Beyond **Rifugio Sandro Pertini** the trail gets rockier and the meadows steepen, affording near-vertical views up Sassopiatto's south face to hang-gliders soaring in

Best for

MOUNTAIN
VIEWS

MOLARJUNG/SHUTTERSTOCK ©

and out among the crags. Near **Plattkofelhütte** – the Friedrich August Weg's official endpoint – the shapely ridgeline of **Sciliar (Schlern)** appears on the western horizon as you pass a turnoff for trail 553A to **Malga Sassopiatto**, a high-country farm selling homemade cheese.

03 From Plattkofelhütte, trail 527 (signs for Langkofelhütte/Rifugio Vicenza) descends along a broad road, then narrows and weaves 30 minutes north through meadows along Sassopiatto's western flank. Near **Piz da Uridl** (2101m), emerge onto a **high shelf with sweeping views** over Saltria and the Alpe di

Siusi. The trail descends through trees, then rises to cross scree-strewn slopes, revealing **fabulous views** northeast to Sassolungo. At a prominent crossroads, trail 527 veers southeast to the legendary climbers' hut, Langkofelhütte, while you follow trail 526 north towards Comici.

04 Trail 526 climbs to a promontory with great views north into Val Gardena. Turn east here to begin circumnavigating Sassolungo's north face, winding through scree at the base of colossal cliffs. Within 40 minutes, killer views over the Sella massif open up at **Rifugio Emilio Comici** (2154m). Complete

the loop with a 45-minute jaunt through the meadows below Sassolungo's eastern face. Starting as a broad track, trail 526 eventually narrows and descends through the rugged City of Rocks to reach the Passo Sella Resort.

 **TAKE A BREAK**

On a high ridge near the hike's midpoint, the Kasseroler family's **Plattkofelhütte** (www.plattkofel. com) has been feeding hungry hikers since 1935. The alpine-Mediterranean menu features many ingredients grown at their nearby farm, Maso Örtlhof.

36

TRE CIME DI LAVAREDO

DURATION	DIFFICULTY	DISTANCE	START/END
3hrs	Moderate	9km	Rifugio Auronzo

TERRAIN	Dirt roads and trails

When the Dolomites attained Unesco World Heritage status in 2009, the Tre Cime (pictured; Dreizinnen) emerged as the region's official symbol. Soaring to nearly 3000m, these three ravishing rock towers exert a magnetic attraction on all who venture near. This popular loop circumnavigates the massif, offering front-row views from multiple angles.

GETTING HERE
Dolomitibus (www.dolomitibus.it) runs buses from Cortina d'Ampezzo (one hour, 22km). Drivers must pay a €30 toll on the SP49 from Misurina.

STARTING POINT
At the foot of the Tre Cime, Rifugio Auronzo offers parking, restrooms, food and lodging.

01 The Tre Cime tower is to your left as you leave Rifugio Auronzo on trail 101, a broad, flat path signposted for Rifugio Lavaredo. Within 15 minutes, pass a **chapel** dedicated to the Italian soldiers who lost their lives here in WWI. Continue another 10 minutes around the mountain's base to **Rifugio Lavaredo** (2344m), a cute two-storey wood-and-stone structure whose bright red shutters contrast vividly with the stark, treeless rockscape. Hikers crowd the front terrace, sipping coffee and beers.

02 The views keep getting better as trail 101 narrows and winds closer to Tre Cime's crags. A steady 10-minute ascent brings you to **Forcella Lavaredo (Paternsattel)**, a high saddle marking the border between Belluno and South Tyrol. **Spectacular Dolomites vistas** unfold in all directions, and a **plaque** commemorates Pope John Paul II's visit to this spot in 1996. The northern horizon is dominated by **Toblinger Knoten**, a blocky tower of rock

Best for
MOUNTAIN
VIEWS

VOYAGEURB/SHUTTERSTOCK ©

jutting above the red roof of the precariously perched Dreizin-nenhütte (Rifugio Locatelli). Trail 101, now a broad unpaved track, snakes gradually downhill for 20 minutes to a junction directly below the *rifugio*.

03 A signpost announces that you've joined the Alta Via 4, one of the Dolomites' legendary 'high routes'. Turn right, following signs steeply uphill towards **Dreizinnenhütte**. In 10 minutes, you're on top of the world, with the *rifugio*'s outdoor terrace offering a supremely **panoramic lunch stop**. Pause to admire the **Laghi dei Piani**, a pair of lonely lakes adjoining

the *rifugio*, then return to the trail junction below. This time head south on trail 105 towards Lange Alm, with the north face of the Tre Cime looming directly ahead. A long descent, partly on log steps, leads steeply into a bowl before climbing back up the opposite side.

04 Arrive at **Langalmhütte** (2283m), a massive stone hut with outdoor seating on rustic wood benches and a menu featuring organic yogurt, homemade cakes, cold cuts, wood-oven bread and local draft beer. Time for another break? Sure, why not! You're now only 40 minutes from Rifugio Auron-

zo. Follow trail 105 past a small lake and over **Forcella Col de Mezo summit** (2315m), completing the loop with a final descent past a whimsical collection of cairns.

 **TAKE A BREAK**

A hikers' beacon of hope amidst Tre Cime's rocky wastes, **Dreizinnen-hütte** (www.dreizinnenhuette.com) sits at the foot of evocatively named Sausage Mountain (Frankfurter Würstl in German, Monolite della Salsiccia in Italian). Feast on regional specialties such as *casunziei con finferli* (Cortina-style half-moon pasta with chanterelles) in the wood-panelled dining room or on the panoramic outdoor terrace.

37
ALPE DI FANES

DURATION	DIFFICULTY	DISTANCE	START/END
7hrs	Hard	20km	Capanna Alpina

TERRAIN	Dirt roads and trails, some very steep

Forming the heart of Parco Naturale Fanes-Sennes-Braies, the Alpe di Fanes is renowned as one of the most evocative settings in the Dolomites. Centuries of potent Ladin legends have their roots in this mystical landscape, and JRR Tolkien is said to have drawn inspiration for *The Hobbit* and *The Lord of the Rings* from this half-ethereal, half-forbidding high country. This epic loop takes you first across the high Fanes plateau, then gives you a taste of the challenging Alta Via 1, one of Italy's most exhilarating long-distance hiking trails.

GETTING HERE

From Corvara, take SAD bus 465 to Sciaré (25 minutes) and walk the 15-minute dirt road to Capanna Alpina, or drive 11km to Armentarola and follow signs 1.5km off the SP37 to the parking lot.

STARTING POINT

Food, drinks, picnic tables, restrooms and paid parking are all available at Capanna Alpina.

01 Fronting a green meadow at the threshold of **Parco Naturale Fanes-Sennes-Braies**, the trailside snack shack of **Capanna Alpina** makes an inspiring spot to launch into your journey. Embark on a broad dirt track, with the rocky sentinels of Piz dl Lech (2654m) and Piz dles Cunturines (3064m) standing watch over the verdant valley before you. Within a couple of minutes, your outbound route (signposted as trail 11) branches left towards Col de Locia, while trail 20 (your eventual return route) branches right to Rifugio Scotoni.

02 **Views back down the valley** get better and better as the trail passes first through grassy meadows, then begins steadily climbing towards **Col de Locia**. About 45 minutes into the walk, a **natural spring** on the right lets you know you're nearing the summit (a climb of nearly 350m from the parking lot). From here, a series of log steps brings you up top, where **amazing views** open up south towards Marmolada from a wood bench and railing at the precipice's edge.

03 Following signs for Gran Fanes, the trail now descends towards a **rocky creek** at the edge of the high Fanes plateau. Within 10 minutes the trail crosses the creek and widens, climbing gently as it parallels the creek bed, then descends again to cross a narrow log bridge, with the Fanes high country opening up in the distance.

04 Just over an hour into the walk, reach a **key junction with Alta Via 1**, one of the Dolomites' fabled high routes (signposted on the right here as trail 20B to Lago Lagazuoi). You'll be taking this trail later in the day, but for now continue straight on trail 11 to Gran Fanes. For the next 40 minutes, **wide-open vistas abound** as the broad, nearly flat trail traverses the high plateau, with larger mountains looming on either side. About halfway along you'll pass a huge expanse of boulders cascading down the slopes of **Piza Nord** (2834m) on the right.

05 Enjoy long views east and downstream across rock-strewn meadows as you cross a bridge and arrive at **Malga Gran Fanes**, a hut at the junction with trail 10 coming up from Cortina d'Ampezzo. The gorgeous vistas continue as trail 11 winds gradually uphill and north towards a low pass. Continue following signs for Fanes and Pederü, and you'll soon reach an **iron cross** on your right memorialising the Tiroler Standschützen, Austrian troops who fought in these remote uplands during WWI.

06 The trail levels off at **Lé de Limo**, a lake on the right, then begins descending

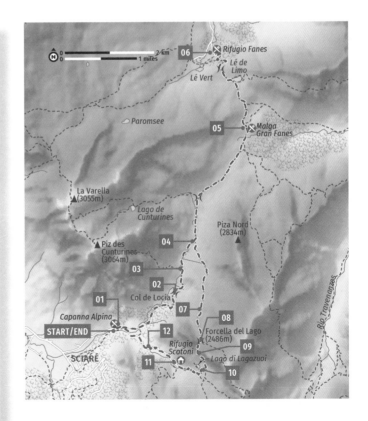

along a wide dirt road with nice views north to a new range of mountains. Within 15 minutes from the lake, follow a crude wooden signpost pointing downhill towards **Rifugio Fanes** on the right. A narrow, steep trail brings you in short order to the front terrace of this rather luxurious mountain hut, which makes an excellent lunch stop.

07 Retrace your steps south across the Fanes plateau to the junction with trail 20B (a walk of 1¼ to 1½ hours). Fork left here and begin following blazes painted on rocks beside the trail. **Dramatic rock faces begin peeking out** above the forested lowlands ahead as the trail climbs – gradually at first, then more steeply – towards the saddle at Forcella del Lago (pictured).

08 Just beyond a **hand-carved wooden memorial plaque** on the left, the trail begins crossing scree slopes towards rock pinnacles. The ensuing 45-minute climb reveals astounding views west towards green valleys and slopes far below. As you near the summit, **Forcella del Lago** comes into view as a distinct notch in the barren rockscape ahead.

09 Nothing you've seen on the north side prepares you for the **jaw-dropping views** south from Forcella del Lago (2486m). Directly ahead, sheer-edged slopes plummet into the valley of Lago Lagazuoi. You now begin an implausibly steep descent on the masterfully engineered Alta Via 1, which runs

150km through the Dolomites from the Pragser Wildsee to Belluno. The views down to Lago Lagazuoi far below (300m to be exact) are riveting as you pick your way down a series of switchbacks anchored by rough-and-ready log and stone steps for the next 45 minutes or so.

10 The trail begins hugging the cliff face to your left as it continues its steady descent towards the lake, with the continuation of Alta Via 1 traversing raw scree slopes visible far ahead. Level off briefly as you finally reach the frigid shores of **Lago Lagazuoi**, then resume your precipitous descent towards Rifugio Scotoni, following signs for trail 20 on your right at a signposted junction.

11 Set in a stunning green valley backed by craggy Dolomites peaks, **Rifugio Scotoni** (pictured p152) is a welcoming sight indeed after your steep 20-minute jaunt down the rocky gorge below Lago Lagazuoi. After so much exertion, the fluffy duvets and well-stocked bar and restaurant here make an overnight stay mighty tempting. Even if you plan to forge on, it's worth grabbing a beer on the front terrace to relish your completion of the walk's most challenging leg.

12 Your return route to Capanna Alpina is steep but scenic, zigzagging down to the parking lot on a wide dirt road through **inviting green meadows**, with the familiar jagged profile of Piz dles Cunturines towering once again before you.

The High Road...

The Dolomites' most legendary hiking routes are the Alte Vie delle Dolomiti (or Dolomiten-Höhenwege) – long-distance 'High Routes' that criss-cross the mountains' rarefied upper reaches, passing by dozens of mountain refuges en route and intersecting periodically with the trails described in this guide.

Here are some basic specs for the four most famous Alte Vie:

Alta Via 1 From Pragser Wildsee to Belluno; 150km

Alta Via 2 From Brixen to Feltre; 185km

Alta Via 3 From Toblach to Longarone; 120km

Alta Via 4 From Innichen to Pieve di Cadore; 90km

For further info, see www.alta badia.org/en/summer -holidays/trekking-hiking/ dolomites-high-routes.html.

TAKE A BREAK

A welcoming oasis in the heart of the mountains, **Rifugio Fanes** (✆348 3900660; www.rifugiofanes.com; mains €9.50-17.50; ⏰9am-6pm) seduces passing hikers with its sunny front terrace and platters of delicious South Tyrolean fare. Go for bratwurst and sauerkraut, goulash with polenta, trout with sautéed veggies or the colourful *Knödeltris* – a trio of beet, spinach and alpine cheese dumplings. Whatever you do, don't leave without sampling at least one dessert (hint: the buckwheat *Torte* is a perennial favourite).

38

PRAGSER WILDSEE

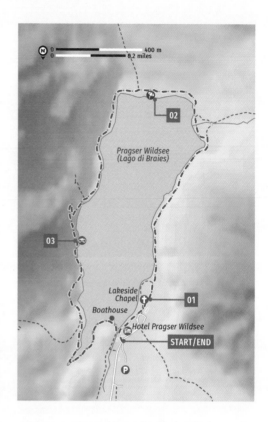

DURATION	DIFFICULTY	DISTANCE	START/END
1¼hrs	Easy	3.5km	Hotel Pragser Wildsee

TERRAIN	Mainly flat, with one short uphill

Traversing forests and beaches, this easygoing loop circles the shores of the gorgeous, mountain-ringed Pragser Wildsee (Lago di Braies). The first half of the walk, along the lake's western shore, readily accommodates strollers and wheel-chairs, while the narrower path along the eastern shore involves one brief climb.

GETTING HERE

From Niederdorf (Villabassa) train station, drive or take bus 442 (20 minutes, hourly) 13km southwest through the Pragsertal to Hotel Pragser Wildsee.

STARTING POINT

The walk starts and ends at the Hotel Pragser Wild-see, where you'll find restaurants, toilets, a paid car park and a wall-mounted trail map.

01 Walk towards the boathouse (pictured p16), 100m south of the parking lot on the lake's northern shore. You're instantly rewarded with your first views of the emerald green Pragser Wildsee, backed by the imposing peaks of Seekofel (2810m), Grosser Rosskofel (2559m) and Herrstein (2447m) in Parco Naturale di Fanes-Sennes-Braies. Head counterclockwise around the lake, following signs for Seeweg (Giro del Lago), a broad flat path skirting the lake's western shore. Within five minutes, you'll reach a large stone barn, famous throughout Italy as a filming location for the TV series *Un Passo dal Cielo*. A few paces further on, stop to admire the thin-steepled **lakeside chapel** (pictured left and on p139), where a plaque commemorates the 133 Allied hostages liberated here at the end of WWII.

02 Continue through a shady wood, catching occasional glimpses of boaters rowing against a backdrop of peaks reflected in the lake's

Lakeside Hospitality

Dominating the lakeshore since 1899, the grand old **Hotel Pragser Wildsee** (Hotel Lago di Braies; ☎ 0474 74 86 02; www.pragserwildsee.com; St Veit 27, Braies; s €109-145, d €174-246, all incl half-board) is a longtime favourite European vacation spot. Its tradition of hospitality dates back to Austro-Hungarian imperial days, when it hosted the likes of Archduke Franz Ferdinand. In the waning days of WWII, the three-storey hotel also offered shelter to several dozen freed prisoners from 17 European countries upon their transfer from Dachau and other Nazi concentration camps.

ANDRII VATSYK/SHUTTERSTOCK ©

placid waters. At a junction with trail 19 to Grünwald Alm, keep left, continuing past signposted toilet facilities towards the broad expanse of **beach** at the lake's southern edge. The pebbly shores here offer a welcome break – and an invigorating swimming spot for those undaunted by the lake's icy waters. Traditional legends of the local Ladin people immortalised this end of the lake as 'Sass dia Porta', the gateway to the underworld.

03 The trail narrows as you continue towards the lake's steeper eastern shore, passing a signposted junction with the Alta Via 1, one of the

Dolomites' legendary 'high routes'. Long-distance backpackers turn right here to reach the high country of Parco Naturale di Fanes-Sennes-Braies – but your easier lakeside route hugs the shoreline as it curves gently left and re-enters the forest. Pass a lovely green cove on the left, cross through a gate with a rather amusing 'Beware of Cows' sign, and zigzag 100m uphill along a wooden railing to reach the trail's **high point**. Benches along this stretch invite you to pause and soak up views of the lake's eastern slopes plunging into the waters below. A 15-minute walk brings you back to the **boathouse**, where you can

extend your visit by renting a handmade 'Lancetta' rowboat.

TAKE A BREAK

Bypass the trailside chalet snack shack and head 25 minutes north to **Durnwald** (☎ 0474 74 68 86; http:// restaurantdurnwald.it; Nikolaus-Amhof-Strasse 6, Pichl, Gsies; meals €30-42; ⏱ noon-2pm & 7-9pm Tue-Sun), a family-run gem in the pastoral Gsiesertal. Seasonal, locally sourced South Tyrolean specialties such as venison goulash with polenta, pork medallions with chanterelles and porcini, spinach dumplings, house-cured meats, smoked trout mousse and homemade apple fritters are all served with a smile.

39

PERCORSO DELLE SEGHERIE

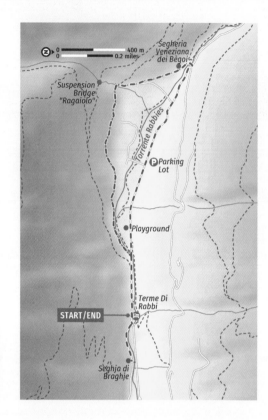

DURATION	DIFFICULTY	DISTANCE	START/END
1½hrs	Easy	4km	Terme di Rabbi

TERRAIN	Level paved and dirt roads

Gentle terrain and outstanding scenery combine on this walk through the verdant Val di Rabbi on Parco Nazionale dello Stelvio's eastern doorstep. The trail, whose name means 'Path of the Sawmills', connects a pair of historic water-driven mills along the Torrente Rabbies.

The signposted **Percorso delle Segherie** starts from **Terme di Rabbi**, the 19th-century spa-hotel complex surrounding Val di Rabbi's natural hot springs. Steep green meadows rise towards pine and larch forest on either side as the paved road follows the valley floor west. Pass a parking lot on the right and continue gently uphill another 700m to a left-hand turnoff marked 'Segheria Begoi'. Here, the trail becomes a wide unpaved path following the rushing **Torrente Rabbiés** downstream.

Immediately on your right is the **Segheria Veneziana dei Bègoi**, a working 18th-century sawmill with an impressive **river-driven water wheel**. In summer, free guided tours offer a close-up glimpse of its ingenious hydraulic mechanisms sawing wood. Continue down the wide footpath through shady forest. About 500m downstream, turn your gaze right (uphill) to see a waterfall and a dizzyingly perched 100m **suspension footbridge** (pictured).

Still paralleling the river, the trail gently rises and falls through forest, rejoining the paved valley road 1km downstream. At the junction, a sprawling **playground** in a grassy field invites kids to get their wiggles out. Continue 500m downstream past the spa hotel and branch right onto a smaller road just beyond the orange village church. Within minutes, you'll reach the **Seghja Di Braghje**, a second historic sawmill. Cross a wooden bridge and turn left, returning along the main road to your starting point.

40

ADOLF MUNKEL WEG

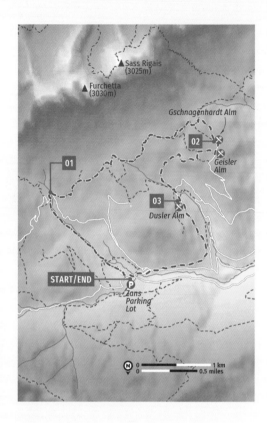

DURATION	DIFFICULTY	DISTANCE	START/END
2½hrs	Moderate	9km	Zans parking lot

TERRAIN	Dirt roads and forest trails

For mesmerising in-your-face views of the Odle group without breaking too much of a sweat, consider this family-friendly loop, which shepherds you through the high country at the base of these peaks in less than three hours.

GETTING HERE

Zans sits in the upper Val di Funes, 50km northeast of Bolzano. SAD buses run here from Brixen (50 minutes). Drivers can follow the squiggly, signposted road 6km uphill from St Magdalena.

STARTING POINT

At Zans, you'll find a parking lot and a cafe-restaurant with restroom facilities.

01 Hit the dirt road east of the Zans parking lot, following signs for trail 6 (Adolf Munkel

Weg). The broad path climbs between fences into the forest, with a creek running parallel and rock spires peeking out between the trees ahead. After 20 minutes, at a clearing with a cluster of signposts, turn right to follow trail 35 (Adolf Munkel Weg) towards Brogles Alm. The trail crosses a creek, narrows and enters the woods, soon yielding **sublime views** of the rocky pinnacles of Sass Rigais (3025m) and Furchetta (3030m) towering overhead. An un-numbered trail on the left leads to the Klettergarten, a popular spot for rock climbers. Keep straight here and at two other intersections on the right for trails 36B and 36A. Throughout this stretch, the views of the Odle group to the left are stupendous, especially when rays of morning sunlight come streaming through the crags.

02 At the next junction, after nearly an hour zigzagging along the rocky face, turn away from the mountains and join trail 36 towards

Fairy-Tale Mountain Chapel

If a single image can sum up the Dolomites' mix of natural beauty and human steward-ship, it's the chapel of **St Johann** (San Giovanni; pictured) in Ranui, just east of St Magdalena Villnöss (Santa Maddalena di Funes), 45km northeast of Bolzano. Sitting alone in a meadow below the Odle group, this teensy baroque church is one of South Tyrol's most icon-ic photo-ops. The surrounding Villnösstal (Val di Funes) is a charmed land of small villages and working farmsteads. For bird's-eye perspectives on the valley, snake uphill towards Würzjoch (Passo delle Erbe, 2006m) on the insanely narrow but staggeringly scenic SP163 and SP29.

Best for

FAMILIES

ACHIM THOMAE/GETTY IMAGES ©

Gschnagenhardt Alm. A staircase climbs into the forest on your right, affording **gorgeous views** back over the Dolomites glowing in evergreen-filtered sunlight. The trail soon levels out and passes through a gate into a vast meadow dotted with evergreens. Moments later, you arrive at **Gschnagenhardt Alm** (Malga Casnago, 2006m), a high-country farmstead with a large front ter-race beckoning you in for a beer. Less than five minutes further on, you'll come to **Geisler Alm**, another high-country hut at the junction of trails 34 and 36. Take the right fork onto trail 36 and cross a boardwalk through the field, reaching a new crossroads

within moments. Here you take the left fork, trail 36 to Dusler Alm and Zans.

03 Trail 36 continues down through the woods, reaching a junction with trail 36B after 15 minutes. Turn left here on a wide dirt road and shortly after enter a clearing where the **Dusler Alm** mountain hut sets a classic South Tyrolean tone with its red eagle flag, wooden shutters, geranium-filled flower boxes and gnomes peeking out from heart-shaped cutouts in the woodpile. Trail 36 leaves Dusler Alm as a narrow path through the meadow, soon entering the woods and reaching

a junction with trail 34B. Turn right and climb through the woods on a root-ridden, rocky stretch of trail; 10 minutes later, turn left, taking trail 33 back to your starting point.

 **TAKE A BREAK**

Boasting panoramic views of the Odle group, the family-run **Gschnagenhardt Alm** (www. gschnagenhardtalm.it) sits sur-rounded by alpine meadows in the high country east of St Magdalena. It makes a festive place to stop for dumplings and beer on a walk through the high country, especially when the live accordion music is in full swing!

Also Try...

MOLARJUNG/SHUTTERSTOCK ©

RODA DE PÜTIA

Encompassing everything from gentle pastures to rugged ravines, this high-altitude loop offers the added bonus of multiple mountain huts where you can recharge your batteries.

Park at Wurzjoch (1987m), one of the Dolomites' most remote passes, and take the signposted Roda de Pütia trail towards Sass de Pütia (Peitlerkofel), the hulking 2875m mountain to your south. At the Malga Fornella hut, branch right on trail 8A (pictured), then continue onto trail 4, proceeding anti-clockwise around the mountain's base and climbing 1¼ hours through a barren, rock-strewn landscape to Forcella de Putia (2361m). East of the pass, a dirt road descends through huge green meadows. Continue circumnavigating Sass de Putia on trails 35 and 8B, passing two welcoming mountain huts – Ütia Vaćiara and Ütia de Göma – to close the loop at Malga Fornella and return to Wurzjoch.

DURATION 4hrs
DIFFICULTY Moderate
DISTANCE 13km

SECEDA TO PIERALONGIA

For top-of-the-world views with limited exertion, nothing beats this family-friendly, gondola-assisted loop through the high pastures and ski slopes above Val Gardena.

Ride the cable car from Ortisei up to Seceda (2518m), where a vast trail network fans out below the ridge separating Val Gardena from Val di Funes. Walk east from the gondola station, following trails 1 and 2B towards the prominent rocky outcrop of Pieralongia. Here you can stop for homemade hot chocolate, buttermilk or beer at family-run Malga Pieralongia. Loop back to Seceda, serenaded by mooing cows and goat bells. First descend trail 4A toward Col Raiser, then climb trail 1, with another optional snack stop at the luxurious Trojer Hütte. For a last-minute thrill, detour up trail 6 towards Furcela de Pana, where views of the knife-edged ridge dropping into Val de Funes are spellbinding.

DURATION 1¾hrs
DIFFICULTY Easy
DISTANCE 5km

ALESSANDRO PERSIANI/SHUTTERSTOCK ©

GIRO DEL BULLACCIA

Europe's largest alpine meadow forms the backdrop for this panoramic loop with wrap-around views of the Dolomites.

From Compatsch's cable-car station, trail 14 meanders north through meadows to Arnika Hütte, revealing views west to Schlern's spiky-toothed profile. Climb 20 minutes further to Hexenbänke (Witches' Benches), a rocky outcrop with bird's-eye perspectives over Val Gardena, then loop back to the cable car via Puflatschhütte, through pastures overlooking Sassolungo and the Seiser Alm (Alpe di Siusi).

DURATION 3hrs
DIFFICULTY Moderate
DISTANCE 10km

GIRO DEI LAGHI

Val di Pejo (pictured) in Parco Nazionale dello Stelvio is home to several famous peaks and glaciers, and the lake-riddled highlands that form the backdrop for this strenuous half-day loop.

From Malga Mare (2031m), climb steadily up trail 102 to Rifugio Larcher (2607m), enjoying views to Monte Cevedale (3769m) and the Careser Glacier. Trail 104 continues to Lago delle Marmotte, then joins trail 123, descending past Lago Lungo and Lago Nero to the dam at Lago Careser before dropping steeply back to Malga Mare.

DURATION 5½hrs
DIFFICULTY Hard
DISTANCE 12km

SENTIERO DELLE CASCATE

At the Brenta Dolomites' western edge, the pristine Val di Genova is great walking country, laced with splendid waterfalls.

The 16km 'Waterfalls Trail' follows the Torrente Sarca di Genova upriver past four mountain huts serving refreshments – Chalet da Gino, Rifugio Fontana Bona, Rifugio Stella Alpina and Rifugio Bedole. From July through early September, private vehicles are banned and a free shuttle runs the length of the valley, facilitating return transport from various points along the trail.

DURATION 6hrs
DIFFICULTY Moderate
DISTANCE 16km

0 ⌐────────────┐ **10 km**
N └────────────┘
0 ⌐────────┐ **5 miles**

Irgoli

Fuile
Mare

Galtelli

Monte
▲Tuttavista

Orosei

Marina di
Orosei

Nuoro

Monte
▲Ortobene
(955m)

Cala
Cartoe

Oliena

Dorgali

Valle di Lanaittu

Cala
Gonone

43

Caletta
Fuili

45

Monte
Tiscali
(515m)

Grotta
del Blue
Marino

Golfo di
Orosei

Monte
Corrasi
(1463m)

Gola di
Gorropu

Cala
Luna

Orgosolo

Monte Oddeu
(1063m)▲

42

Parco Nazionale del
Golfo di Orosei e
del Gennargentu

44

Supramonte

Cala
Sisine

Passo Genna
e Silana

Foresta de Montes

Cala
Mariolu

Cala
Goloritzè

Passo di
Caravai

Urzulei

41

Arcu
Carreboi

Capo di
Monte Santo

Altopiano
del Golgo

Monti del Gennargentu

Talana

Tyrrhenian
Sea

Punta La
▲Marmora
(1834m)

Baunei

Villagrande
Strisaili

Santa Maria
Navarrese

Lago Alto della
Flumendosa

Lotzorai

Isola
dell'Ogliastra

Monte Perda Liana
(1293m)▲

Arzana

Tortoli

Arbatax

SARDINIA

41 **Cala Goloritzé** Descend through ancient oaks to a secluded turquoise cove. **p168**

42 **Gola di Gorropu** Follow a river valley into one of Europe's deepest canyons. **p170**

43 **Tiscali** Climb to a mysterious abandoned village in a collapsed cave. **p172**

44 **Cala Sisine to Cala Luna** Explore one of Italy's most secluded and dramatic coastlines. **p176**

45 **Monte Corrasi** Survey the rugged Supramonte from a windswept limestone summit. **p178**

Explore
SARDINIA

Lapped by seductively beautiful blue-green waters and crowned by sparsely vegetated limestone highlands, Sardinia is one of Italy's most unique and eye-catching regions. The island's remote mid-Med location – roughly equidistant from Tunisia, Spain, France and Italy – has left Sardinia with a culture, cuisine and language all its own. Hikers here will find a world of intrigue, from gorgeous coastal walks to mysterious archaeological sites, isolated mountaintops and deep canyons. Of particular interest is Parco Nazionale Gennargentu, sprawling from the Golfo di Orosei across the vast limestone massif of the Supramonte to Sardinia's highest peak, Punta La Marmora.

CALA GONONE

Reached by a long descent through hairpin bends and boasting grandstand views of the dazzling blue Golfo di Orosei, the seaside resort of Cala Gonone has a low-key, family-friendly vibe. A slew of boat operators based at Cala Gonone's port run tours down the glorious coastline, granting access to the gulf's most pristine and secluded beaches. Outside of August, conditions are relatively uncrowded and rates affordable at Cala Gonone's glut of hotels and restaurants. In winter, the resort slumbers, closing from November until Easter.

BAUNEI

Clinging to a high ridge on the tortuous road between Arbatax and Dorgali, the old stone shepherds' village of Baunei is an agreeable mountain outpost on the Supramonte's south-eastern edge. Just above town sits the Altopiano del Golgo, an otherworldly plateau where goats, pigs and donkeys graze in the *macchia* (Mediterranean scrub), and where you'll find the trailhead for the magnificent walk to Cala Goloritzé. Services in Baunei are limited to a handful of hotels and restaurants, but in this lonely corner of the island, it feels like a welcome oasis indeed.

DORGALI

Dorgali is a workaday town with a grandiose backdrop, nestled at the foot of Monte Bardia and framed by vineyards and olive groves. Limestone peaks rear above the centre's pastel-coloured houses and steep, narrow streets, luring hikers and climbers to their summits. While the town itself is not particularly prepossessing, the sparkling Golfo di Orosei and spectacular Supramonte are within easy striking distance, making it a convenient base, especially for trips to nearby Gola di Gorropu.

NUORO

About 40km inland from the coast, Nuoro is Sardinia's

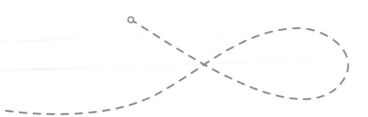

sixth-largest city, home to a university and a good ethnographic museum. A hodgepodge of modern buildings sprawls down Nuoro's hillsides, backed by the granite peak of Monte Ortobene (955m). With a full range of tourist services, it makes a good base for exploring the nearby Supramonte.

☀ WHEN TO GO

The best period for walking is springtime, when days are lengthening, wildflowers are in bloom and there are frequent patron saint feast days in the local villages. Autumn is also a pleasant time to walk. Winter is too cold, and summer – when the beaches get packed with tourists – is far too hot for walking.

✈ TRANSPORT

Sardinia has commercial airports at Cagliari in the south, Olbia in the northeast and Alghero in the northwest. Ferries serve the island from Corsica, Toulon and Marseille (France), Sicily, Genoa, Livorno, Civitavecchia and Naples (Italy), and Barcelona (Spain). Train service on the island is slow

and limited to a few main routes connecting urban centres such as Cagliari, Oristano, Sassari and Olbia. Buses operated by **Azienda Regionale Sarda Trasporti** (ARST; ☎800 865042; www.arst.sardegna. it) offer service to smaller towns around the island. However, to really explore Sardinia and reach the most interesting trailheads, you'll need to have your own wheels.

🛎 WHERE TO STAY

Sardinia offers a variety of attractive accommodation options, from beach hotels to family-run B&Bs to *agriturismi* (farm stays). Top choices include **Casa Solotti** (☎328 6028975, 0784 3 39 54; www.casasolotti.it; Località Monte Ortobene; per person €26-35; P ❄ 🛜) in Nuoro, where hosts Mario and Frédérique offer a wealth of walking advice, and the side-by-side *agriturismi* of **Codula Fuili** (☎340 2546208, 328 7340863; www.codulafuili.com; Località Pranos; r per person incl breakfast €35-60, half-board €65-90, camping 2 people, car & tent €16-20) and **Nuraghe Mannu** (☎0784 9 32 64, 328 8685824; www.agriturismo nuraghemannu.com; Località Pranos; r per person incl breakfast €29-36, half-board €48-55, camping per per-

Resources

Sardegna Turismo (www.sardegnaturismo.it) Sardinia's official tourism website.

Parco Nazionale Gennargentu (www.parcogennargentu.it) Website for Parco Nazionale Gennargentu.

Namaste (☎0784 9 37 23; Viale Colombo 11; ⊗8am-1pm & 4-8pm) Great source for hiking maps and guides in Cala Gonone.

son €10-12) in Cala Gonone, both picturesquely perched above the Golfo di Orosei and regaling hikers with fabulous multi-course home-cooked dinners.

👍 WHAT'S ON

Settimana Santa Holy Week in Sardinia is a big deal, with solemn processions and Passion plays all over the island.

Sagra del Redentore (Festa del Redentore) Horsemen and dancers accompany Sardinia's grandest costumed parade in August, a pilgrimage to the statue of Christ the Redeemer on Nuoro's Monte Ortobene.

Autunno in Barbagia Rural villages in Barbagia host foodie events, craft fairs and workshops at this autumn festival, held from September to December.

41

CALA GOLORITZÉ

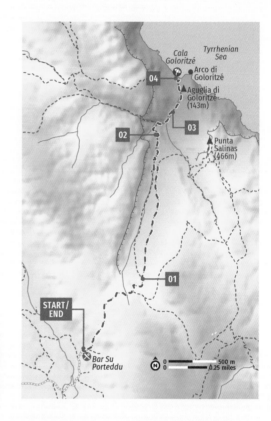

DURATION	DIFFICULTY	DISTANCE	START/END
2½hrs	Moderate	7.5km	Bar Su Porteddu

TERRAIN	Wide rocky path, moderately steep

Descending to the sea through a canyon replete with ancient oaks and sheer limestone outcrops, this trail is a Sardinian classic. The walk culminates at one of Sardinia's most dazzling coves, where limpid turquoise waters compete for your attention with a long sweep of coastal cliffs and a dagger-shaped pinnacle popular with climbers.

GETTING HERE

Climb from Baunei onto the Altopiano del Golgo. After 8km, turn right on a dirt track, following signs 1.2km to the trailhead.

STARTING POINT

The trailhead at Su Porteddu has a ticket kiosk, restrooms, parking and a bar-restaurant serving drinks and snacks.

01 Start with a gradual but steady 10-minute ascent from the **Su Porteddu ticket booth**. Scurrying pigs add a dose of atmosphere as the rocky trail climbs through scrubby vegetation, then levels out, rounding a bend along the hilltop ridge to reveal first glimpses of Aguglia, the distinctive rocky pinnacle on the shoreline far below. At an unmarked junction 15 minutes from the trailhead, a trail to Punta Salinas heads uphill on your right. The main trail bears left here – watch for a stone engraved with the word 'Goloritzé' – and begins descending a rock-strewn canyon, passing between low stone walls and under a succession of ancient oaks. Moments later, amidst a heavily eroded section of trail, another rock engraved 'Goloritzé' offers reassurance that you're on the right track.

02 Chirping birds accompany your descent into the canyon, through a landscape regularly punctuated by grand oaks growing among boulders.

Google Maps Goof-Ups

In 2019, Baunei mayor Salvatore Corrias made an impassioned plea to all tourists travelling through Sardinia's sparsely populated Supramonte region: don't rely on Google Maps! The problem? Way too many hapless visitors were putting their faith in Google and getting lost in the Supramonte on remote roads unsuited even for donkey traffic; official tallies counted 144 stranded vehicles in a two-year period, including some with 4WD! Corrias's solution? Put up dozens of official signs on local roadways warning people not to follow Google's instructions. The signs were in place by late 2019 and expected to stay up until Google sends out a new research team.

Best for

COASTAL SCENERY

MARCIN KRZYŻAK/SHUTTERSTOCK ©

Occasional shepherds' dwellings are built into the rocky outcrop on your right, while a pronounced cliff face towers across the valley to your left. Half an hour into the descent, just beyond a section bordered by low moss-covered stone walls, arrive at **a clearing with dramatic perspectives** on the Aguglia pinnacle framed by trees.

03 Continuing downhill, pass under a giant oak below a sheer white rock wall on your right, then come to another clearing with views of cavelike depressions on the canyon wall to the north. You're now deep into the canyon, with rock walls

looming on all sides, and a low stone fence defining the edges of the rocky path. The trail passes through a rock archway, then re-enters shady woods. After a final flat and easy stretch through the forest, you get your first close-up **views of the coastline** ahead.

04 Moments later, reach the fence and wooden staircase that mark the end of the trail, and zigzag on down to the beach at **Cala Goloritzé** (pictured above and on p5). A ravishing landscape of **white rocks and turquoise seas** greets you at this secluded cove accessible only by foot or boat. The beach is espe-

cially splendid early morning or late afternoon, when the absence of tour boats allows you to fully absorb Goloritzé's raw natural beauty. Linger as long as you like, then retrace your steps to Su Porteddu.

 TAKE A BREAK

Set in a huge parking lot directly opposite the Cala Goritzè trailhead, **Bar Su Porteddu** (☏ 320 7481158; www.facebook.com/pg/suporteddu; Altopiano del Golgo; ⏰ 7am-2am) is a welcome stop for morning cappuccinos, trail snacks or homemade sandwiches and drinks after your hike. There are also basic camping facilities here.

42

GOLA DI GORROPU

DURATION	DIFFICULTY	DISTANCE	START/END
4½hrs	Moderate	14km	Chiosco Sa Barva

TERRAIN	Wide multi-surface road, dirt trails

Sometimes touted as Sardinia's Grand Canyon, the precipitous Gorropu gorge is flanked by limestone walls towering up to 500m. This popular approach along a scenic stretch of river offers opportunities for a swim and/or a picnic along the way.

GETTING HERE

Turn off the SS125 3km south of Dorgali and follow the signposted dirt road 10km southwest to Chiosco Sa Barva (on your right just before a bridge).

STARTING POINT

Selling drinks and snacks, Chiosco Sa Barva is a simple kiosk with a dirt parking area. ('Sa Barva', also spelled 'S'Abba Arva', means 'white water' in Sardinian.)

01 Cross the Flumineddu at the bridge below the parking lot, turning left at the Ponte S'Abba Arva (200m) signpost to head upstream on a wide flat road. At the next junction (Sa Roda), pass through a wooden gate and enjoy nice views over a bend in the river as you climb along cobblestones and concrete pavement to **S'Arcu 'e Dispensa** (255m). A rough descent marked by sand, protruding rocks and rutted dirt leads to **Su Balladorzu** (225m), where picnic tables and a pretty beach invite you to pause by the riverside. The road eventually peters out completely at a rocky outcrop where only red-and-white blazes mark the route.

02 The trail narrows and enters the woods, soon arriving at shady **Cantaru Orruos** (275m), a natural spring surrounded by stone walls. Five minutes beyond the spring, a 'Jeep Transfer' sign points left to a river crossing used by jeeps coming in from the SS125 (steeply uphill to your east). Over the next half-hour

COOLR/SHUTTERSTOCK ©

climb through shady forest, then zigzag up an embankment to a high, open **viewpoint** near the signposted Sant'Anna junction (375m). Fine views of the gorge walls loom ahead, and you soon descend steeply to the entrance booth on the valley floor.

03 Enter the boulder-choked canyon and begin exploring. The dry river bed is accessible for 1.5km here, with the Flumineddu flowing through unseen subterranean channels. Flora and fauna in the gorge includes **golden eagles, mouflons, foxes,** and a rare endemic species of **Aquilegia** (columbine). Green arrows and paint dots mark the route for the first 500m. Cross improvised wooden bridges and climb towards a cave-like overhang on the right, where a surprising burst of greenery contrasts with the gorge's otherwise barren landscape. The canyon walls, which towered 350m above you at the entrance, rise to 500m at the gorge's narrowest, most vertiginous point, a 5m-wide gap that you'll reach within 15 minutes. Beyond this point, yellow paint marks the 500m intermediate section, with bigger rocks and more slippery footing. The last 500m section of the gorge, marked with red blazes, is only open to experienced climbers with equipment. The most famous spot for climbing is called **Hotel Supramonte**, a 400m climb rated 8B at the foot of an 888m peak. When you've reached your limit, retrace your steps to Sa Barva.

TAKE A BREAK

Snacks are available at Chiosco Sa Barva, but hungry hikers should hold out for dinner and panoramic sunset views at **Ristorante Ispinigoli** (www. hotelispinigoli.it), in the countryside northeast of Dorgali. Linger over local delights such as black ravioli with mullet roe, herb-infused roast kid and a waistline-expanding selection of cheeses.

43

TISCALI

Best for

HISTORY & CULTURE

DURATION	DIFFICULTY	DISTANCE	START/END
3hrs	Moderate	9km	Su Ruvagliu

TERRAIN	Dirt road and rocky trails

Hidden in a mountaintop cave high above the Valle di Lanaittu, the mysterious nuraghic village of Tiscali is one of Sardinia's must-see archaeological highlights. Dating from the 6th century BC and populated until Roman times, the village was re-discovered in the late 19th century. At that time it was relatively intact, but since then grave robbers have done a pretty good job of looting the place, stripping the conical stone-and-mud huts down to the skeletal remains that you see today.

GETTING HERE

You'll need your own wheels. Leave the SP46 between Oliena and Dorgali, following signs to Su Gologone, then continuing 7km south through the remote Lanaitto valley on a rough dirt road.

STARTING POINT

Near the southeastern end of the Lanaitto valley road, Su Ruvagliu (180m) is nothing more than a dirt parking area. Services are 7km north at Su Gologone.

01 From the parking lot, follow signs for trail 410 to Tiscali, heading uphill (southeast) along a continuation of the same broad dirt road you drove in on. After a few switchbacks, just beyond a bend where the park ranger often parks his vehicle, continue ascending steadily on a stony old woodcutters' path marked by red-and-white blazes on rocks and trees. The trail passes through a **forest** of holm oak (*Quercus ilex*) and mastic (*Pistacia lentiscus*), with occasional switchbacks as you climb.

02 Straight ahead, about 40 minutes into the walk, is a huge exposed white rock commanding **exceptional views over the Valle di Lanaittu** below. The sun-baked landscape that spreads before you – seas of olive groves backed by the stark limestone profile of Monte Corrasi – served as a film location for John Huston's 1966 film *The Bible: In the Beginning*. The valley is also home to some important prehistoric archaeological sites, most notably the 5-hectare **Sa Sedda 'e Sos Carros**, whose circular Temple of the Sacred Well – surrounded by stone spouts that would have fed spring water into a huge central basin – is unique in Sardinia.

03 Be careful not to continue straight (south)

beyond the white rock; rather, watch on the left (east) side of the road for a pair of stones with well-defined red-and-white stripes and a faded red arrow; these mark the continuation of trail 410, which branches off the main road here and begins climbing, with roots and rocks underfoot, towards an imposing orange-and-grey outcrop clearly visible above the trees to the northeast. Wooden steps ease your progress through a forest punctuated with wind-sculpted ancient junipers. About 20 minutes after leaving the white rock, reach the signposted Curtigia 'e Tiscali junction (485m), where trail 410 meets up with trail

480. Turn left at the signpost, following trail 410 up a series of rocky steps to a **secret cleft** in the rock face. A narrow passage takes you straight through to the other side of the crevice, where the trail begins descending.

04 You now skirt a wide **rocky ledge** (pictured p174) bordered on your right by an impressive vertical wall of wind- and water-sculpted grey-and-orange limestone. After passing a prominent gnarled juniper on your left (one of several such trees along this stretch), pay careful attention to stay on the trail and avoid a drop-off on the right. The path

Nuraghic Culture

Sardinia's unique prehistoric culture remains mysterious, even to scholars. Starting in the second millennium BC, the island's nuraghic people evolved from Bronze Age farmers into skilled metallurgists and stonemasons. Their upland settlements featured distinctive conical towers, so sturdily built that over 7000 of them still remain. Nuraghic civilisation also fashioned human-like statuettes known as *bronzetti* from locally produced bronze, and traded them with societies in the Balearics, Greece, Crete and Sicily. Nuraghic culture mysteriously began fizzling out around 500 BC with the arrival of the Phoenicians. Its final trouncing came with the Romans' arrival in 238 BC.

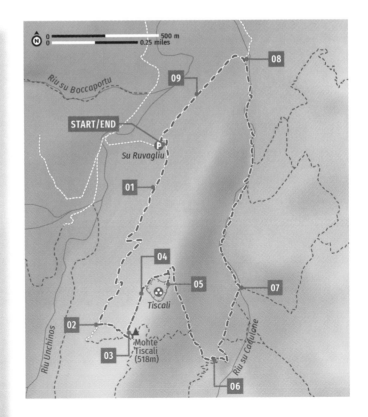

becomes uneven, with stones clinking underfoot as you descend, but remains well marked with frequent red-and-white blazes. Round the corner of the mountain, soon reaching Tiscali junction (420m).

05 A spur trail branches right here, climbing to the ruins of **Tiscali**. Within five minutes, cross the lip of the cave and continue down a stone staircase with wood and rope handrails to the entrance gate, where you pay a €5 fee. Despite the fragmentary condition of the ruins themselves, Tiscali is an awe-inspiring sight, with jumbled stone foundations amid holm oak and turpentine trees huddled in the eerie twilight of the limestone overhang. The inhabitants of nearby Sa Sedda 'e Sos Carros used this remote outpost as a hiding place from the Romans, and its inaccessibility ensured that the Sards were able to hold out here until well into the 2nd century BC.

06 Leave Tiscali on trail 481 towards Dolovèrre, descending steeply at first through a labyrinth of juniper forest before levelling out after about 15 minutes. You'll soon come to a junction labeled **Pala Úporo** (305m), where trail 480A branches southeast towards Su Praicarzu, S'Arcu 'e Doronè and Donanigoro. Stay on trail 481 and continue gradually downhill, north towards Dolovèrre and Ponte S'Abba Arva. The packed earth and stone trail widens and weaves gently downhill below the junction.

The Alternate Route to Tiscali

Hikers can also reach Tiscali from Ponte Sa Barva, the trailhead described in the Gola di Gorropu hike (p170). Upon crossing the Sa Barva bridge, turn right for Tiscali (as opposed to left for Gola di Gorropu) and walk 15 minutes north on trail 481 to the signposted Sùrtana junction (195m). A left turn here takes you up the Scala de Sùrtana, a rather steep and rocky section of trail that climbs 25 minutes to Palas de Puntale (295m). From here it's another 40 minutes through a tree-shaded valley to Dolovèrre junction, where you join the loop trail from the Valley di Lanaittu (see stop 07 of the main hike).

07 Just past a weather-beaten, hand-carved sign pointing towards Oddoene and Dorgali, reach **Dolovèrre junction** (240m), an open clearing with a more reassuring CAI sign atop a brand-new post. Take the left fork, following trail 411 west towards Budurrài and leaving trail 481, which branches east here to Ponte Sa Barva (the alternate route to Tiscali).

08 For the next half-hour stay on trail 411, ignoring a couple of new trail junctions on your right. Pass a clearing with old stone foundations on your left, followed by a pair of caves traditionally used as shelters by herdsmen and their animals, and stay left at the next fork. You'll soon come to **Bilichinzos junction** (160m), where trail 411 branches right towards Buddurài, while trail 410A branches left towards Su Ruvagliu.

09 A 10-minute jaunt on trail 410A – a broad dirt road climbing gently at first through Mediterranean scrub forest and then into denser woods – returns you to your starting point.

☕ TAKE A BREAK

Nestled at the foot of mountains, the rural retreat of **Su Gologone** (☎0784 28 75 12; www.sugologone.it; Località Su Gologone; meals €35-50; ⊙12.30-3pm & 8-10pm) is a delightful spot for lunch or dinner, with a terrace for sunny afternoons and balmy evenings. The local Cannonau red goes well with regional classics such as *culurgiones* (Sardinian ravioli stuffed with ricotta and mint) and *seadas al miele* (light pastries served with bitter honey).

44

CALA SISINE TO CALA LUNA

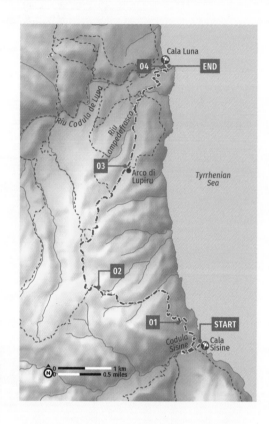

DURATION	DIFFICULTY	DISTANCE	START/END
4hrs	Moderate	12km	Cala Sisine/ Cala Luna

TERRAIN	Dirt trails, some steep sections

A northward extension of Sardinia's legendary Selvaggio Blu climbing route, this stunning coastal walk connects two of Golfo di Orosei's dreamiest beaches. En route, you'll cross the Supramonte's lonely, lovely limestone uplands and visit Arco di Lupiru, an extraordinary natural stone arch.

GETTING HERE

From Cala Gonone's port, boat operators cruise the coast between April and October (€35 one way to Cala Sisine). Arrange pickup from Cala Luna at day's end, or hike another 9km north to Cala Gonone.

STARTING POINT

Cala Sisine is accessible only by boat or by 4WD from the Altopiano di Baunei. In season, Bar Su Coile serves snacks just inland from the beach.

01 Follow the riverbed inland from **Cala Sisine**, turning right at a tree-shaded camping area and climbing onto the slopes north of the beach. You're soon rewarded with **stunning views up and down the coast**. Within 15 minutes the trail, still climbing, curves hard left away from the sea, then doubles back and levels out on a rocky ledge. Lovely views continue to unfold over Cala Sisine's distinctive hat-shaped promontory and the *macchia*-clad outcrops stretching north towards Cala Gonone.

02 An hour into the journey, after a 15-minute ascent through forest, the trail enters a heavily eroded clearing, then climbs to a second clearing with an amazing pigsty made of driftwood at its centre. The sturdy stone wall here makes a pleasant **picnic spot** – provided you can keep the hungry pigs at bay. Climb another 15 minutes through rocky terrain, watching for a series of cairns that signal your impending arrival at a T-junction with a larger

Selvaggio Blu

It's not Italy's longest hike, but Sardinia's four- to seven-day Selvaggio Blu ('Savage Blue') is a definite contender for the nation's toughest trail. Stretching 40km from Pedra Longa to Cala Sisine, the 'Blu' preserves a network of old charcoal burners' and shepherds' paths criss-crossing the high cliffs above the Golfo di Orosei. UIAA technical ratings ranging from EE to IV+ put it out of reach for all but experienced climbers or those traveling with a professional guide – but mere mortals can appreciate the same vertigo-inducing landscape from below at Cala Goloritè and Cala Sisine, where the coastal hiking trails described in this guide intersect with the Selvaggio Blu.

GREGOR CLARK/LONELY PLANET ©

north–south trail. Turn right onto the new trail, bordered by a low rock wall.

03 Meander through open high country, enjoying long views west over the Supramonte's vast limestone uplands. Towards the coast, a sea of *macchia* initially obscures all but a sliver of distant blue – but soon after passing a 'Cala Luna' sign engraved on a rock, you're greeted by **all-encompassing views of the shoreline** stretching north and south. Moments later begin a steady descent along a shrub-shaded section of trail. Half an hour down the hill, a cairn marks the short right-hand detour

to **Arco di Lupiru**, a symmetrical natural stone arch (pictured) already visible above the trees. The views are spellbinding once you emerge onto the open, rocky shelf below the arch, and a short scramble up the hillside reveals full-on **vistas of the north coast**, seen through the enormous 15m-tall hole in the rock.

04 Resume your descent on the main trail, eventually entering a lonesome canyon where rock walls loom above a dry stony riverbed. Soon after exiting the canyon, arrive at a **viewpoint** with sweeping views north over the sandy beach at Cala Luna (pictured p165). Zig-

zag downhill, passing through a tunnel of trees, to reach a restaurant at the bottom. The trail turns towards the sea, paralleling a stream channel to your left, and within five minutes crosses a pontoon bridge to deposit you on the **beach**.

TAKE A BREAK

Nestled amid silvery olive groves on a high bluff above Cala Gonone (a 10-minute drive from the port), **Agriturismo Nuraghe Mannu** (www.nuraghemannu.com) puts on a feast of home-produced pecorino, salami, olives and wine, followed by handmade pasta, succulent roast kid or lamb, and Sardinian sweets.

45

MONTE CORRASI

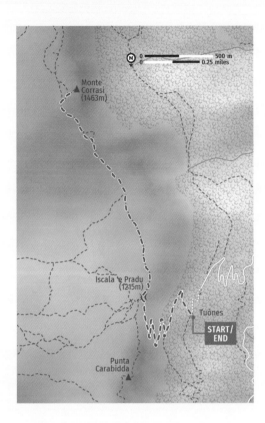

DURATION	DIFFICULTY	DISTANCE	START/END
2½hrs	Moderate	7km	Tuònes

TERRAIN	Wide dirt road and rocky path

Standing proud at the pinnacle of Sardinia's rugged Supramonte region, the limestone peak of Monte Corrasi (1463m) commands amazing perspectives over the eastern reaches of the island. The fairly straightforward climb to its summit yields great scenic rewards.

To reach the trailhead at **Tuònes** (1025m), follow signs for Albergo Monte Maccione off the SP22 south of Oliena, then switchback up a rough dirt road, parking near a **stone circle** 4km past the hotel. Trail 401, marked with red-and-white blazes, starts as a well-graded dirt track climbing past grand old oaks, with an imposing ridge towering overhead. Over the next half hour, the trees disappear as you navigate a series of six switchbacks, dead-ending atop the high exposed saddle of **Iscala 'e Pradu** (1215m).

A **forbidding landscape of whitish-grey stone dotted with junipers** opens up as your trail branches right (south), leaving the road between an unmarked pole and a statuette of the Virgin Mary (watch for a red-and-white '401' painted on a nearby rock). Descending into a vast karst basin, the rocky trail briefly levels out opposite a circular stone-walled sheep pen and some weather-sculpted rocks, then begins climbing steadily, marked by occasional red-and-white blazes.

After 25 minutes, reach a false summit marked **Corrasi** (1430m). Wonderful long views unfurl northeast to the Mediterranean, while sheep jingle their bells on the surrounding crags. To reach the true summit, zigzag five more minutes uphill, following signs for **Punta Corrasi**. Atop the windswept peak, cliffs drop off to the southwest. Enjoy the **magnificent 360-degree views**, then retrace your steps to Tuònes.

Also Try...

TRAVELWILD/SHUTTERSTOCK ©

CALA FUILI TO CALA LUNA

Linking two of the Golfo di Orosei's prettiest beaches, this out-and-back coastal hike makes an easy half-day trip from Cala Gonone (pictured).

At the vehicle turnaround where the paved coastal road dead-ends, 4km south of Cala Gonone, descend a staircase to cross Codula Fuili, a long, deep gorge extending inland from the pleasant beach of Cala Fuili. Continue south, climbing the opposite side of the gorge along a route marked sporadically by green arrows. The stony path cuts through high bushes and low trees with occasional peek-a-boo glimpses of the sea. Descend past the rocky entrance of the Oddoana cave into the gorge of Codula Oddo-ana, then climb back out. Beyond the hill known as Fruncu Nieddu, begin a steep switchbacking descent to the gravel riverbed of the captivating Codula di Luna. A short walk east brings you to magnificent Cala Luna beach.

DURATION 3¾hrs
DIFFICULTY Moderate
DISTANCE 10.5km

MONTE ENTU

This half-day excursion climbs to the summit of Monte Entu (1024m), one of the highest peaks in western Sardinia.

You'll need a car to get to the start, which is by the Nuraghe Ruju picnic area, 9km northwest of Seneghe. Join the path a few metres down from the car park, in the wood to the left of the stone wall. Heading upwards, you'll arrive at an opening, marked by a holm oak tree, where you should go left. Carry on past the wooden gate until you reach a second metal gate. Go through it and continue to a fork in the trail. Head left for some marvellous views of the coast, as far as Alghero on a clear day. From here you can continue onwards to the foot of the volcanic cone that marks the summit of Monte Entu.

DURATION 4hrs
DIFFICULTY Moderate
DISTANCE 12km

WERNER SPREMBERG/SHUTTERSTOCK ©

CAPO TESTA

Resembling a vast sculpture garden, the lighthouse-topped headland of Capo Testa (pictured) is an appealing spot for a day hike.

Set off from the isthmus 4km west of Santa Teresa Gallura, flanked by the twin beaches of Rena di Levante and Rena di Ponente. Circle the cape clockwise, passing through boulder-strewn scrub and admiring the weird and wonderful rock formations created by centuries of wind erosion. Along the way, you can stop to swim and gaze across the Strait of Bonifacio to not-so-distant Corsica.

DURATION 3½hrs
DIFFICULTY Easy
DISTANCE 10km

PUNTA LA MARMORA

This classic ascent leads through treeless high country to Sardinia's highest summit, Punta La Marmora (1834m).

Follow signs from Rifugio S'Arena (off the SP7 south of Fonni) to Arcu Artilai (I1660m), a pass with fine views south across Parco Nazionale Gennargentu Bear right across the slopes of Bruncu Spina (1828m), passing the ruins of Rifugio La Marmora. Beyond the summits of Arcu Gennargentu (1659m) and Genna Orisa (1782m), it's another 15 minutes to Punta La Marmora, whose top-of-the-world credentials are marked by a large cross.

DURATION 5hrs
DIFFICULTY Moderate
DISTANCE 14km

MONTE NOVO SAN GIOVANNI

Seek out this off-the-beaten-track peak, which towers above the rugged landscape of Sardinia's Supramonte.

From Funtana Bona, 15km south of Orgosolo in the Foresta di Montes holm oak preserve, climb east through oak woods, bald hills and rocky outcrops, skirting the base of Monte Fumai to reach Monte Novo San Giovanni. Railings and steps ease your ascent of this intriguing limestone table mountain. Enjoy breathtaking 360-degree views of Sardinia's rock-strewn highlands up top.

DURATION 3hrs
DIFFICULTY Moderate
DISTANCE 9km

UMBRIA & LE MARCHE

46 **Passo del Lupo** Enjoy riveting views of Le Marche's rugged Adriatic coast. **p186**

47 **Gola dell'Infernaccio** Hike through a deep river gorge in Parco Nazionale dei Monti Sibillini. **p188**

48 **Monte Subasio** Climb to St Francis's spiritual retreat high above Assisi. **p190**

49 **Around the Pian Piccolo** Explore vast, lonely grasslands on the Umbria–Le Marche border. **p194**

50 **Bosco di San Francesco** Descend through re-claimed woodland into the olive groves. **p196**

Explore
UMBRIA & LE MARCHE

Umbria bills itself as the 'Green Heart of Italy' for good reason. The rolling verdant landscape makes this a dreamy walking destination, and the region's *centralissimo* location between Rome, Florence and Venice makes it an easy addition to any northern Italian itinerary. Neighbouring Le Marche gets far less press but shares a similar topography, with a long Adriatic coastline thrown in for good measure. For serious walkers, the top draw here is the Parco Nazionale dei Monti Sibillini. Straddling the Umbria–Le Marche border, this little-visited national park boasts some hauntingly lovely landscapes, with wildflower-carpeted plateaus and sheep pastures rising abruptly to craggy peaks.

ASSISI

With the Umbrian plains spreading picturesquely below, and Monte Subasio rearing steeply above, the sight of Assisi in the rosy glow of dusk is enough to send pilgrims' souls spiralling to heaven. When the day trippers have left and the town is shrouded in saintly silence, the true spirit of St Francis of Assisi, born here in 1181, can be keenly felt. As befits a pilgrimage destination, accommodation options and restaurants are abundant and relatively well-priced. However, you don't have to be religious to be struck by Assisi's beauty and enjoy its pristine *centro storico* (historic centre) and Unesco-listed basilica.

CASTELLUCCIO

Severely damaged by earthquakes in 2016, the hilltop town of Castelluccio has been steadily rebuilding its tourist infrastructure and remains a mecca for hikers and hang-gliders thanks to its stunning setting at the heart of the Piano Grande, an ethereal high plateau that explodes with colourful floral displays every spring. Castelluccio is also a popular gateway for hikes through the mountains and gorges of neighbouring Parco Nazionale dei Monti Sibllini. The village has only a limited handful of accommodations (best booked well in advance), and local restaurants mostly operate out of provisional structures along the main road below the earthquake-shattered heart of town. Still, nothing compares to the magic of spending a night in this remote, peaceful outpost, especially when the moon is full.

ANCONA

More a transport hub than a destination in its own right, Le Marche's seafront capital offers ferries across the Adriatic and train connections throughout Italy. For hikers, it's the gateway to the Conero Riviera, a scenic stretch of cliffs and beaches just south of the city that breaks the monotony of the otherwise flat Adriatic shoreline. Founded by Greek settlers from Syracuse around 387 BC, Ancona's old

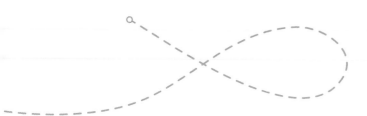

Resources

Umbria Tourism (www.umbria tourism.it) Umbria's official tourism website.

Le Marche Tourism (www.turismo.marche.it) Le Marche's official tourism website.

Parco Nazionale dei Monti Sibillini (www.sibillini.net) Information on Sibillini National Park.

town is crowned by a theatrically sited cathedral, and there are enough archaeological artefacts, Roman arches, Romanesque churches and Renaissance *palazzi* to keep you busy before and after a day of hiking.

WHEN TO GO

Spring and fall are gorgeous times to experience Umbria's green rolling hills and the coastal paths of Le Marche without full-on summertime heat and crowds. Late spring is peak season for viewing wildflowers on the Piano Grande. If you plan to hike at higher elevations in the Monti Sibillini, the summer months (between June and September) are ideal.

TRANSPORT

Umbria International Airport San Francesco d'Assisi (☎ 075 59 21 41; www.airport.umbria.it; Via dell'Aeroporto, Sant'Egidio) outside Perugia and **Marche Airport** (☎ 071 2 82 71; www.aeroportomarche.it; Piazzale Sandro Sordoni, Falconara Marittima) in Ancona are the main international gateways to Umbria and Le Marche respectively. Trains serve the two regions on

the Rome–Ancona and Rome–Florence lines. By car, the A14 autostrada and slower SS16 run down Le Marche's coastline while the A1 and SS3bis connect Rome with Umbria's capital, Perugia. If driving to Perugia from Florence and the north, take the A1 and RA6 *(raccordo autostradale)*. To properly explore the Parco Nazionale dei Monti Sibillini, you really need your own wheels.

WHERE TO STAY

B&Bs, hotels and *affittacamere* (simple rooms for let) make up the bulk of accommodation in most hilltop villages, but the best way to experience Umbria and Le Marche's pastoral scenery is to stay at one of the regions' many *agriturismi* (farm stays). Assisi offers a fair share of pilgrimage and/or religiously affiliated sleeps as well, and there's plenty of camping on Le Marche's coast and around Umbria's Lago Trasimeno.

WHAT'S ON

Corsa dei Ceri (www.ceri.it) Gubbio's centuries-old race features three teams carrying

massive wooden pillars bearing the statues of saints through the city's medieval streets in May.

Umbria Jazz (www.umbriajazz.com) Perugia's swinging 10-day festival in July has put the city firmly on the world jazz map, with international headliners and events held all over town.

Festa del Duca (www.urbino festadelduca.it) Every August, Urbino time-travels back to the Middle Ages, with medieval fun in the form of costumed pageants, markets and the re-enactment of a horseback tournament.

Macerata Opera Festival (www.sferisterio.it; Arena Sferisterio) Macerata's Arena Sferisterio provides the stage for the one of Italy's foremost musical events, attracting the cream of the operatic world every summer.

46

PASSO DEL LUPO

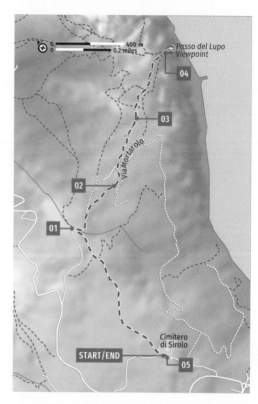

DURATION	DIFFICULTY	DISTANCE	START/END
1½hrs	Easy	4.5km	Cimitero di Sirolo

TERRAIN	Mostly level dirt roads and paths

Much of Italy's Adriatic coast is flat as a pancake, so Le Marche's spectacular Conero Riviera comes as a welcome surprise. Notable for its chalky white cliffs and limpid turquoise waters, this rugged 20km stretch of shoreline rises dramatically to the summit of Monte Conero (572m). The eponymous 6011-hectare Parco Regionale del Conero shelters a network of family-friendly hiking trails, including this short jaunt to an immensely scenic coastal overlook.

GETTING HERE

Reni (www.anconarenibus.it) runs buses (35 minutes) from Ancona to Via Giulietti in Sirolo – a 750m walk from the trailhead. Drivers can park opposite the cemetery.

STARTING POINT

At the cemetery, you'll find nothing more than a parking lot. For other services, head south to Sirolo's town centre.

01 Start uphill from the parking lot, keeping the wall of the **cemetery** on your right as you follow the gently ascending dirt road. About 900m up the hill, turn right at a T-junction with another dirt road, following signs for Belvedere Sud.

02 You'll encounter two **Y-intersections** in the next 400m. At the first, just a stone's throw down the road, take the downhill (right) fork, ignoring the signposted left fork for Belvedere Sud. About 250m further along, take the uphill (left) fork onto a dirt road with a circular red 'motor vehicles prohibited' sign.

ANDREA COM/GETTY IMAGES ©

03 You're now on the trail to Passo del Lupo. The wide dirt road continues without much change in elevation, passing a villa on the left before narrowing to a packed dirt walking path. Here you'll enter a **pleasant shady forest**, with the sea below you to the right obscured by trees. Another 500m along, pass a junction with a trail descending steeply from the Belvedere Sud above. Continue straight through the forest here, and within a couple hundred metres arrive at a rocky clearing with a heart-stopping view.

04 Dazzling perspectives open up over the deep blue Adriatic and surrounding cliffs at the **Passo del Lupo viewpoint**, marked only by an interpretive signboard with Italian-language explanations of local geology. Views to the north are especially breathtaking, with the blindingly white offshore rocks known as the **Due Sorelle** (Two Sisters; pictured) adding exuberant punctuation to a steep limestone promontory.

05 A **rough and very steep trail** continues from here towards the beach below, but for safety's sake resist the temptation and retrace your steps to the parking lot.

 TAKE A BREAK

A 1km walk south from the Passo del Lupo trailhead brings you to Sirolo's main square, where you'll find **Osteria Sara** (📞 071 933 07 16; Corso Italia 9, Sirolo; ⏱ 12.30-2.30pm & 7.30-9.45pm Thu-Tue), an old-school *osteria* serving excellent seafood. The small dining room here, all white walls and ageing framed pictures, fills quickly as diners pour in to sample marinated anchovies and tuna carpaccio starters, followed by seafood risotto and mains such as grilled catch of the day.

47

GOLA DELL' INFERNACCIO

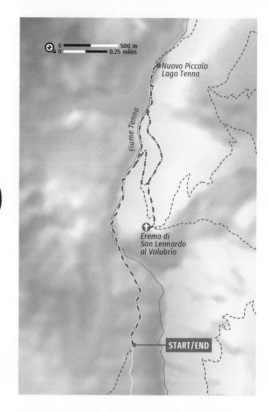

DURATION	DIFFICULTY	DISTANCE	START/END
2½hrs	Moderate	7km	Infernaccio parking area

TERRAIN	Dirt roads and paths

On the Monti Sibillini's eastern edge, this classic trail (pictured right and on p183) leads through the Gola dell'Infernaccio (Hell's Gorge), a thrilling canyon wedged between vertiginous rock walls. The silence here is broken only by birdsong and the rush of the fast-flowing Fiume Tenna.

Starting from a dusty parking lot off the SP83 north of Montefortino, the trail (initially a broad dirt track) descends to meet the **River Tenne**. Enjoy a free shower as drops cascade from the cliff face above.

Cross the river and climb the steep, narrow trail to your left. For the next 20 minutes, you'll traverse the most striking part of the gorge via a series of **four bridges** spaced at five-minute intervals, with limestone walls towering overhead on both sides.

After the last river crossing, enter a **shady beech forest**, watching for a signposted right-hand turnoff for San Leonardo; this will be your return route. For now, follow the valley floor 10 minutes upstream to cross a culvert; just beyond is an **eerie lake** created by the region's 2016 earthquakes, filled with the vestiges of submerged trees.

Turn back the way you came. Two minutes after re-crossing the culvert, an un-signposted but distinct trail on your left climbs into the forest: follow this for 15 minutes to a junction with a dirt road ascending from below. Continue 10 minutes uphill on this 'new' road (it's actually the 'San Leonardo' road you passed previously) to reach the **hermitage church of San Leonardo al Volubrio**, tucked into a sunny clearing with fine mountain views. Your return route to the parking lot descends the dirt road through three switchbacks to the river, then retraces your steps through the gorge.

48

MONTE SUBASIO

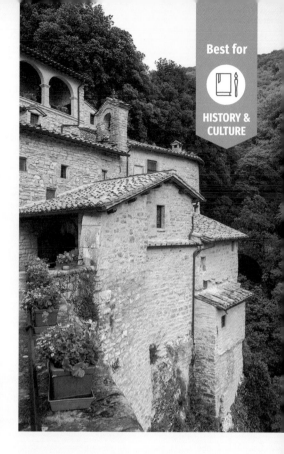

DURATION	DIFFICULTY	DISTANCE	START/END
6½hrs	Moderate	18km	Porta dei Cappuccini, Assisi

TERRAIN	Dirt roads and trails

St Francis of Assisi spent much of his life walking through the Umbrian hills. Few spots held as much spiritual sway for him as Monte Subasio, the half-forested, half-meadowy mountain due east of his native village. Halfway up Subasio's slopes, the Eremo delle Carceri – a mountain hermitage built around a cluster of caves – was a place of frequent spiritual retreat for Francis, lovingly preserved to this day. This hike retraces Francis's route from Assisi to the hermitage and beyond, onto the celestial summit of Subasio itself.

GETTING HERE

Buses from Assisi's train station drop you at Piazza Matteotti, 400m west of the trailhead. Drivers can park in the adjacent Matteotti lot.

STARTING POINT

Porta dei Cappuccini is just 300m east of Assisi's medieval centre, where you'll find parking, restrooms, restaurants, bars, shops and cultural attractions.

01 Leave Assisi through the northeastern town gate **Porta dei Cappuccini**, heading towards the olive-clad hills above town. Immediately after passing through the gate, look for a dirt road framed by rows of cypresses on your left, signposted 'Regione Umbria, Sistema dei Parchi, Parco del Monte Subasio, Sentiero dei Rifugi'.

02 Turn left onto the dirt road and continue through the row of trees for about five minutes till you reach the 14th-century stone tower of the **Rocca Minore** (pictured p192) on your left. From here, there are **excellent views** along Assisi's town walls to the Rocca Maggiore, a larger castle crowning the hills to the west.

03 Opposite the Rocca Minore, the road – now marked with yellow-and-blue signs for the Via di Roma and Via Francigena pilgrimage routes to Rome – curves right and begins climbing into the hills. Within five minutes you reach **Rocchicciola junction** (altitude 500m), where an official metallic CAI signpost indicates that you're on trail 350, one hour from the Eremo delle Carceri. Continue east, bearing right 10 minutes further along at hand-painted signs for Via di Roma and Eremo Carceri (do not turn left onto trail 51 here). The

path narrows and continues east through the forest for the next 45 minutes, with **pretty views over Assisi's southern hills** occasionally opening up to your right.

04 At the next junction – signposted Montarone (797m) – turn right onto a wider dirt road, as more impressive **views** open up across a grassy clearing to the valley below. Re-enter the forest, passing trees with red-and-white blazes and a picnic area on your right.

05 After 10 or 15 minutes, emerge onto a wider paved road, where you again turn right following signs for the

Eremo. Within five minutes, the tile rooftops, stone walls and arcaded galleries of the **hermitage** come into view, peeking out of the deep green forest ahead.

06 Take at least half an hour to explore the **hermitage** (pictured; admission free, silence requested). After soaking up the sun on the upstairs patio with its flowerpots and photogenic views of the ancient stone building and surrounding forest, you can descend a set of narrow stairs to the claustrophobic confines of St Francis's **grotta** (cave), where he prayed and slept on a stone bed in his later years. The oak woods around the Eremo

🥾 Gubbio's Corsa dei Ceri

Walking Umbria's hilly landscape is sufficient exercise for most people – but some hearty souls take things a step further in Gubbio, 50km north of Assisi. The town's favourite springtime festival culminates in the Corsa dei Ceri, a centuries-old race held each 15 May to celebrate Gubbio's patron, Sant'Ubaldo. It involves three teams, each carrying *a cero* (a massive wooden pillar weighing 300kg) bearing the statue of a saint (Sant'Ubaldo, St George or St Antony). Participants race through the city's medieval streets, making a final push up the steep slopes of Monte Ingino to the hilltop Basilica di Sant' Ubaldo.

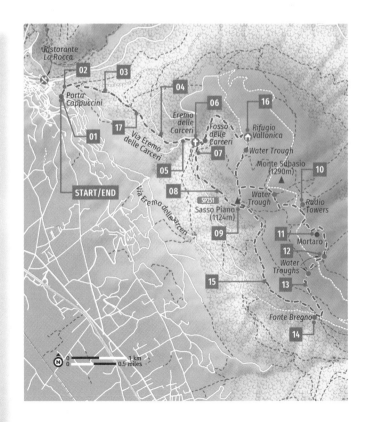

are criss-crossed by several additional hiking trails, dotted with **bronze statues** of St Francis (kicking back on the ground, sandals off) and two friars, Ginepro and Leone, staring at the constellations. As you exit toward the main road, a small shack serving coffee and snacks invites you to linger before resuming your journey.

07 Rejoining the main paved road outside the Eremo, turn right (uphill), following signs for SP251 San Benedetto. Yellow, blue, white and red stripes painted on the metal signpost let you know you're also still on CAI trail 350 and the Via di Roma/Via Francigena pilgrimage route. Follow the pavement through **shady forest** for 15 minutes; about halfway along you'll pass a junction labeled Fosso delle Carceri (830m) on your left – this will be your return route. For now, continue straight and gradually uphill along the paved road.

08 At a junction on your left marked Rinboschimento (868m), leave the paved road and join the rocky trail 360, signposted for Sasso Piano (45 minutes). After 20 minutes climbing steadily uphill through the forest, the trees begin to thin. As the trail emerges above the tree line 10 minutes later, look back to the north, where **views** open up to Sasso Piano, a high promontory with a large wooden cross. The trail doubles back on itself here, bringing you up to the cross in about five minutes.

STEFANO_VALERI/SHUTTERSTOCK ©

09 Linger a few minutes atop **Sasso Piano** to enjoy the amazing views down over Assisi. At the base of the cross is a metal box containing a book where pilgrims are invited to write messages. From here, head 100m or so uphill to the signposted Sasso Piano trail junction (1124m), and continue uphill into the surrounding pastureland, following signs for trail 350 towards the grazing cows and horses silhouetted on the high ridgeline above.

10 The radio antennae atop **Monte Subasio** come into view as you near the crest of the hill. After passing an animal watering trough marked with red-and-white blazes on your left (15 minutes above Sasso Piano), continue climbing another 15 minutes through the fields, reaching a T-intersection with a dirt road opposite the radio towers.

11 Bear right on the dirt road, following it south past fenceposts marked with red-and-white blazes and the trail number 350. In 10 minutes, turn left off the road at a signpost marked 'Mortaro 10 min; Fonte Bregno 50 min' and continue through open fields to reach the **Mortaro**, a deep *dolina* (sinkhole) on the right. With a spiral of stones at the bottom, this symmetrical cavity of sunken pastureland has a mystical feel, especially when mists are swirling through the surrounding hills.

12 The trail gets fainter for the next 10-minute stretch through high meadows; watch for stones at ground level painted red and white. When you reach a long **animal trough**, scan the ridgeline ahead for a prominent signpost and head towards it.

13 Turn right at the signposted junction – marked Prati di Pizzo (1128m) – and stay on trail 350 towards Fonte Bregno. Within a couple of minutes you'll cross a dirt road, continuing through high meadows marked with painted stones to reach an animal trough on a hill crest. The next 15 minutes are all downhill, with **fabulous long views** across pastures and the valley far below. Take care to follow the blazes, which will point you left and then right as you descend.

14 Turn right as the trail dead-ends into a dirt road (watch for a tree with waymarks near the junction). Within a minute you'll reach **Fonte Bregno**, a natural spring (sometimes dry) where trail 360 comes in from the north.

15 Head north for 45 minutes on trail 360, initially contouring the lower edge of a large meadow, with trees along the left side offering shade. After 20 minutes, break into open meadows and begin climbing, eventually turning east to parallel a river gully visible to your left. Beyond a small thicket of bushes and a metal pole painted with yellow, blue, white and red stripes, the trail turns north to cross the gully. Soon the **cross at Sasso Piano** comes into view on the promontory ahead, and the trail rises to meet it within 10 minutes.

16 Back at the signposted Sasso Piano junction, continue north, following signs for trail 350 towards Rifugio Vallonica, Eremo Carceri and Assisi. The trail descends through cow and horse pastures, passing a water trough and the abandoned **Rifugio Vallonica** on the right within 15 minutes. Turn left at the signposted junction beyond the *rifugio* to stay on trail 350, soon leaving the high pastures and beginning a sustained 20-minute descent through the woods.

17 Just beyond some picnic benches on the left, reach the familiar **Fosso delle Carceri junction** that you passed a few hours ago. Here, trail 350 dead-ends into the paved road coming up from Eremo delle Carceri. Turn right and retrace your steps for 1¼ hours or so downhill to Assisi.

TAKE A BREAK

Just inside the town walls on Assisi's northeastern edge – a stone's throw from the Porta dei Cappuccini – family-run **Ristorante La Rocca** (📞 075 81 22 84; www.hotelarocca.it/ristorante; Via Porta Perlici 27; fixed price menus €13-16, meals €25-35; 🕙 noon-2pm & 7-9pm) serves a full lineup of Umbrian classics at bargain prices. The large interior dining room is a bit sterile and formal (and noisy when packed with fellow diners), but both the food and the atmosphere are pure bliss if you can snag a spot on the breezy upstairs terrace.

49

AROUND THE PIAN PICCOLO

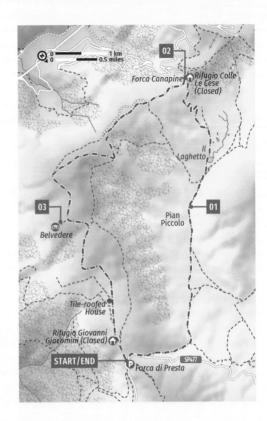

DURATION	DIFFICULTY	DISTANCE	START/END
4½hrs	Moderate	14km	Forca di Presta

TERRAIN	Dirt roads and trails

The lonely high plateaus around Castelluccio take on an otherworldly beauty each spring during the annual explosion of poppies, cornflowers and other blooms. This walk leads you across one such plateau and climbs into the surrounding hills for spellbinding views of the Monti Sibillini.

GETTING HERE

Summer-only buses from Ascoli Piceno to Castelluccio pass by Forca di Presta – but given the region's remoteness, your own vehicle is more dependable.

STARTING POINT

Straddling the Umbria–Le Marche border, lonely Forca di Presta (1550m) offers only a parking lot. Head 6km west to Castelluccio for other services.

01 Descend west from Forca di Presta on the paved SP477. Just beyond a right-hand bend, turn left at a concrete culvert painted with red-and-white blazes and the faded trail number 207. Continue gently downhill on a faint trail paralleling a gully to your right, with a **beech-forested hillside** above to your left. At a T-junction 15 minutes along, turn left onto a wider dirt road and round the edge of the hillside to your left, emerging onto the vast grassy expanses of the **Pian Piccolo**. For the next hour, continue southwest across the plateau, slowly approaching a second ridge of hills to the west. Trail markings here are nonexistent; simply stay on the valley floor between the two ranges of hills. After half an hour, near the valley's western edge, a new dirt road merges in from the north. Branch left and continue past an animal watering trough; 15 minutes further on, branch onto a faint road along the valley's eastern edge, keeping the aptly named **Laghetto** – a small lake – on your right.

Umbria's Piano Grande

Tucked into Umbria's far-eastern corner, the 1270m-high Piano Grande (pictured) is a karstic plateau framed by the bare-backed peaks of the Sibilline mountains. It's an alluring sight at any time of the year but is especially enchanting between May and June when the snows have melted and wildflowers carpet the grassy plain. Poppies, cornflowers, wild tulips, daisies, crocuses and narcissi produce an extraordinary display of reds, golds, violets and whites to add to the greens and browns of the surrounding slopes. It's a florist's heaven, a hay-fever sufferer's hell and an endless source of fascination for walkers, who flock here for strolls through the meadows.

Best for

👍

AVOIDING THE CROWDS

02 Ten minutes beyond Il Laghetto, branch left onto a grass-covered dirt road at a junction marked with a short pole, green paint and barbed wire. Begin steadily uphill, crossing in and out of beech forest. After 30 minutes of climbing, arrive at **Forca Canapine**, where the abandoned **Rifugio Colle le Cese** sits surrounded by sheep pastures. Turn left onto a broad dirt road, following signs for Forca di Presta. Red-and-white blazes mark the trail from here on. About 15 minutes along, branch left at a low post onto a smaller, ascending trail, with the main road still visible below to your right. **Views over the Sibillini** stretch clear to the southern horizon.

03 The trail dips gently, passing to the left of some beeches. Watch for an arrow painted on a stone here, and follow it left onto a new dirt road into the forest. About 10 minutes later, the road rises to enter another meadow, where you branch right at a post and begin climbing a narrower trail across the flank of a bald hill. **Ravishing views** north towards Monte Vettore soon open up on your left. The trail levels out and within 15 minutes joins a wide dirt road curving north. Moments later, you reach a right-hand turnoff where an optional detour along a boardwalk leads to a scenic **belvedere**. From this junction, continue straight on the main dirt road to reach Forca di Presta within an hour.

☕ TAKE A BREAK

After a walk on the Piano Grande, there's no more satisfying place for a snack than **Panino allo Scarafischio**, a humble food truck parked at Castelluccio's main crossroads and named for the region's traditional spicy sausage sandwich. Everything is served with a smile by the friendly proprietor, who has been feeding hungry hikers here since long before the Castelluccio earthquakes.

50

BOSCO DI SAN FRANCESCO

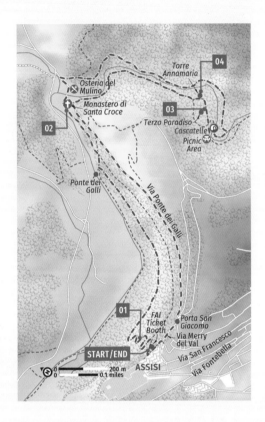

DURATION	DIFFICULTY	DISTANCE	START/END
2hrs	Moderate	5km	Piazza di San Francesco, Assisi

TERRAIN	Dirt roads and trails, paved road

In 2008, Fondo Ambiente Italiano (FAI) – the Italian counterpart to Britain's National Trust – began recuperating 64 hectares of long-neglected, donated woodland on the slopes below Assisi's world-famous Basilica di San Francesco. The result is a lovingly maintained nature preserve threaded with peaceful walking trails, ideal for a meditative half-day stroll.

GETTING HERE

Buses from Assisi's train station drop you 500m from the basilica and the FAI ticket booth.

STARTING POINT

Assisi's medieval centre, directly adjacent to the trailhead, has restaurants, parking and restrooms.

01 Pay admission and pick up a trail map at the **FAI entrance booth**, reached through a signposted gate just uphill from Assisi's basilica. A broad, well-maintained path switchbacks gently down into the forest, with **staircases and wooden railings** easing your progress.

02 **Beautiful views** open up back to the basilica as the trail levels out at the base of the hill. Shortly, an optional detour to the left leads to **Ponte dei Galli**, an arched medieval bridge named for the passage of Charlemagne's troops through here in the 8th century. Continue north on the main trail through olive trees to the lovely gardens of the **Monastero di Santa Croce** (pictured), a harmonious ensemble of cypresses, grapevines, fruit trees and stone walls draped with trailing rosemary. The restored stone buildings of this 13th-century Benedictine convent now serve as FAI's headquarters and info centre, while the **12th-century stone mill**

SALLIANN/SHUTTERSTOCK ©

just across the river has been converted into a restaurant.

03 East of the convent walls, take the path marked 'Terzo Paradiso'. A short jaunt up the riverbed brings you to the *calcinaie* – wood-fired kilns historically used to process local limestone. Continue upstream, soon arriving at the **Terzo Paradiso open-air art project**. In the clearing before you, 10-dozen olive trees arrayed in three interlinked rings spread across the grassy slopes. Artist Michelangelo Pistoletto envisioned this 'Third Paradise' as a sanctuary for contemplating the bonds between humanity and nature.

Gracefully curving paths run between the rows of tightly interwoven olive trees, inviting you to enter this calming refuge.

04 For a bird's-eye view of it all, climb the **Torre Annamaria**, a stone tower at the northeastern end of the clearing. South of Terzo Paradiso, the main trail continues to an inviting picnic area near a more traditional olive grove. Cross the Torrente Tescio on stepping stones to return along the river's eastern bank to Santa Croce. From here, you can either retrace your steps uphill through the Selva di San Francesco, or climb the slightly steeper paved

road, Via Ponte dei Galli, to re-enter Assisi via the Porta San Giacomo gate.

 TAKE A BREAK

Housed in a converted mill on Assisi's northern outskirts, **Osteria del Mulino** (www.facebook.com/ OsteriaDelMulino) makes a tasty halfway break on a walk through the Bosco di San Francesco. Seasonal specialties such as *umbricelli al boscaiolo* (Umbrian-style thick spaghetti with wild mushrooms) are a hiker's delight, and carnivores will rejoice at Il Mulino's lineup of meat grilled on the open fire, from locally raised lamb to Black Angus beef with rock salt and rosemary.

Also Try...

FABRIZIO GIARDI PH/SHUTTERSTOCK ©

ABOVE THE PIANO GRANDE

This hike climbs high into the hills above Castelluccio (pictured), affording views of the Monti
Sibillini and the Piano Grande. It's beautiful
year-round, but uncommonly so in June, when the
infioritura (wildflower bloom) is in full swing.

Just north of Castelluccio's main crossroads, turn
left (northwest) onto a side road past Agriturismo
Valle delle Aquile. Sheep pastures and pretty stands
of beech trees alternate for the next hour as you
follow the unpaved road west. Pass a blue EU sign
on the left, and continue uphill, soon bypassing
a right-hand junction marked only with a cairn.
Climb 20 minutes through a high grassy meadow
to a T-intersection with a major dirt road, and turn
left. A long, winding hour-long descent brings you
to a junction with the signposted E13 trail; turn left,
enjoying phenomenal Piano Grande views all the
way back to Castelluccio.

DURATION 3hrs
DIFFICULTY Moderate
DISTANCE 10km

TRAVERSATA DEL CONERO

This delightful hike south of Ancona skirts the
slopes of Monte Conero (572m), affording expansive views along Le Marche's Adriatic coastline.

From the roadside Osteria del Poggio restaurant,
head east on trail 301. The broad dirt track climbs
gently through shady forest to a viewpoint overlooking the Piano Grande, a coastal shelf beneath Monte
Conero's chalky cliffs, punctuated by a Napoleonic
fort, Santa Maria di Portonovo church and a pair of
lakes.

Branch left onto trail 301A, soon reaching the
Belvedere Nord, with more fine views north over
the Adriatic. From here, the road turns south to the
Convento dei Camaldolesi, a historic-monastery-
turned-hotel whose bar offers a welcome break.
Descend east along trail 301 to the Belvedere Sud
for east- and south-facing coastal perspectives, then
continue 1½ hours to Fonte d'Olio, the trail's southern terminus near the seaside village of Sirolo.

DURATION 4hrs
DIFFICULTY Moderate
DISTANCE 11km

LUCIANO PIERANTONI/SHUTTERSTOCK ©

MONTE VETTORE

Peak-baggers will love this classic climb from Forca di Presta (1550m) to Monte Vettore (2476m), the Monti Sibillini's highest summit.

Ascend the grassy slopes north of the SP477. The gradient is moderate at first but soon steepens, climbing past Monte Vettoretto (2052m) and Rifugio Tito Zilioli to fantastic views over Lago di Pilato. Large switchbacks culminate near Monte Vettore's summit, where the northern Sibillini's great bald summits and ridges are revealed; on a clear day, you can make out the Adriatic coast.

DURATION 4–4½hrs
DIFFICULTY Hard
DISTANCE 10km

LAGO DI PILATO

This walk leads to Lago di Pilato, a hauntingly remote lake long associated with necromancy and reputed to be Pontius Pilate's final resting place.

The path (pictured; signposted as trail 151) begins where the road ends in the village of Foce, 7km southwest of Montemonaco. Elevation gain is 995m, but it's well worth the effort, as you pass through the grassy Piano della Gardosa into the awe-inspiring Valle del Lago, with Monte Vettore (2476m) to your left and the sheer rock walls of Pizzo del Diavolo (2410m) towering to your right.

DURATION 5½hrs
DIFFICULTY Hard
DISTANCE 12km

GUBBIO HILLS LOOP

Climb high above the charming town of Gubbio for views over the medieval centre and the surrounding Apennines.

From Gubbio's crenellated 14th-century Palazzo dei Consoli, head southeast, leaving town via Strada San Gerolamo and climbing the slopes of Monte d'Ansciano on trail 253. About 1¼ hours into the hike, break for snacks at Ristorante Parco Coppo, then loop back southwest to Gubbio on trail 257, enjoying fabulous views from the heights of Monte Ingino (908m) and Basilica di Sant'Ubaldo en route.

DURATION 2½hrs
DIFFICULTY Moderate
DISTANCE 8km

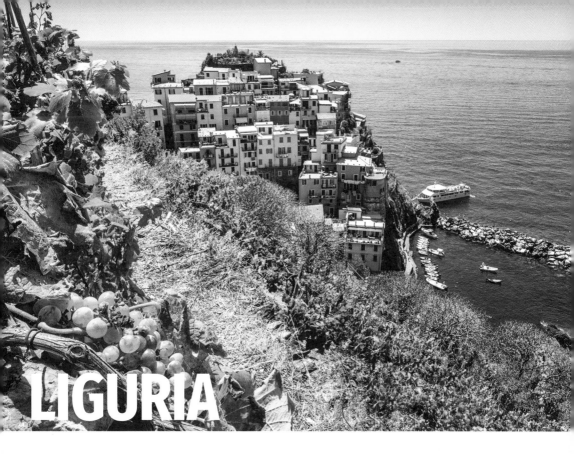

LIGURIA

51 **Levanto to Monterosso** Epic ramble between two of Liguria's finest beach towns. **p204**

52 **Portofino to San Fruttuoso** Deluxe resort meets hidden monastic hamlet on the protected Portofino peninsula. **p206**

53 **Manarola to Corniglia** Spectacular meander between two of Cinque Terre's pastel-hued villages. **p208**

54 **Sentiero Azzurro** A historic journey along the Ligurian coast on old mule paths. **p210**

55 **Porto Venere to Riomaggiore** Wander atop precipitous cliffs and dip down to classic Riviera harborfronts. **p214**

Explore
LIGURIA

For centuries an eastern outpost of the Most Serene Republic of Genoa, Liguria's history is written all over its steep-sided cliffs in diminutive chapels, hidden coves, and deftly terraced olive groves. It is also preserved underfoot on an intricate network of narrow paths that have been trodden down by generations of farmers, monks, sailors, townsfolk and – more recently – tourists.

CINQUE TERRE

Set amid some of the most dramatic coastal scenery on the planet, these five ingeniously constructed fishing villages can bolster the most jaded of spirits. A Unesco World Heritage site since 1997, Cinque Terre isn't the undiscovered Eden it once was but, frankly, who cares? Sinuous paths traverse seemingly impregnable cliff sides, while a 19th-century railway line cut through a series of coastal tunnels ferries the footsore from village to village. Thankfully, cars were banned over a decade ago.

Rooted in antiquity, Cinque Terre's five villages date from the early medieval period. While much of this fetching vernacular architecture remains, Cinque Terre's unique historical draw is the steeply terraced cliffs bisected by a complicated system of fields and gardens that have been hacked, chiselled, shaped and layered over the course of nearly two millennia. The extensive *muretti* (low stone walls) can be compared to the Great Wall of China in their grandeur and scope.

MONTEROSSO AL MARE

The most accessible Cinque Terre village by car and the only one of the five settlements to sport a proper stretch of beach, Monterosso, the westernmost village, is the least quintessential of the quintet. Notwithstanding, the village, known for its lemon trees and anchovies, is delightful. Split in two, its new and old halves are linked by an underground tunnel burrowed beneath the blustery San Cristoforo promontory.

PORTOFINO PENINSULA

Even the trees are handsome in Portofino, a small but perfectly coiffured coastal village that sits on its own peninsula, 35km east of the gritty city of Genoa. Hotels here are hushed and headily priced establishments and a walk around the yacht-filled harbour and adjacent designer shops can be a largely vicarious experience unless you have rock-star connections. But you don't need to be a Rolling Stone to enjoy the abundant trails. Protected within a regional park, the crinkled hills and indented coast of the peninsula contains 60km of walking paths that link isolated churches, old mills, abandoned WWII coastal batteries and the gorgeous little monastic hamlet of San Fruttuoso.

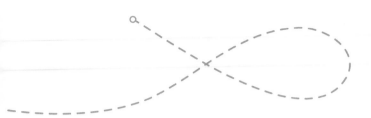

Resources

www.parconazionale5terre.it
Official website of Parco Nazionale delle Cinque Terre with comprehensive information about hiking trail closures.

www.cinqueterre.com Route descriptions of all the main Cinque Terre walking paths.

www.parks.it/parco.portofino Website for the Parco Naturale Regionale di Portofino.

BEYOND CINQUE TERRE

If you can't stomach the crowds in the Cinque Terre, there are some fine options further afield. Less-crowded Porto Venere has obvious appeal with a dramatic setting at the tip of a peninsula, an island just offshore to explore and some pretty walks right from town. Across the gulf of La Spezia, the villages of San Terenzo, Lerici and Tellaro also make charming bases in the region, with good beaches, dining and walking nearby. Even easier to reach is the seaside town of Levanto, which has a fine beach, and a historical centre sprinkled with medieval sites. Further up the coast, Sestri Levante is another captivating option, and it remains more popular with Italian rather than foreign visitors.

AVOIDING THE CROWDS

The glorious Sentiero Azzurro is perennially popular and it gets frustratingly crowded at peak times. To avoid the mayhem, get out early in the morning or later in the day (after 6pm in the summer). Alternatively, take one of the less famous trails in the national park, which see far fewer visitors – though it's still best to get an early start if you don't enjoy hiking with crowds.

 WHEN TO GO

The crowd-shy would be wise to avoid the Cinque Terre during the peak summer months of July and August, when the area becomes inundated with hordes of tourists keen to experience its much-famed beauty first-hand. September and October are arguably the best months. Many businesses close in winter and paths can be wet and slippery.

 TRANSPORT

The Cinque Terre walks in this chapter are all within steps of the coastal railway line that runs from Ventimiglia through Genoa to La Spezia. Connect in Genoa for Turin, and La Spezia for Florence and Milan. The Portofino peninsula is accessible from Camogli or Santa Margherita Ligure train stations.

 WHERE TO STAY

Overnighting in Cinque Terre is truly special but note that .hotels can book out for the entire April-to-October season and almost all are closed outside of that. Book well ahead and be willing to pay if you want something special. Alternatives are apartment rental or making a base in either La Spezia or Levanto.

Hotels in Portofino are stratospherically priced (if beautiful). Nearby Santa Margherita Ligure has cheaper options.

 WHAT'S ON

Sciacchetrail (www.sciacche trail.com) Held in early April, this challenging long-distance foot race takes to the hills of Cinque Terre following a rocky path along cliff edges, through terraced vineyards and looping past five iconic villages.

51

LEVANTO TO MONTEROSSO

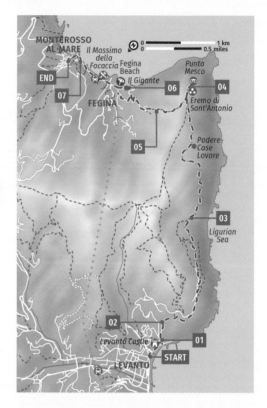

DURATION	DIFFICULTY	DISTANCE	START/END
2½hrs	Moderate	7km	Levanto/ Monterosso al Mare
TERRAIN	Mostly firm coastal paths with some undulations		

This walk takes in Mediterranean forest, sea cliffs and overlooks. It also offers a window into the past, with stops at a 13th-century castle and the ruins of a medieval monastery. The highlight is the view from atop Punta Mesco, where you'll be able to see all five Cinque Terre villages tucked along this jagged stretch of coast (pictured).

GETTING HERE

Frequent regional trains run along the coast to Genoa (€6, 51 minutes) and La Spezia (€4, 30 minutes). From late March to October, boats sail from Levanto to Cinque Terre villages.

STARTING POINT

Begin the walk on the shoreline of Levanto. Walk towards the southern end of the promenade and admire the view from this underrated coastal town. Take the marked stairway just past the stone columns on your left.

01 The stairs go up through an old part of the village and past Levanto's **beautifully preserved 13th-century castle**. This hunky fortification, complete with crenellated towers, fulfilled many roles over the years – including as a prison in the 18th century. Today it is privately owned.

02 Beyond the castle, the route briefly joins a paved road before branching off to track the coast. Cultivated land and holm oak forest bisect the gradual ascent to Punta Mesco. Just before arriving, you'll encounter the terracotta-coloured **Podere Case Lovara**.

03 The path ascends along rocky soil, through pines, holm oaks and Mediterranean scrub,

Podere Case Lovara

Less than 1km northwest of the Punta Mesco, the FAI (the National Trust for Italy) is restoring an abandoned agricultural site overlooking the Ligurian Sea. Olive groves, new drystone walls, fruit trees and vegetable gardens, and rebuilt farm dwellings are transforming this ruin into a place of beauty and productivity. If volunteers are around, you're welcome to take a look at the work that they're doing or have a picnic on the property (small donation requested).

SASHA64F/SHUTTERSTOCK ©

with the views becoming ever more majestic over the cliff faces. You'll soon be at a prime panoramic spot on the **Punta Mesco**. Atop this lofty promontory you'll be able to see both the bay of Levanto and the bay of Monterosso.

04 The ruins of a **hermitage dedicated to St Anthony** lie at the end of a short 300m spur off the main trail. The site dates back to the 1300s, and was gradually abandoned over the centuries. The brothers here kept an eye out for pirate ships on the horizon and lit signal fires to warn nearby villages of approaching corsairs.

05 You'll have **fabulous views** as you begin the descent towards Monterosso. After many stairs, the **beach** comes into view, with Fegina, Monterosso's modern half just beyond.

06 Before rejoining civilisation, walk to the beach and check out the huge statue known as **Il Gigante** set into the cliff face. The 14m statue, which depicts the sea god Neptune, dates from 1910 and once adorned a picturesque villa, though storms have removed his arms and trident.

07 End your walk in **Monterosso's historic centre**,

reached by taking the **car-pedestrian tunnel** located a few hundred metres past the train station.

TAKE A BREAK

Just below the train station, **Il Massimo della Focaccia** (Via Fegina 50; focaccia €2-5; ⏰9am-6pm Thu-Tue) is a strategically placed takeaway firing up the best focaccia in all of Cinque Terre. You can order that perfectly crisped bread topped with pesto, tomatoes and olives, sweet onions, with cheese or in various other fashions. There's also quiche-like *torta* (savoury pie) and a few sweet dessert items.

52

PORTOFINO TO SAN FRUTTUOSO

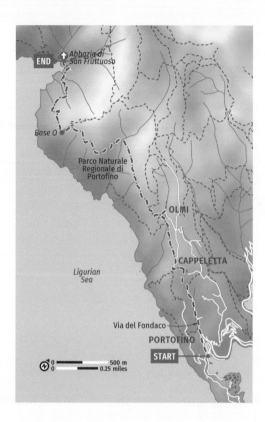

DURATION	DIFFICULTY	DISTANCE	START/END
2hrs	Moderate	4.5km	Portofino/ San Fruttuoso

TERRAIN	Stone steps and well-marked coastal and forest trails

The Portofino peninsula, just east of Genoa, is a pocket of ruggedness on the otherwise elegant Italian Riviera. This short coastal rollercoaster dips into both its wild and deluxe sides.

Follow Via del Fondaco away from Portofino's small harbour. The town quickly disappears behind you as the street turns to steps. Head up, go left at a fork and pass through a couple of gates to reach the cluster of buildings known as **Cappeletta**.

Go right here and head down the dirt road forking left after 300m in the hamlet of **Olmi**. This trail, marked by two red dots, zigzags around a scattering of houses and quickly enters a wilder domain with **epic coastal scenery**. This is the **Parco Naturale Regionale di Portofino**, where pines and Mediterranean *macchia* dominate the headlands, and broad-leaved vegetation abounds in the gullies.

The next landmark is a park junction known as **Base 'O'**, which served as a military post in WWII. Soon after this you'll cross a concrete helipad and begin the descent through forest to **San Fruttuoso** nestled in a cove below.

The hamlet's sensitively restored **Benedictine abbey** (pictured) was built as a final resting place for Bishop St Fructuosus of Tarragona, martyred in Spain in AD 259. It was rebuilt in the mid-13th century with the assistance of the Doria family. Today, its calm simplicity and charming everyday collection of ancient monkish things feels touchingly close and human. The hamlet has several restaurants, a sheltered pebble beach and regular boats back to Portofino.

53

MANAROLA TO CORNIGLIA

DURATION	DIFFICULTY	DISTANCE	START/END
2½hrs	Moderate	5km	Manarola/Corniglia

TERRAIN	Narrow hillside paths and many steps

A more than adequate substitute for the closed section of the Sentiero Azzurro between Manarola and Corniglia, this spectacular walk links the Cinque Terre towns via the lofty village of Volastra, passing through terraced vineyards and lush forest along the way.

GETTING HERE
Manarola is on the main train line for the Trenitalia Cinque Terre Express trains.

STARTING POINT
Reach the start of the trail by walking uphill along Manarola's main street, Via Discovolo. Just around the bend – and before you reach the church – take the ramp leading off to the left, with a makeshift sign indicating 'Volastra'.

01 After about a 20-minute climb, the path intersects a set of **stairs**. Take these up to the left, following the red-and-white blazes for the rest of the hike. You'll get a serious workout as you walk up hundreds of steps, passing **fig trees, olive groves, blackberry brambles and old stone fences**.

02 The path continues uphill for another 1km before arriving in the peaceful hamlet of **Volastra**. Older than Manarola, Volastra was founded by the Romans in 177 BC as a staging post for changing horses. Settlers quickly realised the agricultural potential here; the town's name comes from 'Vicus Oleaster' – the land of the olive trees.

03 The **village church** was likely built in the late 12th century, and has a plain gabled facade, and an image of the Madonna that is particularly venerated. According to legend, the church bells were hidden during a time of Saracen raids, and

Manarola

Bequeathed with more grapevines than any other Cinque Terre village, Manarola (pictured p201) is famous for its sweet Sciacchetrà wine. It's also awash with priceless medieval relics, supporting claims that it is the oldest of the five. The spirited locals here speak an esoteric local dialect known as Manarolese. Due to its proximity to Riomaggiore (852m away), the village is heavily trafficked, especially by Italian school parties along with the regular tourists.

MSTUDIOIMAGES/GETTY IMAGES ©

never recovered. It is said that the bells still toll on stormy nights.

04 You'll leave the village by following signs to Corniglia along trail 586. This stretch offers **brilliant views over land and sea**, and passes right through a patchwork of terraced vineyards. Volastra has an ideal microclimate for winemaking. As you leave town, you might see locals hard at work in the surrounding fields – cultivating the DOC Le Coste, one of Cinque Terre's best wines.

05 As you descend, you'll enter a forest of **maritime pines**. This lush area was once cultivated – you'll see abandoned terraces, rusting water tanks and moss-covered stone walls which have now been reclaimed by the forest.

06 The descent gets steeper and rockier as you near **Corniglia** (pictured), Cinque Terre's 'quiet' middle village that sits atop a 100m-high rocky promontory surrounded by vineyards. Trail 586 intersects with 587 (signed 'Corniglia'), which you'll take into the village. You'll arrive at a T-intersection, practically behind the **Chiesa San Pietro**. Turn right and follow the lane onto Via Fieschi, Corniglia's

main street – and fine place to find refreshments.

TAKE A BREAK

The casual **KMO** (www.facebook.com/KMOCorniglia; Via Fieschi 151; mains around €8; 🕙11am-10pm Wed-Mon) on Corniglia's main drag serves simple but delicious market-fresh fare. Think well-balanced seafood risotto, tomato and mozzarella salad, hearty plates of ravioli, and good beers and wines. You can dine in the flower-fringed courtyard just across the lane from the restaurant.

54

SENTIERO AZZURRO

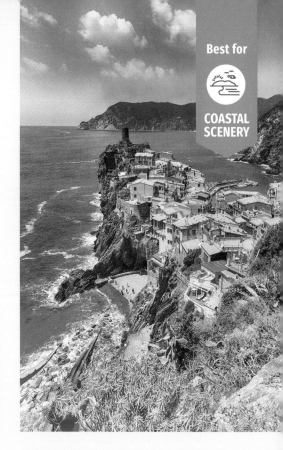

Best for
COASTAL SCENERY

DURATION	DIFFICULTY	DISTANCE	START/END
3hrs	Moderate	7.5km	Monterosso al Mare/ Corniglia

TERRAIN	Narrow but well-used coastal trails with steep ascents and descents, including steps

Cinque Terre's most emblematic and popular walk follows the course of an age-old path that theoretically connects all five villages. However, due to recent weather damage, only the two sections between Monterosso and Corniglia remain open. Short but steep in parts, the trail is a conveyor belt of fabulous scenery, with views over terraced vineyards, olive groves, steep mountains and pastel-hued villages.

GETTING HERE

Monterosso is on the main train line for the Trenitalia Cinque Terre Express trains. It also has the largest parking area of all the villages.

STARTING POINT

Exit Monterosso train station and turn left, passing through the shared pedestrian-car tunnel. After the tunnel, stick to the main road that parallels the beach. About 400m from town, you'll reach the staffed entrance to the trail where you'll need to purchase a trekking pass.

01 The ascent begins gently, passing by **vineyards** to right and left, with **periodic lookouts** back to Monterosso. Soon, the climbing begins in earnest as the route incorporates copious flights of steps (there are over 1000 throughout the walk). Keep an eye out for the sign announcing **Vétua**, a small family-run vineyard of just 6000 sq metres. Here Bosco, Albarola and Vermentino are cultivated to create classic varieties of Cinque Terre DOC white wine. Aside from grapes, Vétua also grows lemons, artichokes, capers and herbs – all nurtured sustainably.

02 About halfway between Monterosso and Vernazza, the trail winds its way back to the coast, affording **dramatic views** over the seaside. In contrast to the manicured lands you've just passed through, the landscape here is wild and untouched, with a view stretching far off into the distance to the steep mountainsides that intersect with the foaming waters surrounding the wave-battered shore. In parts, the drop-off is sheer, so watch your footing and keep children close.

03 The worst of the climbing is now in the bag, with only a few gentle ups and downs over the rest of the walk.

A **mesmerising perspective of Vernazza** (pictured) comes in and out of view as the cliff-side trail winds down. At first glance, the seaside village seems like something from a fable: tiny pastel-coloured buildings nestled amid the imposing mountainsides rising above at near-vertical angles. The details come more into focus as you round the final bend: the harbourfront buildings standing tightly together, with the geometric block of a medieval tower set on the sea cliff just behind them. The tiny **beach**, watched over by the bell tower of the **church**, sits beside the small **waterfront piazza**, hardly visible beneath the yellow, red, blue and green umbrellas of the square's al fresco restaurants and cafes. And behind the waterfront, **terraced vineyards** (pictured p212) rise steeply above the village.

04 Nearing the village, cultivated fields materialise once more. Olive groves, vineyards, lemon trees and vegetable gardens grow just beyond the rock walls skirting the trail. Soon you'll pass the ticket booth for Monterosso-bound hikers, and a popular panorama of Vernazza dominated by the cupola of **Santa Margherita d'Antiochia**. People not up for doing the full hike often come up to this viewpoint for the inspiring perspective.

Weather-Beaten Trail

The 12km-long Sentiero Azzurro is an old mule path that dates back to the early days of the Republic of Genoa in the 12th and 13th centuries. Until the opening of the railway line in 1874, it was the only practical means of transport between Cinque Terre's five main villages.

Owing to bad storms and landslides over the last decade, only two sections of the trail remain open: from Monterosso to Vernazza and Vernazza to Corniglia. The trail between Riomaggiore and Manarola (the famed Via dell'Amore) remains closed, though it may reopen in the years ahead. The path between Corniglia and Manarola was so badly damaged by landslides that it will likely never reopen.

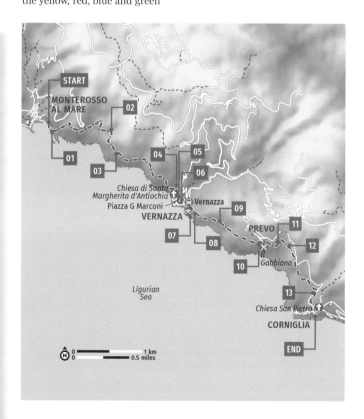

05 After passing the church, the path turns into Via Ettore Vernazza. Take the first set of stairs leading down to the right. These put you right onto the waterfront **Piazza Guglielmo Marconi**, where you can have a drink or a meal, or refresh over some gelato while sitting on the breakwall. Be sure to take a peak inside the **Chiesa di Santa Margherita d'Antiochia**, a few steps from the waterfront. The atmospheric Ligurian-Gothic church is one of the finest in all of the Cinque Terre.

06 To rejoin the Sentiero Azzurro, head away from the waterfront along Via Roma, and take the first right just before the pharmacy. Look for the small sign with red arrows labelled 'Sentiero per Corniglia' on the wall. Head up the steps and follow this *carrugi* (narrow street) as it winds up through the back parts of town. Veer left up the stairs at the first T-intersection; after another 200m, you'll see a well-worn stone staircase up to the right, with a 'Corniglia' sign pointing the way beside red-and-white blaze (these are used everywhere in the Cinque Terre as trail markers).

07 The stairs take you up to a **lookout** with a stop-in-your-tracks view over Vernazza. From here, it's possible to peer over wildflowers and cacti clinging to the hillside just below your feet, down to the tiny **beach** below the cliffs.

JORDAN SIEMENS/GETTY IMAGES ©

08 Continue on the path to reach the checkpoint for the next section of the hike. The walk starts off with gentle ascents, following the cliff edge along the sea with superb views at every turn. You'll start out above the open train tracks. Around 500m up the track, you'll begin climbing up uneven stone steps which zigzag past **olive trees** and stretches of **bushy forest**. You'll also pass **terraced gardens** that have long since been abandoned. The path is compacted dirt or flat stones in places, with plenty of stairs throughout. Along the cliffs, wooden railings provide added protection, but the trail suffers significant wear and tear during the rainy months.

09 Soon you'll reach a wild part of the coast with **views** of densely forested slopes of distinct Mediterranean vegetation stretching ahead, and the cliffs to the right thick with Indian fig opuntia and agave plants.

10 At around the midpoint between Vernazza and Corniglia, the path skirts the hamlet of **Prevo** off to your left. According to tradition, the tiny settlement was founded in the 16th century by families of mountain shepherds who migrated here in the winters to shelter with their flocks. Protected by dry stone walls, the terraces here nurture **vegetable gardens, and lemon and pomegranate trees**, as well as **cherries and quince**.

Cinque Terre Card

If you plan to hike between villages, the best way to get around Cinque Terre is with a **Cinque Terre card**.

Two versions of the card are available: with or without train travel. Both include unlimited use of walking paths and electric village buses, as well as cultural exhibitions. The basic one-/two-day card for those aged over four years costs €7.50/14.50. With unlimited train trips between the towns, the card costs €16/29. A one-day family card for two adults and two children (under 12) costs €42/20 with/without train travel.

Both versions of the card are sold at all Cinque Terre park information offices and each of Cinque Terre's train stations. You can also purchase trail admission at each of the trailheads.

11 It's worth slowing down to admire the view here: this is one of the highest points of the Sentiero Azzuro, at an elevation of 208m. On clear days, the fine vantage point affords **views over the distant islands of Corsica, Elba, Gorgona and Capraia**. There's also a spectacular **view of Corniglia**, a jumble of soft-hued buildings huddling tightly together atop the steep, seemingly vertical cliffs above the sea. Terraced gardens have modified the hillside just behind the village; while farther along the coastline, the village of Manarola is partially visible.

12 The **knee-killing descent** into Corniglia begins at the outskirts of town with a seemingly endless stretch of stairs. After this you'll cross several bridges over mountain streams before reaching the main road into town.

13 Cross the pavement and look for the connecting path, which continues a few metres up on the left. The path winds its way into the village, past **vineyards** (pictured) to right and left, eventually reaching the top of Via Fieschi, near the steps of the **Chiesa di San Pietro**. Turn right onto this lane, which will lead into the heart of **Corniglia**.

TAKE A BREAK

One of the only places where you'll find refreshment on the Sentiero Azzuro sits alongside the trail (on the Mediterranean side) in Prevo. **Il Gabbiano** (Prevo; snacks from €4; ☺9am-6pm) serves up cold drinks (smoothies, iced coffee, *granite*) as well as *panini* and other snacks. Perched right over the cliff, the shaded outdoor tables have magnificent views.

55

PORTO VENERE TO RIOMAGGIORE

DURATION	DIFFICULTY	DISTANCE	START/END
4½hrs	Hard	13km	Porto Venere/ Riomaggiore

TERRAIN	Mountain paths with some dirt tracks and paved sections

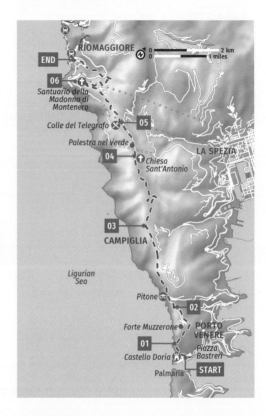

Just a few kilometres shy of a full-blown marathon, the 38km Alta Via delle Cinque Terre from Porto Venere to Levanto is beyond the capabilities of most day-walkers. A less-demanding option is to partake in the first epic third of the walk. For every 100 people you see on the Sentiero Azzurro, you'll spy only one or two up here.

GETTING HERE

Porto Venere is served by daily buses from La Spezia. From late March to October, **Consorzio Marittimo Turistico Cinque Terre Golfo dei Poeti** (☎0187 73 29 87; www.navigazionegolfodeipoeti.it) sails from Porto Venere to Cinque Terre villages.

STARTING POINT

Find your way to the Piazza Giacamo Bastreri in

Porto Venere and take the stairs leading up to the Castello Doria.

01 Ascend alongside the castle walls to emerge onto a narrow rocky path that skirts the coast. Behind lies the castle and the island of Palmaria. Leaving the views temporarily behind, enter a scrubby forest and continue up the rocky path which skirts the ruins of **Forte Muzzerone**, a 19th-century fortification used in both world wars.

02 Leaving the fort behind, the Alta Via steepens as it passes a **marble quarry** above the Muzzerone cliffs. There are some steep drop-offs in places. Keep climbing and you'll reach one of the most striking lookouts over Porto Venere. Known as **Pitone**, this ledge juts out above the hilltop, providing a natural balcony high above the sea. Here, one can admire the diminutive islands of **Palmaria**, **Tino** and **Tinetto**.

Local Marble

The stone found on this part of the coast with its valuable black marble and goldish-yellow streaks is called *marmo portoro* (portoro marble). Marble extraction near Porto Venere dates back to the Roman era, and in the 1860s there were 30 active quarries throughout the region (including five on the island of Palmaria). Today, however, the quarry at Muzzerone near the start of this walk is the only one still in operation.

Best for

👍

AVOIDING THE CROWDS

ELOI_OMELLA/GETTY IMAGES ©

03 The ascent continues, at times crossing over boulders and jagged rocks, and through dense Mediterranean vegetation. It's another 40 minutes or so of climbing to reach the small village of **Campiglia**, passing the ruins of a **17th-century windmill** on the way. Several other paths intersect in the village. Look for the AV5T signs and continue straight through.

04 Up is the only way to go as the route climbs past orchards and vineyards. **Views over La Spezia bay** offer some cool relief as the path enters a forest of pine, chestnut and oak.

Around 2.3km from Campiglia is the Valico di Sant'Antonio, another trail intersection. Here, there's a small **chapel**, a **fountain** and a wooded *Palestra nel Verde* (open-air gym).

05 It's a fairly flat stretch up to **Colle del Telegrafo**, so named for the telegraph wires that used to be strung here. You'll know you've arrived when you reach the restaurant named after the spot.

06 From the Colle, take trail 593 (SVA3) down to Riomaggiore. The path descends first through scrub and, later, cultivated gardens

to the 18th-century **Santuario della Madonna di Montenero**. From the church, continue on 593 as it crosses the provincial highway, contours a wide gully and deposits you in the top end of **Riomaggiore** (pictured above and on p13).

☕ TAKE A BREAK

You can refuel with plates of bruschettaand cold drinks, while relaxing on the terrace overlooking the sea, at **Colle del Telegrafo** (📞0187 76 05 61; Località Colle del Telegrafo; meals €25-35; ⏰9am-8pm Tue-Sun), a walker's favourite located two-thirds of the way into this walk.

Also Try...

ROSTISLAV GLINSKY/SHUTTERSTOCK ©

CAMOGLI TO SAN FRUTTUOSO

The Portofino peninsula is littered with trails –
60km of them. Many are absolutely remote and
a galaxy away from the sinuous sports-car-lined
roads inland.

From the fishing town of Camogli (pictured), one
of the more popular routes leads over the coastal
escapements to the road-less fishing hamlet of
San Fruttuoso. The trail, initially marked with two
red circles, heads south, climbing copious steps to
the chapel of San Rooco. From here it divides: the
red-dot path takes a vertiginous 'expert-only' route
around the cliff-sides to San Fruttuoso, while an
easier inland path, marked by a single red ring,
journeys through chestnut, pine and olive trees to
a path junction called Pietre Strette. Here, a rockier
path switchbacks down to the hidden hamlet with
its Benedictine abbey and sheltered pebble beach.
You can catch a boat back to Camogli.

DURATION 2½hrs
DIFFICULTY Moderate
DISTANCE 8.5km

ALTA VIA DELLE CINQUE TERRE

The antidote to the Sentiero Azzurro, the Alta Via
traverses the Cinque Terre coastline at a higher
altitude. It is thus more isolated from the historic
villages and a lot less crowded.

Due to its length (38km), the path is often tackled in
smaller chunks. The middle section from Colle del
Telegrafo to Foce Drignana is a sizeable bite for a
day walk, although you'll need to get on and off the
trail by using public transport or other trails.

The scenery oscillates from open, scrubby terrain
to dense forest, with the Mediterranean just a blue
suggestion through the thick foliage. Along the way,
you'll pass the ruins of an old fortress, a weathered
menhir signed just off the path and the lofty slopes
of Mt Malpertuso, the highest point of Cinque Terre
at 815m.

DURATION 4½hrs
DIFFICULTY Moderate
DISTANCE 13.5km

TATSUO NAKAMURA/SHUTTERSTOCK ©

MONTEROSSO TO SANTUARIO DELLA MADONNA DI SOVIORE

From Monterosso, follow trail 509 up through forest and past the ruins of an old hexagonal chapel to an ancient paved mule path that leads to Soviore, the Italian Riviera's oldest sanctuary ,dating from the 11th century.

Here you'll find a bar, a restaurant and views as far as Corsica on a clear day. It's a 1½-hour walk to get there. Reach the trailhead by taking Via Roma up through town; just after the roundabout, take the stairs (signed with trail markers) off to the left.

DURATION 1½hrs
DIFFICULTY Moderate
DISTANCE 2.5km

RIOMAGGIORE TO SANTUARIO DELLA MADONNA DI MONTENERO

You'd better like stairs to tackle the short, sharp uphill grunt to Riomaggiore's hilltop chapel.

Trail 593V starts harbourside in Cinque Terre's most easterly village and ascends well-worn steps past walled gardens to a restored 18th-century chapel (pictured) with a frescoed ceiling, which sits atop an astounding lookout high above the coastline. The walk includes a short 400m stretch along the main SP370 coast road. The total 300m of ascent is condensed over a short distance.

DURATION 1hr
DIFFICULTY Moderate
DISTANCE 1.5km

PORTOFINO TO SANTA MARGHERITA LIGURE

The elegant, manicured eastern side of the Portofino peninsula is very different to the precipitous south.

Head up the steps behind Portofino's harborside church and turn right following the trail marked with three red dots. After sailing past elegant Riviera mansions, you will be delivered briefly to the coast road in the hamlet of Paraggi before ascending steps to the San Gerolamo chapel in Gave. From here it's a straightforward descent to deluxe Santa Margherita and its classy marina. The train station is at the far end of the promenade.

DURATION 1hr
DIFFICULTY Easy
DISTANCE 5km

WESTERN & MARITIME ALPS

56 **Tour du Mont Blanc** Explore the Italian side of Europe's most majestic mountain. **p222**

57 **Sella-Herbetet Traverse** Visit a royal hunting lodge in Italy's oldest national park. **p226**

58 **Gran Balconata del Cervino** Glimpse the iconic Matterhorn from meadows along the Italian–Swiss border. **p228**

59 **Vallone di Grauson** Walk upriver amid waterfalls, high pastures and stone villages. **p232**

60 **Rifugio Garelli** Climb to an alpine refuge high in the Maritime Alps. **p234**

Explore
WESTERN &
MARITIME ALPS

Sweeping up to spectacular alpine summits along the French and Swiss borders, north-western Italy is a paradise for mountain walks. This region is home to world-renowned icons like Mont Blanc (Monte Bianco) and the Matterhorn (Cervino) – but it also shelters plenty of lesser-known natural attractions. Tucked into the northern region of Valle d'Aosta, Italy's oldest national park – Parco Nazionale Gran Paradiso – presents a landscape of rushing rivers, high pastures, stone huts and snow-capped peaks, while further south, the Mediterranean-influenced Alpi Marettimi offer equally enticing walking opportunities at slightly lower elevations.

COGNE

Gazing up at the 4061m summit of Gran Paradiso (Italy's seventh-highest peak), Cogne (1534m) is the main stepping stone into Parco Nazionale Gran Paradiso. It's a low-key place with a dependable collection of hotels, restaurants and shops catering to outdoors-oriented tourists. The adjacent national park was created in 1922 after Vittorio Emanuele II gave his hunting reserve to the state, ostensibly to protect the endangered ibex. The park preceded the rise of the modern ski resort and has so far resisted the lucrative mass tourist trade. Its tangible wilderness feel is rare in Italy.

COURMAYEUR

Flush up against France and linked by a vertigo-inducing cable-car ride to its cross-border cousin in Chamonix, Courmayeur is an activity-oriented Aosta village that has grafted upmarket ski facilities onto an ancient Roman bulwark. Its pièce de résistance is lofty Mont Blanc, Western Europe's highest mountain – 4810m of solid rock and ice that rises like an impregnable wall above the narrow valleys of northwestern Italy. In summer, the Società delle Guide Alpine di Courmayeur is bivouacked here and the town is an important staging post on the iconic Tour du Mont Blanc (TMB) long-distance hiking trail.

BREUIL-CERVINIA

One of the Alps' most architecturally incongruous resorts, Breuil-Cervinia is a rather dull collection of high-rise hotels and ski lifts redeemed only by its gorgeous mountain backdrop, smack at the foot of the Matterhorn. Less than 10km from Zermatt, Switzerland, as the crow flies, it crowns the far end of Valtournenche, a side valley running north off the Valle d'Aosta. Ugly or not, Cervinia's facilities are second to none, with a plethora of accommodation and restaurants, and gondolas that can whisk you up to trails in the surrounding high country.

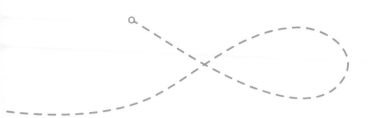

Resources

Parco Nazionale Gran Paradiso
(www.pngp.it) Website for
Italy's oldest national park,
founded in 1922.

**Parco Naturale delle Alpi
Marettime** (www.parcoalpi
marittime.it) Info about this
well-run regional park near the
French border.

Parco Naturale del Marguareis
(www.parcomarguareis.it) Info
about the Alpi Marettimi's
other most important park.

CUNEO

Sitting on a promontory between two rivers, stately Cuneo
provides excellent mountain
views framed by the high
pyramid-shaped peak of Monte
Viso (3841m) in the Cottian
Alps. There are a raft of reasons
to visit this pleasant provincial
capital, not least being the food,
the bike friendliness, the hiking
possibilities nearby and, last
but certainly not least, the city's
signature rum-filled chocolates.

WHEN TO GO

Summer is prime time for exploring the Western and Maritime
Alps, though conditions vary
widely from year to year. While
most high-country walks should
be accessible from June through
September, snow can remain
above 2500m until mid-June, or
even later. From mid-July until
late August, the area is very busy
and accommodation is at a premi-
um. Public transport services are
more frequent during summer;
camping areas and *rifugi* are
generally open from late May to
mid-September.

Thanks to their lower altitude
and proximity to the Mediterranean, the Maritime Alps become
free of snow somewhat earlier
than more northerly parts of the
Alps, though heavy snow cover
in winter is a certainty.

TRANSPORT

This large region is serviced by
airports in Turin and Genoa, and
is convenient to Milan Mal-
pensa, too. Frequent trains run
from Turin, Genoa and Milan
to mountain gateways such as
Cuneo, Aosta and Courmayeur.
Buses serve many side valleys,
including SVAP (www.svap.it) to
Cogne in Valle d'Aosta, Arriva
Savda (www.savda.it) to Breuil-
Cervinia in Valtournenche and
Grandabus (www.grandabus.it)
around Cuneo. Even so, having
your own wheels is advanta-
geous for reaching the region's
more remote trailheads.

WHERE TO STAY

There's a big variety of places to
stay in this diverse region, from
luxury hotels to *agriturismi* (farm
stays) – but for many hikers,
nothing compares to the romance
of overnighting in a trailside
rifugio (mountain hut). Hotels in
Valle d'Aosta range from rustic
family-run places to the ultra-lux-
urious. Most of them utilise the
vernacular architecture of the region, with stone and wood playing
an atmospheric part. Piedmont
does pared-back, quiet elegance
with aplomb and tends to be
better value than elsewhere in the
north, with a host of welcoming
B&Bs and farm stays.

WHAT'S ON

Festa delle Guide Alpine At
this annual mountaineering
festival in August, alpine guides
demonstrate their climbing skills
at locations throughout Valle
d'Aosta.

Terra Madre Salone del Gusto
Hosted by the locally based Slow
Food Movement in October, this
biennial gathering in Turin celebrates sustainable agriculture
and regional cuisine, drawing
chefs and producers from 150
countries.

56

TOUR DU MONT BLANC

DURATION	DIFFICULTY	DISTANCE	START/END
9hrs	Hard	20km	Rifugio Maison Vieille

TERRAIN	Dirt roads and trails, some very steep

Europe's highest mountain, Mont Blanc (Monte Bianco in Italian) exerts a magnetic appeal over hikers, who flock here every summer to complete the 170km Tour du Mont Blanc. The long day hike described here (easily split in two with an overnight at Rifugio Elisabetta) focuses on an especially scenic section of the TMB, all on the Italian side of the mountain near Courmayeur. It's a memorable way to feel the excitement of this legendary loop and rub shoulders with through-hikers, without committing to the entire multiday trek.

GETTING HERE

In July and August a *funivia* (gondola) and *seggiovia* (chairlift) run from Courmayeur up to Maison Vieille (www.courmayeur-montblanc.com). Otherwise it's a two-hour walk.

STARTING POINT

Rifugio Maison Vieille has restrooms, a bar-restaurant and dormitory accommodation, making it an ideal stopover before hitting the trail.

01 Bid farewell to the red plastic cow and Tibetan prayer flags outside **Rifugio Maison Vieille** and lace up your boots for an exhilarating adventure. From the low saddle of **Col Chécrouit** (1956m) the trail starts climbing instantly, heading straight uphill past ski lifts and meadows full of grazing horses. Diamond-shaped TMB symbols and triangular signs for trail 2 regularly appear alongside the route, letting you know you haven't lost your way.

02 Half an hour up the mountain, pass sparkling **Lac Chécrouit** (2165 m) on the left. The **views** – north into the forested depths of Val Vény, west to the hulking massif of Mont Blanc and southwest to the undulating outwash of the Lex Blanche glacier – just keep getting more majestic as you climb the now treeless slopes.

03 After 1¾ hours of steady climbing from Maison Vieille, a final set of switchbacks leads up to **Arête du Mont-Favre** (2435m), where the trail mercifully levels out, revealing **grand views** into the next valley south, with the Lex Blanche glacier looming on the far horizon.

04 For the next hour or so, the trail heads down, down, down through a broad side valley off Val Vény, initially tracing a zigzag descent from the pass, with a creek on the left-hand side, to reach the stone huts of **Arp Vieille Dessus**. On the outskirts of this high mountain outpost, watch for black-on-yellow trail symbols for the TMB and trail 2 painted on rocks. Another 10 minutes of walking brings you to a bridge across the creek, and 15 minutes further on, with Val Vény now in plain view ahead, you'll pass a **picturesque decaying shed** on the right, its roof beams overgrown with grasses and wildflowers. From here it's another 15 minutes to the valley floor.

05 The trail flattens out at a prominent signposted junction beside the milky grey-blue glacial meltwaters of **Val Vény** (pictured p225). Signs here point southwest to Rifugio Elisabetta, northeast to Rifugio Monte Bianco, and northwest to Cabane du Combal (1968m, a lakeside *rifugio* 10 minutes across the valley). Take the left fork and emerge into the blissfully flat **Plan Vény**, with wonderful close-up views of Mont Blanc's pinnacles reflected in the wetlands to your right. To your left, a curious bilingual (French-Italian) placard on a tree commemorates the September 1975 disappearance of a 23-year-old gem collector, last seen near here with his orange Volkswagen and never heard

🥾 Hiking the TMB

If hiking a one-day segment of the TMB just whets your appetite for more, perhaps it's time to join the 30,000 souls who pass through Courmayeur each summer on the unforgettable 170km odyssey around the base of Mont Blanc. Most people spend one week to 12 days circumnavigating the mountain, passing through Italy, France and Switzerland and stopping to sleep and eat at *gîtes* and *rifugi* at the nine hiker-friendly villages en route. It's possible to do the hike solo, but if you're unfamiliar with the area, hooking up with a local guide is a good idea as the route traverses glacial landscapes. The Società delle Guide Alpine di Courmayeur is a great place to arrange a trek.

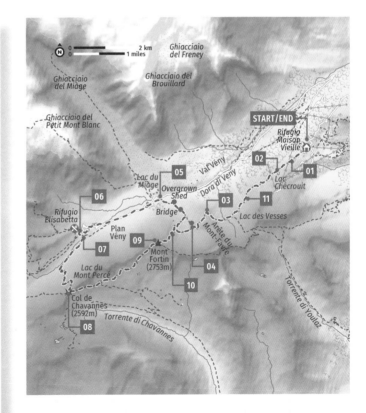

from again. After half an hour of flat walking along a wide dirt road, begin climbing again via a series of switchbacks towards Rifugio Elisabetta, now visible on a dauntingly high hillside directly above you.

06 After a 25-minute climb, the dirt road levels off at a right-hand turnoff for **Rifugio Elisabetta**, marked by a sign on a nearby building (La Lex Blanche, 2282m). It's well worth the 10-minute uphill detour to the *rifugio*, where hearty lunches come accompanied by **amazing Mont Blanc views** from the outdoor deck. If you prefer to split the journey over two days, there are reasonably priced dorms and private rooms upstairs

07 The main TMB trail continues straight ahead (southwest) from La Lex Blanche junction towards the French border at Col de la Seigne (2516m; pictured p222). A few metres ahead, near a **freshwater spring** pouring into a log trough, trail 2 forks to the left, marked by a yellow-and-black triangle and signs for Col de Chavannes/La Thuile. Branch off here, almost immediately crossing a simple wood bridge across a creek and beginning a gradual climb up the opposite slope.

08 Trail 2 continues relentlessly uphill for the next 1¼ hours, revealing **ever more expansive views** of the grassy slopes of Mont Fortin dropping into the braided gravel riverbed below, with the hulking backdrop of Mt Blanc dominating the northern horizon. The terrain gets more rugged as you climb, switchback-

ing up into a forbidding world of scree and boulders as you near the summit. Identified by a trail marker, **Col de Chavannes** (2592m) is a high saddle at the foot of a long ridgeline. Pause to admire views in all directions, then turn left here along trail 2 towards Courmayeur, following the eastern edge of the ridge.

09 After about 10 minutes, take a left fork onto the smaller trail 11B (signs for Mont Fortin). You'll soon pass **Lac du Mont Percé**, a high mountain lake backed by stark peaks on the left side of the trail. Following circular black-on-yellow symbols for trail 11A painted on stones, continue climbing another 40 minutes to a promontory just below the summit of **Mont Fortin** (2753m). From here, the north-facing perspectives across deep Val Vény to Mont Blanc's *aiguilles* (needle-sharp pinnacles) are truly awe-inspiring.

10 Following signs for trail 9 to Ponte Combal, branch left over the edge of the ridge and begin a steep descent into the valley below. Take your time navigating the scree and boulder fields along the trail's higher reaches. Far below you lie the stone huts and meadows of Arp Vieille Dessus, which you passed on your earlier descent towards Val Vény. The trail gets less steep as you near the valley floor, ultimately joining up with the TMB trail after about an hour.

11 Turn right on the TMB and retrace your steps to **Rifugio Maison Vieille**, about 1¾ hours to the northeast.

Melting Glaciers

Global warming has started to hit close to home in Italy's western Alps. In September 2019, scientists were alarmed to see a massive chunk of ice beginning to detach from the Planpincieux glacier on the Grandes Jorasses peak north of Courmayeur. Daily ice movements of up to a metre a day (vs its normal daily rate of 10cm) spurred Italian authorities to order the evacuation of homes and roads in the area, fearing that a 250,000-cubic-metre section of the glacier was in danger of collapse. While the glacier in question poses no threat to the section of trail described in this guide, it's a sobering wake-up call to the real-world implications of global climate change.

TAKE A BREAK

For a memorable lunch with front-row views of Mont Blanc and the Lex Blanche glacier, head for the ample sun terrace at **Rifugio Elisabetta** (📞0165 84 40 80; www.rifugio elisabetta.com; Località Lex Blanche, Val Veny; meals €25; ⏰noon-3pm), high on the mountainside near the French–Italian border. The menu features a mix of Italian and alpine specialties, followed by local desserts such as chestnuts with homemade whipped cream.

57

SELLA-HERBETET TRAVERSE

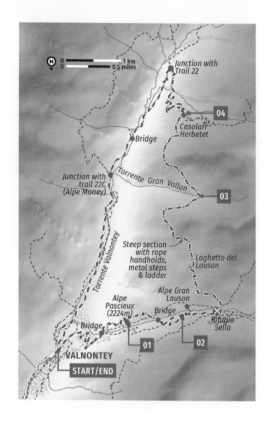

DURATION	DIFFICULTY	DISTANCE	START/END
7½hrs	Hard	15km	Valnontey

TERRAIN	Dirt trail; steep, tricky sections

This incredibly exhilarating and scenic traverse follows the precipitous slopes high above Valnontey, with plenty of wildlife to keep you company.

GETTING HERE
Several daily buses run from Aosta to Cogne (50 minutes), from where you can walk (3km) or catch a free shuttle (five minutes) to Valnontey.

STARTING POINT
Tiny Valnontey offers restaurants, bars, restrooms and paid parking at a lot in the village centre.

01 Head west across the bridge from **Valnontey village** and follow signs for trail 18 towards Rifugio Sella. After half an hour climbing through evergreen forest, cross a bridge and emerge into a meadow with a collapsed farm structure and a water trough. Zigzag another 15 minutes uphill to reach **Pascieux** (2224m), where a stone hut sits astride sloping pastureland, commanding **amazing views over distant mountains**. About half an hour above Pascieux, the trail dips to cross a rushing creek above a waterfall, then continues up the opposite bank.

02 The trail switchbacks relentlessly up the creek canyon, traversing rugged treeless slopes. About 30 minutes along, the attractively clustered stone houses of Alpe Gran Lauson appear across the creek. Soon thereafter you'll reach a signposted junction opposite the old stone **Casotto del Lauson** (2588m), in a mountain bowl ringed by unforgiving-looking rocky slopes. Before you stands **Rifugio Sella**, a perfect lunch stop.

03 Continue through the open high country, following circular black-on-yellow markers

Best for

MOUNTAIN VIEWS

KEN WELSH/GETTY IMAGES ©

for trail 18B. The sinuous route climbs through stone-strewn pastures, passing an austere mountain lake and affording **ever more amazing views** into the steep-walled Valnontey valley. About 45 minutes past the *rifugio*, a series of rope handholds, metal steps anchored in the rock and a short ladder help you navigate a particularly steep section. No technical skills are required; simply watch your step and take your time. You're soon rewarded with **magnificent vistas of the towering snow-capped peaks** at the valley's far end. After briefly veering right to cross a creek, the trail doubles back through a boulder field with painted arrows indicating the way. Ethereal views of the valley far below continue for another hour as you emerge on a high rocky shelf and pick your way towards the mountain meadow of Herbetet.

04 Massive slate roofs crown the **Casolari Herbetet** (2437m), a cluster of stone houses flanked by a spring where you can replenish your water supply. Trails 18B and 22G converge here; follow the latter towards the valley floor (signs for Alpe Money), switchbacking steadily down the mountainside for the next hour to reach another crossroads. The day's final stage back to Valnontey is a meandering, relatively level 1½-hour walk downstream along the verdant banks of the Torrente Valnontey, traversing a wonderland of enormous boulders, rocky spires and deep green forest.

 **TAKE A BREAK**

The high country's uncontested lunch pick is **Rifugio Sella** (www. rifugiosella.com), King Vittorio Emanuele II's former hunting lodge. Set on a high plateau at the hike's midpoint, surrounded by stark mountain walls, it offers hearty lunches of homemade minestrone, followed by polenta served with local fontina cheese or *carbonada* (veal stewed with onions and white wine).

58

GRAN BALCONATA DEL CERVINO

DURATION	DIFFICULTY	DISTANCE	START/END
6hrs	Moderate	15km	Chamois/ Breuil-Cervinia

TERRAIN	Dirt trail, meadows and rocky slopes

Spellbinding views of the Matterhorn – seen from the less-familiar Italian side – are the star attraction on this 15km section of the 73km Gran Balconata del Cervino, one of the Alps' classic loop hikes. For most of the walk you'll be traversing rocky ridgelines and grassy meadows high above the pastoral Valtournenche valley, with the shapely 4478m triangular peak (known to Italians as Cervino; pictured p219) towering high above it all.

GETTING HERE

From Buisson on the SR46, the year-round Funivia Buisson-Chamois cable car (www.funiviachamois.it) climbs to Chamois in five minutes. At trail's end in Cervinia, Arriva Savda (www.savda.it) runs buses back to Buisson (€2.20, 30 minutes).

STARTING POINT

Near the upper cable car station in Chamois are a couple of bar-restaurants with restrooms, but no parking (cars are prohibited in Chamois).

01 From the **upper cable-car station**, walk straight ahead (east) through **Chamois village** – also known as Corgnolaz. Shortly after passing Bar Chamois on your right, yellow-and-black signs for trail 107 point you left up the hill. Opposite the turnoff, a fountain with a cute ibex-head spout makes a good place to fill your water bottles.

02 Zigzag up the hill on a mix of stone steps, paved road, dirt road and single-track trail. Signposts are frequent along this stretch, but make sure to stick to trail 107, as several other trails branch off here. Pass a kids' playground and a variety of stone houses on Chamois' outskirts, then merge onto a wide **larch-shaded path**, ignoring signs for Rifugio Ermitage as you cross a road and continue straight uphill between low stone walls.

03 Arrive at **Lago di Lod**, a mountain lake flanked by ski lifts, after a 35-minute climb from Chamois. The small lakeside park here offers picnic tables, drinking water and restroom facilities. Note that between late June and early September you can reach this same point via chairlift from Chamois. At the three-way junction to the right of the

lake, trails 3 and 34 branch right and left, respectively, while you take the narrower central route marked 107 in black-and-yellow paint on a pylon. Starting as a faint path running parallel to the ski lift, the trail passes briefly through larch forest, then opens onto a wider dirt road climbing steeply up the ski slopes, with **pretty views over the lake and mountains below**.

04 You've reached the 'no pain, no gain' part of the trail – but rest assured, Matterhorn views are coming soon! At the top of the ski slope, as chairlift pylons

disappear off to the right, trail 107 branches left off the grass-covered dirt road onto a narrow, steep path with signs for Cheneil. The trail continues climbing steadily, eventually levelling out a bit as it passes through low juniper scrub, meadows and larch forest.

05 Sunlight floods in as the trail leaves the forest, re-enters a meadow and bears left to reach the summit at **Col Cheneil**. Follow signs for **Cheneil village** (pictured) along a broad, grass-covered road to your left. Begin a gentle descent, with **fantastic views** of the Matterhorn to the

Climbing the Matterhorn

Some 3000 alpinists summit Europe's most photographed peak (4478m) each year. You don't need to be super-human to do it, but you do need to be a skilled climber in tip-top physical shape and have a week in hand to acclimatise beforehand to make the iconic ascent up sheer rock and ice. No one attempts the Matterhorn without local know-how: mountain guides charge around €1500 per person for the eight-hour return climb. Client:guide ratios are 1:1. Mid-July to mid-September is the best time of year to attempt the ascent. You'll probably be required to do training climbs first, just to prove you really are 100% up to it. The Matterhorn claims more than a few lives each year.

north and a mountain ridge framing the deep valley of Valtournenche to the west. A bench surrounded by wood railings makes a pleasant spot to take it all in. From here it's mostly downhill to the village of Cheneil, where the **Hotel Panorama al Bich restaurant** makes another welcome rest stop.

06 Exit Cheneil to the north, following signs for trail 107, and climb through the forest to the **tiny hilltop church of Notre Dame de la Guérison**. Tantalising glimpses of the Matterhorn reappear as you continue beyond the church into the high country, weaving through meadows and stands of larch forest. About 40 minutes past the church, pass a left-hand turnoff for Champlève (trail 28) and continue straight on trail 107, following the clear indications painted in yellow on the rocks.

07 After cresting a ridgeline, the trail descends to cross the ski slopes around **Dzandzoevé** and **Cime Bianche** (also shown as Desert on some maps). A couple of bar-restaurants offer refreshments here, including **Willy Bar** at the top of the Salette gondola, and **La Roisette**, in an old stone house near the base of the Motta chairlift.

08 Trail 107 continues north through high open country for the next half-hour, passing occasional stone houses and widening from a single-track path to a dirt road. Just beyond the **picturesque lichen-covered ruins** of an old stone house on the left, at a T-intersection signposted Tramail di Mande (2310m), turn right onto a paved road. About 10 minutes further on, turn left at a **long stone barn (Alpe Manda)** to stay on trail 107.

09 Five minutes beyond the stone barn, at a Y-intersection of two dirt roads, branch left (signs for Breuil-Cervinia) and begin an hour-long descent to the valley floor. Pass a **pretty stone building** backed by fabulous **mountain views**, cross a **wooden bridge** over an old funicular railway, then snake your way across a large rockslide. **Bewitching glimpses of the Matterhorn** framed by trees greet you for the next 15 minutes as you descend more steeply through larch forest.

10 The trail levels out at a clearing signposted Layet (2045m), where you'll find a **natural spring** with drinking water and the two-storey **Baita Layet restaurant**. From here, it's all downhill to **Lago**

Blu (Lac Bleu, 1981m), just 10 minutes below. This piercingly blue mountain lake (pictured) is one of Valtournenche's **most photographed spots** thanks to the perfect reflections of the Matterhorn mirrored in its waters.

11 You've now reached the valley floor, where a 25-minute walk parallel to the main road leads past a picnic area to the ski village of **Breuil-Cervinia** – home to a plethora of restaurants and a bus stop where you can hop a ride back to the base station of the Buisson-Chamois cable car.

☕ TAKE A BREAK

Conveniently placed opposite the bus stop on Breuil-Cervinia's lower traffic circle, **Birdy Bakery** (📞348 6617235; www.facebook.com/BirdyBakery; Piazza Guido Rey 17, Breuil-Cervinia; snacks & mains €2.50-16; 🕖7am-8pm Wed-Mon) is a perfect trail-ender. This friendly corner bakery and all-around local hangout serves tasty homemade pizza, sandwiches, focaccia and pastries, along with great cappuccinos. At lunchtime, check out the daily specials such as homemade pasta or delicious Swiss-style *rösti* (pan-fried potatoes with cheese, prosciutto and/or a fried egg).

59

VALLONE DI GRAUSON

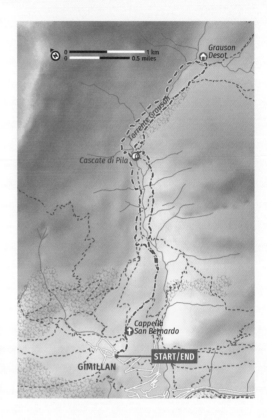

DURATION	DIFFICULTY	DISTANCE	START/END
3½hrs	Moderate	10km	Gimillan

TERRAIN	Dirt trail, some steep sections

Reaching deep into the mountains northeast of Cogne, the beautiful Grauson valley (pictured) shelters small meadows, larch woodlands and thundering cascades in its precipitous lower reaches, while its grassy highlands are dotted with stone huts, some still used by herdsmen during midsummer grazing.

From **Gimillan's village centre**, follow signs for trail 8 towards Grauson Desot. Climbing past electrical pylons, the trail reaches a meadow with fine **views** over Gimillan's wooden chalets and slate rooftops.

Trail 8 soon branches right, descending to cross the **Torrente Grauson** at Tschezeu junction (1910m). Begin climbing the opposite side of the valley, with views ahead to a **dramatic waterfall (Cascate di Pila)**. Beyond the falls, the trail climbs a steep embankment and passes through larch forest to reach a

hilltop shrine with a cross about 1¾ hours from your starting point.

From here, a gentle stroll of less than 10 minutes descends to the tumbledown stone chalets of **Grauson Desot**. Refill your water bottles at the freshwater spring on your right just before the village bridge, and consider a picnic on the stone benches along the town's lone thoroughfare.

Return via trail 8E along the opposite side of the river, making sure not to miss the picturesque views back to the village as you leave. After initially climbing high above the Grauson valley, with **splendid long vistas** towards the snowy peaks of Parco Nazionale Gran Paradiso, the trail spends the next hour descending parallel to the river gorge. Beyond a large meadow, turn left at a junction for trail 3C, which reconnects with the path you came in on (trail 8) about 20 minutes outside of Gimillan.

60

RIFUGIO GARELLI

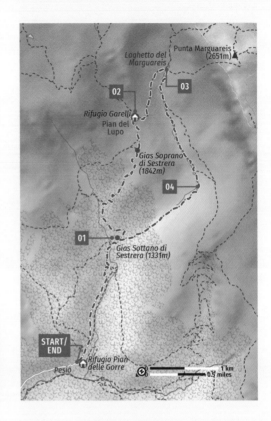

DURATION	DIFFICULTY	DISTANCE	START/END
5hrs	Moderate	12km	Rifugio Pian delle Gorre

TERRAIN	Dirt roads and trails, sustained climbs

Experience the primeval essence of the Marguareis range on this delightful day hike into the wide-open high country surrounding Rifugio Garelli. This fleeting taste of the Maritime alpine wilderness gets you up and back in five hours, with an optional lunch stop at the trail's midpoint.

GETTING HERE

Grandabus (www.grandabus.it) runs buses from Cogne via Chiusa di Pesio to Certosa di Pesio, 3km north of the trailhead. Drivers can park at the trailhead.

STARTING POINT

You'll find paid parking, restrooms and a bar-restaurant at Rifugio Pian delle Gorre, directly adjacent to the trailhead.

01 From **Rifugio Pian delle Gorre**, head uphill on a broad unpaved road signposted for Rifugio Garelli. The going is easy and pleasant, traipsing through forest and past a waterfall on the left to reach a clearing with a large signboard in about 30 minutes. Leave the dirt road here, branching left onto trail H8 (marked Gias di Sestrera/Rifugio Garelli) and zigzagging up through giant evergreen forest. In about 20 minutes, emerge from the trees at **Gias Sottano di Sestrera** (1331m), a gloriously green meadow with a natural spring pouring into a stone trough. Trail H1 to Laghetto del Marguareis (your eventual return route) branches right here; continue left instead on trail H8 to Rifugio Garelli.

02 A sustained climb ensues, as you make your way into open high country. After an hour or so, you reach the stone barn of **Gias Soprano di Sestrera**, where a wall plaque relates the WWII history surrounding this mountain outpost. A further

FEDERICO LANDRA/SHUTTERSTOCK ©

15 minutes of climbing brings you to **Pian del Lupo** (2000m), a windswept summit made hospitable by the sleek, solar-powered **Rifugio Garelli** (pictured).

03 Leaving the *rifugio*, follow signs for Sentiero F Sordella, a narrow trail that leads gradually downhill to the frigid waters of **Laghetto del Marguareis**. At the next trail junction (about 20 minutes past the lake, 40 minutes from Rifugio Garelli), ignore the trail straight ahead for Passo del Duca, turning right instead to follow signs for Rifugio Pian delle Gorre. Begin steadily descending a long valley running parallel to a

creek on your right, traversing a rugged, treeless high country landscape. Occasional stone shepherds' huts painted with red-and-white blazes offer the only hint of civilisation. About half an hour into the descent, ignore a trail junction on your left marked 'GTA' (Grand Tour des Alpes) and continue descending straight ahead through the sheep pastures.

04 An hour or so after leaving Laghetto del Marguareis, the trail finally drops back below the tree line, first passing through a **maple-fringed meadow**, then following the rushing creek into a full-fledged **deciduous**

forest. Cross a bridge over the creek, and you'll soon find yourself back in the clearing at Gias Sottano di Sestrera. Turn left at the familiar water trough and retrace your steps down the hill to Rifugio Pian delle Gorre.

TAKE A BREAK

Perched in a mountain meadow at 1970m, **Rifugio Garelli** (☎ 0171 73 80 78; www.rifugiogarelli.com; Al Pian del Lupo; dm €26, with half-board €49; ⏱ mid-Jun–mid-Sep) makes a welcoming spot for a hearty mountain lunch, with specialties including mushroom risotto and grilled trout. If you're wiped out from your long climb, you can even spend the night!

Also Try...

SBELLOTT/SHUTTERSTOCK ©

LAGO DI VALSCURA CIRCUIT

Near the French border, this superb walk to glacial lakes at the head of a picturesque alpine valley (pictured) affords fine Alpi Marettime views.

From Terme di Valdieri, climb an hour to Piano del Valasco, a rock-strewn high plateau where you can refuel with snacks at a historic royal hunting lodge. Continue up through a glacial valley to reach Lago Inferiore di Valscura (2274m) within 1½ hours, then follow the GTA (Grand Tour des Alpes) – here an old military road built between the world wars – towards Lago del Claus.

Passing some lakelets, the trail enters the cliff-fringed glacial basin of Lago del Claus (2344m), then zigzags down to a signposted junction for Rifugio Questa, which serves home-cooked lunches and offers accommodation. Red-and-white squares mark the GTA as it descends to rejoin your earlier route. Go right, descending two hours back to Terme di Valdieri.

DURATION 6hrs
DIFFICULTY Moderate
DISTANCE 21km

ALPE DI MOŃEY

This outstandingly panoramic walk through Parco Nazionale Gran Paradiso leads to traditional alpine grazing huts below the edge of a glacier.

From the bridge in Valnontey village, follow trail 22 upstream along the rushing Torrente Valnontey. Turn left after about 50 minutes onto trail 22C and weave steeply up through a series of cliffs, enjoying magnificent valley and mountain views.

The trail levels off after another hour, crossing huge rock slabs to Alpe di Money (2325m), where several slate-roofed stone farm structures contrast picturesquely with the stunning backdrop of Gran Paradiso and its glaciers. The path continues south through the high country, then descends to a bridge over Torrente Valnontey about two hours from Alpe Money. Bypass a left-hand junction with trail 22G and continue downstream on trail 22 all the way to Valnontey, with the Torrente Valnontey rushing beside you and mighty cliffs soaring above.

DURATION 5¾–6¼hrs
DIFFICULTY Hard
DISTANCE 15km

AMY CORTI/SHUTTERSTOCK ©

CASCATE DI LILLAZ

This short climb from Lillaz village leads to a series of gorgeous waterfalls (pictured) at the edge of Parco Nazionale Gran Paradiso.

Cross a pedestrian bridge from the village parking lot, turning left past Bar Cascate to reach the Parco Geologico. Signs for 'Cascate' lead onto a flat, paved riverside path, then up stairs to the lower falls. Continue uphill to two more waterfalls before rejoining the main path, crossing a bridge over the falls and paralleling your original route back down to Lillaz.

DURATION 1hr
DIFFICULTY Easy
DISTANCE 3km

TORRENTE VALNONTEY

The river is your constant companion on this easygoing ramble through the valley of the Torrente Valnontey.

From Valnontey village, follow signs for trail 22 south. Beginning as a broad track, the level trail parallels the rushing river through conifer forest and cow pastures, narrowing as it continues upstream. About an hour into the hike, cross the river at Ponte dell'Erfaulet and continue 30 minutes up the forested, boulder-strewn valley, turning around at a junction with trail 22G and returning downriver.

DURATION 3hrs
DIFFICULTY Easy
DISTANCE 10km

CHAMOIS TO LA MAGDALEINE

Stroll the verdant slopes above Valtournenche on this relatively flat section of the Gran Balconata del Cervino, one of northwestern Italy's classic hikes.

From Buisson on the main road, take the gondola up to Chamois, then follow signs for trail 107 towards La Magdaleine. Exiting Chamois village towards the south, the wide trail meanders through forests and meadows for about an hour to La Magdaleine, where you can retrace your steps back to Chamois.

DURATION 2hrs
DIFFICULTY Easy
DISTANCE 8km

Language

Italian pronunciation isn't difficult as most sounds are also found in English. The pronunciation of some consonants depends on which vowel follows, but if you read our pronunciation guides below as if they were English, you'll be understood just fine. Just remember to pronounce double consonants as a longer, more forceful sound than single ones.

To enhance your trip with a phrasebook, visit **lonelyplanet. com**. Find Lonely Planet iPhone phrasebooks in the Apple App store.

BASICS

Hello.
Buongiorno./Ciao.   bwon·jor·no/chow
(pol/inf)

How are you?
Come sta?   ko·me sta

I'm fine, thanks.
Bene, grazie.   be·ne gra·tsye

Excuse me.
Mi scusi.   mee skoo·zee

Yes./No.
Sì./No.   see/no

Please. (when asking)
Per favore.   per fa·vo·re

Thank you.
Grazie.   gra·tsye

Goodbye.
Arrivederci./   a·ree·ve·der·chee/
Ciao.   chow (pol/inf)

Do you speak English?
Parla inglese?   par·la een·gle·ze

I don't understand.
Non capisco.   non ka·pee·sko

How much is this?
Quanto costa?   kwan·to ko·sta

ON THE TRAIL

How many more hours to ...?
Restano quante ore a ...?

We're walking from ... to ...
Andiamo da ... a ...

Does this path go to ...?
Questo sentiero arriva a ...?

Can you show me on the map?
Può mostrarmi sulla carta?

Where have you come from?
Da dove è venuto/a?

How long does it take?
Ci vuole quanto tempo?

How much snow is there on the pass?
Quanta neve c'è sul passo?

Can the river be crossed?
Si può attraversare il fiume?

DIRECTIONS

Go straight ahead.	Si va sempre diritto.
Turn left/right.	Gira a sinistra/destra.
the first left/ right	il primo a sinistra/ destra
direction	direzione
round trip	(viaggio di) andata e ritorno
turnoff	bivio
ahead	avanti/davanti
behind	dietro
above	sopra
below	sotto
before	prima di/davanti a
after	dopo
beginning	inizio
end	fine

downstream	a valle
upstream	a monte
flat	piatto
steep	ripido
high	alto
low	basso
near	vicino
far	lontano
beside	accanto a
between	tra
level with	alla pari di
opposite	di fronte
north	nord
south	sud
east	est
west	ovest

WEATHER

What's the forecast?
Come sono le previsioni?

Tomorrow it will be ...
Domani sarà ...

good weather	bel tempo
bad weather	brutto tempo
cloudy	nuvoloso
cold	freddo
flood	alluvione
fog/mist	nebbia
hot	caldo
ice (it's icy)	ghiaccio (è ghiacciato)
lightning	fulmine
rain (it's raining)	pioggia (piove)
snow (it's snowing)	neve (nevica)

storm	tempesta
sunny	soleggiato
thunderstorm	temporale
wind (it's windy)	vento (c'è vento)

CLOTHING & EQUIPMENT

backpack	zaino
(walking) boots	scarpone
compass	bussola
gloves	guanti
(walking) map	carta
pocket knife	temperino
rain jacket	impermeabile
sleeping bag	sacco a pelo
socks	calzini
sunglasses	occhiali da sole
tent	tenda
toilet paper	carta igienica
torch/flashlight	torcia elettrica
walking pole	bastone da passeggio
water bottle	borraccia

GEOGRAPHIC FEATURES

bend (in road)	curva
bridge	ponte
cable car	funivia
cairn	tumolo (di peitre)
farm	fattoria
fence	recinto
footbridge	passerella
ford	guado
forest	foresta/bosco
house/building	casa/edificio
hut	rifugio
path	sentiero
quarry	cava
road	strada
shelter	bivacco
signpost	cartello indicatore

spring (of water)	sorgente
town	città
tree	albero
village	frazione/paese/villagio
way marker	segnale

LANDFORMS

bay	baia
cape/headland	capo
cave	caverna/grotta
cliff	scogliera scoscesa/rupe
coast	costa
crater	cratere
gap	passo/valico
glacier	ghiacciaio
gorge	gorge
hill	collina/colle
island	isola
junction (in river or stream)	confluenza
lake	lago
landslide	frana
mountain	montagna
mud	fango
pass	passo/forcella
peninsula	peninsola
plateau	altipiano
ridge	cresta
river	fiume/rio/torrente
riverbank	riva
rockfall	caduta di pietra/caduta massi
saddle	sella
scree/talus	ghiaione
slope	versante
snowfield	nevaio
stream	ruscello/torrente
summit/peak	cima/sommità
valley	valle/val/vallon
volcano	vulcanoe
waterfall	cascata

ACCOMMODATION

I'd like to book a room.
Vorrei prenotare una camera. — vo·ray pre·no·ta·re oo·na ka·me·ra

How much is it per night?
Quanto costa per una notte? — kwan·to kos·ta per oo·na no·te

EATING & DRINKING

I'd like ..., please.
Vorrei ..., per favore. — vo·ray ... per fa·vo·re

What would you recommend?
Cosa mi consiglia? — ko·za mee kon·see·lya

That was delicious!
Era squisito! — e·ra skwee·zee·to

Bring the bill/check, please.
Mi porta il conto, per favore. — mee por·ta eel kon·to per fa·vo·re

I'm allergic (to peanuts).
Sono allergico/a (alle arachidi). (m/f) — so·no a·ler·jee·ko/a (a·le a·ra·kee·dee)

I don't eat ...
Non mangio ... — non man·jo ...

fish	pesce	pe·she
meat	carne	kar·ne
poultry	pollame	po·la·me

EMERGENCIES

I'm ill.
Mi sento male. — mee sen·to ma·le

Help!
Aiuto! — a·yoo·to

Call a doctor!
Chiami un medico! — kya·mee oon me·dee·ko

Call the police!
Chiami la polizia! — kya·mee la po·lee·tsee·a

Behind the Scenes

Send us your feedback

We love to hear from travellers – your comments help make our books better. We read every word, and we guarantee that your feedback goes straight to the authors. Visit **lonelyplanet.com/ contact** to submit your updates and suggestions.
Note: We may edit, reproduce and incorporate your comments in Lonely Planet products such as guidebooks,websites and digital products, so let us know if you don't want your comments reproduced or your name acknowledged. For a copy of our privacy policy visit lonelyplanet. com/privacy.

WRITERS' THANKS

GREGOR CLARK

Heartfelt thanks to all of the many Italians and fellow travellers who shared their recommendations and enthusiasm for walking in Italy – especially Fabiana, Fausto, Micol, Stefano, Mario, Frédérique, Diego, Patrizia, Marisin, Francesco, Sandro, Paula and Jörg. I'm also indebted to fellow author Brendan Sainsbury for all of his excellent recommendations in the Western and Maritime Alps. Last but not least, huge thanks and hugs to Gaen for coming to help me research Umbria – my favourite part of the whole trip.

BRENDAN SAINSBURY

Grazie mille to all the rural bus drivers who got me to the start points of the most isolated trails (and always on time!), the great B&Bs in L'Aquila and Sulmona, the gelaterias in Tuscany, and the coffee and pizza makers pretty much everywhere.

ACKNOWLEDGMENTS

Digital Elevation Model Data

© European Union, Copernicus Land Monitoring Service 2019, European Environment Agency (EEA), produced with funding of the European Union

Cover photograph Santa Maddalena di Funes, Dolomites, Janoka82/Getty Images ©

Photographs pp6–11 Vladislav Pichugin/Shutterstock ©; e55evu/Getty Images ©; Gregor Clark/Lonely Planet ©; canadastock/Shutterstock ©; fokke baarssen/Shutterstock ©; gnoparus/Shutterstock ©; DaLiu/ Shutterstock ©; zorattifabio/Getty Images ©; REDMASON/ Shutterstock ©; Nicole Kwiatkowski/Shutterstock ©

THIS BOOK

This book was researched and written by Gregor Clark and Brendan Sainsbury. It was produced by the following:

Product Editor Rachel Rawling

Book Designer Katherine Marsh

Regional Senior Cartographer Anthony Phelan

Cartographers David Connolly, Hunor Csutoros, Katerina Pavkova

Assisting Editors Andrea Dobbin, Carly Hall, Victoria Harrison, Kate James

Product Development Imogen Bannister, Liz Heynes, Anne Mason, Dianne Schallmeiner, John Taufa, Juan Winata

Design Development Virginia Moreno

Cover Design & Researcher Ania Bartoszek

Cartographic Series Designer Wayne Murphy

Thanks to Kerry Christiani, Piotr Czajkowski, Barbara Di Castro, Daniel Di Paolo, Tina Garcia, Shona Gray, Martin Heng, Chris LeeAck, Jennifer McDonagh, Campbell McKenzie, Darren O'Connell, Piers Pickard, Wibowo Rusli, Kate Sullivan, Glenn van der Knijff, Steve Waters

By Difficulty

EASY

Castellina to Radda..............98
Certaldo to San Gimignano..............100
Greenway al Lago di Como..............32
Oasi Faunistica di Vendicari..............130
Orrido di Sant'Anna..............30
Panzano to Radda..............96
Passo del Lupo..............186
Percorso delle Segherie..............158
Pragser Wildsee..............156

MODERATE

Above Pescasseroli..............74
Adolf Munkel Weg..............160
Around the Pian Piccolo..............194
Bosco di San Francesco..............196
Cala Goloritzé..............168
Cala Sisine to Cala Luna..............176
Campo Imperatore Ridge..............76
Chianti Classico..............102
Fossa di Vulcano..............132
Gola dell'Infernaccio..............188
Gola di Gorropu..............170
Gran Balconata
del Cervino..............228
Hans & Paula Steger Weg..............142
La Rocca di Cefalù..............124
La Strada del Ponale..............36
Le Tre Marine..............60
Levanto to Monterosso..............204
Manarola to Corniglia..............208
Medieval Towns & Villages..............110
Monte Corrasi..............178
Monte Isola Loop..............38
Monte Subasio..............190
Necropoli di Pantalica..............122
Passegiata del Pizzolungo..............50
Portofino to San Fruttuoso..............206
Punta Campanella..............52
Punta Troia..............134
Rifugio Garelli..............234
Riserva Naturale
dello Zingaro..............126
Santa Maria del
Castello Circuit..............64
Santo Stefano di Sessanio
to Rocca Calascio..............72
Sassolungo Circuit..............148
Sentiero Azzurro..............210
Sentiero degli Dei..............54
Stromboli..............120
Tiscali..............172
Tre Cime di Lavaredo..............150
Tuscan Hill Crests..............106
Valle del Sambuco..............58
Valle delle Ferriere..............62
Vallone di Grauson..............232

HARD

Alpe di Fanes..............152
Monte Baldo:
Sentiero del Ventrar..............42
Monte Mileto..............82
Passo Gardena to Vallunga..............144
Porto Venere
to Riomaggiore..............214
Rocca Ridge..............78
Sella-Herbetet Traverse..............226
Sentiero della Libertà..............86
The Slopes of Monte Grona..............40
Tour du Mont Blanc..............222

Index

A

Abruzzo 69-91
  accommodation 71
  events 71
  festivals
  resources 71
  transport 71
  travel seasons 71
accessible trails 16-17
accommodation
  agriturismo 94
  Hotel Pragser Wildsee 157
  language 239
  Lido Palace 37
  Pensione Tranchina 129
  rifugi 19, 22
  Rifugio Elisabetta 224
  Rifugio Garelli 235
  Rifugio Menaggio 41
  Villa della Quercia 55
Adolf Munkel Weg 160-1
agriturismi 94
Alicudi 136
Alpe di Fanes 10, 152-5
Alpe di Money 236
alps, *see* Western & Maritime Alps
Alta Via delle Cinque Terre 216
Alta Vie delle Dolomiti 154
Amalfi 48-9, 62
Amalfi Coast 47-67
  accommodation 49
  events 49
  festivals 49
  resources 49
  transport 49
  travel seasons 49
Ancona 184-5
animals 23, 80

Apennines 70
Appian Way 20
archaeological sites
  Anàktoron 122
  Apennine castle-fortress 73
  Castel Mancino 74
  Castelvecchio 111, 112
  Ercole Curino 90
  Podere Case Lovara 205
  Segesta 129
  Tempio di Diana 125
Arco Naturale 50
Assergi 91
Assisi 184, 190-1, 196-7
Atrani 67

B

Baia di Ieranto 53
Baunei 166
beaches
  Baia di Ieranto 53
  Cala Berretta 128
  Cala Capreria 127
  Cala della Disa 127
  Cala dell'Uzzo 128
  Cala Goloritzé 169
  Cala Tonnarella dell'Uzzo 129
  Calamosche beach 131
  Marina di Praia 60
  Positano 57
Boccaccio, Giovanni 101
Bolzano 140
Bomerano 54
borghi 108
Bosco di San Francesco 196-7
Bozzanigo 34
Breglia 40
Breuil-Cervinia 220

C

Cadenabbia 35
Cala Fuili 180
Cala Goloritzé 168-9
Cala Gonone 166
Cala Luna 8, 176-7, 180
Cala Sisine 8, 176-7
Camogli 216
Campania 47-67
  accommodation 49
  events 49
  festivals 49
  resources 49
  transport 49
  travel seasons 49
Campiglia 215
Campo 78 89
Campo Imperatore Ridge 76-7
Campocecina 115
Cannobina 30
Cannobio 45
Cansano 87
Cantaru Orruos 170
Capo d'Acqua 64
Capo di Milazzo 137
Capo Testa 181
Cappelletta 206
Capri Town 50
Caramanico Terme 91
Carmine Superiore 45
Carzano 39
Cascate di Lillaz 237
Casolari Herbetet 227
Castellina in Chianti 98
Castelluccio 184
Castelpoggio 115
Castelvecchio Nature Reserve 112
Catania 118

cathedrals, *see* churches & cathedrals
Cefalù 118, 124-5
Certaldo 100-1
Chamois 228, 237
chapels, *see* churches & cathedrals
Chianti 8, 94, 102-5
children, travel with 14
Chiosco Sa Barva 170
churches & cathedrals
   Basilica di San Francesco 196
   Chapel of St Johann
     (San Giovanni) 161
   Chiesa di Santa Margherita
     d'Antiochia 212
   Chiesa di Santa Maria delle Pietà 73
   Chiesa di Sant'Anna 30
   Collegiata di Santa Maria 58
   Pieve di Cellole 101
   Pieve di San Giusto in Salcio 103
   Pieve di Santo Stefano a Campo 114
   San Gimignano cathedral 107
   Santuario della Madonna del
     Soccorso 33
   Santuario Madonna della Ceriola 38-9
   St Johann 161
   Volastra village church 208
Cime Bianche 230
Cinque Terre 202
Cinque Terre card 213
Cisternulo 55
climate 19
clothing 18-19
   language 239
Club Alpino Italiano 22, 25
coastline walks 12
Cogne 220
Col Chécrouit 222
Col de Chavannes 224
Colma di Malcesine 42
Colonno 32
Compaccio 142-3
Compatsch 142-3
Conca dei Marini 61
Conero Riviera 186-7
Convento San Nicola 59
Corniglia 208-9, 213

Corno Grande 90
Corsa degli Zingari 83
Corsa dei Ceri 191
Cortina d'Ampezzo 140
Corvara in Badia 140
Courmayeur 220
Croce della Conocchia 66
culture 12
Cuneo 221

D

dangers, *see* safe travel
disabilities, travellers with 16-17
Dolomites & Stelvio 139-63
   accommodation 141
   events 141
   festivals 141
   resources 141
   transport 141
   travel seasons 140-1
Dorgali 166
drinking, *see* food & drink
Dzandzoevé 230

E

evironmental issues 23-4, 224
equipment 18-19
   language 239
Etna 137

F

family travel 14-15
festivals & events, *see individual
   locations*
Fiordo di Crapolla 67
Fiordo di Furore 60, 61
Fiume Calcinara 122
food & drink
   Agriturismo Nuraghe Mannu 177
   Bar Dante 105
   Bar Su Porteddu 169
   Birdy Bakery 230
   Caffè Sicilia 131

C'era Una Volta 65
Colle del Telegrafo 215
Da Armandino 61
Dolceria Corrado Costanzo 131
Dolomites cuisine 145
Dreizinnenhütte 151
Durnwald 157
Gelateria Dondoli 101
Gostner Schwaige 143
Gschnagenhardt 161
Il Duca degli Abruzzi 81
Il Gabbiano 213
KMO 209
La Capannina 43
La Fabbrica del Gelato 35
La Forgia Maurizio 133
La Scarpetta di Venere 89
language 239
Lapillo Gelato 121
L'Incontro 113
Lo Scoglio 53
Locanda al Lago 39
Locanda Sotto gli Archi 73
Mandralisca 16 125
Ostello Lo Zio 77
Osteria del Mulino 197
Osteria delle Catene 109
Osteria Sara 187
Panino allo Scarafischio 195
Plattkofelhütte 149
Ponale Alto Belvedere 37
Relais Villa Miraglia 136
Rifugio Fanes 154
Rifugio Menaggio 41
Rifugio Puez 147
Rifugio Sella 227
Ristorante Ispinigoli 171
Ristorante La Rocca 193
Ristorante-Pizzeria Majella 85
Ritrovo Ingrid 121
Sal de Riso 59
Sicilian cuisine 131
Su Gologone 175
Trattoria Il Mulino 63
Trattoria Il Veliero 135

food & drink *continued*
   Trattoria Santa Croce 57
   Zi Peppe 65
Forato 114
Forcella de Ciampei 146
Forcella de Crespeina 145
Fossa di Vulcano 132-3
Francis of Assisi 190-2

G

Galenda 103
German language 153
Gias Soprano di Sestrera 234
Gimillan 232
Giro dei Laghi 163
Giro del Bullaccia 163
glaciers 224
Gola dell'Infernaccio 188
Gola di Gorropu 170-1
Gorropu gorge 170-1
Gran Balconata del Cervino 228-31
Gran Sasso Raid 77
Grauson Desot 232
Greenway al Lago di Como 9, 32-5
Greve in Chianti 114
Grotta del Biscotto 54
Grotta del Genovese 135
Grotta dell'Uzzo 128
Grotta di Matermània 50
Gubbio 191

H

Hans & Paula Steger Weg 142-3
Herbetet 226-7
history 12, 20-3, 77

I

internet resources, *see* websites
Ischia 66
Italian Lakes 27-45
   accommodation 29
   events 29
   festivals 29
   resources 29
   transport 29
   travel seasons 29
Italian language 238-9

L

La Magdaleine 237
La Rocca di Cefalù 124-5
La Strada del Ponale 36-7
La Tese trail 65
Laghetto del Marguareis 235
Lago Blu 230
Lago di Biviere 136
Lago di Braies 156-7
Lago di Como 9, 28, 32-5
Lago di Garda 28-9, 36-7
Lago di Pilato 199
Lago di Valscura 236
Lago d'Iseo 29, 38-9
Lago d'Orta 45
Lago Maggiore 28
lakes, *see* Italian Lakes, *individual lakes*
languages 153, 238-9
L'Aquila 70
Le Marche 183-99
   accommodation 185
   events 185
   festivals 185
   resources 185
   transport 185
   travel seasons 185
Le Tre Marine 60-1
Levanto 203, 204-5
Liguria 201-17
   accommodation 203
   events 203
   resources 203
   transport 203
   travel seasons 203
Lipari 118
Lucca 115

M

Maiori 58, 67

Malcesine 42
Manarola 208-9
maps 18, 169
marble 215
Marettimo 134-5
Marguareis 234
Marina di Furore 61
Marina di Praia 60
Maritime Alps 219-37
   accommodation 221
   events 221
   festivals 221
   resources 221
   transport 221
   travel seasons 221
Massa 39
Matterhorn 229, 230
medieval architecture 110-12
Mezzegra 34
Minori 59
Minuta 63
Montauto 109
Mont Blanc 6, 23, 222-4
Monte Baldo 42-3
Monte Bolettone 45
Monte Corrasi 178
Monte delle Croci 73
Monte Entu 180
Monte Epomeo 66
Monte Grona 40-1
Monte Isola 38-9
Monte Mileto 7, 82, 84
Monte Mottarone 44
Monte Novo San Giovanni 181
Monte Pietroso 79
Monte Portella 77
Monte San Costanzo 53
Monte Sant'Angelo 64
Monte Subasio 190-3
Monte Tranquillo 79
Monte Tuoro 50
Monte Vettore 199
Montepertuso 56
Monterosso 204-5, 210, 217
Monterosso al Mare 202

Morrone di Pacentro 83
mountains 13, *see also individual mountains*
Mt Etna 137
museums
  Casa Chianti Classico 98
  Centro di Visita di Pescasseroli 79
  Museo della Carta (Paper Museum) 63
  Museo della Cultura Contadina 129
  Museo della Manna 127
  Museo delle Attività Marinare 128-9
  Museo dell'Intreccio 128
  Museo Etrusco Guarnacci 111
  Museo Naturalistico 127

N

national parks & nature reserves 23-4
  Castelvecchio Nature Reserve 112
  Gran Sasso-Laga National Park 91
  Majella National Park 86-7
  Parco Naturale Fanes-Sennes-Braies 152-5
  Parco Naturale Puez Odle 144
  Parco Naturale Regionale di Portofino 206
  Parco Nazionale d'Abruzzo, Lazio e Molise 70-1
  Parco Nazionale del Gran Sasso e Monti della Laga 71
  Parco Nazionale della Majella 71
  Parco Nazionale Gran Paradiso 236
  Parco Regionale del Conero 186
  Riserva Naturale dello Zingaro 126-29
nature reserves, *see* national parks & nature reserves
Necropoli di Pantalica 122
Nerano 53
Nocelle 55
Noto 118
Nuoro 166
Nuraghic people 173

O

Oasi Faunistica di Vendicari 130-1
Olzano 39

Orfento Gorge 91
Orrido di Sant'Anna 30
Orta San Giulio 45
Ossuccio 33

P

Pacentro 82, 84, 85
Palazzina 112
Palena 89
Pancole 101
Pania della Croce 114
Pantalica 122
Panzano in Chianti 96
Parco Naturale Puez Odle 144
Parco Nazionale d'Abruzzo, Lazio e Molise 70-1
Parco Nazionale del Gran Sasso e Monti della Laga 71
Parco Nazionale della Majella 71
parks, *see* national parks
Pascieux 226
Passeggiata del Pizzolungo 50
Passo del Lupo 186-7
Passo Gardena 9, 144-7
Percorso delle Segherie 158
Pescasseroli 74, 78
Peschiera Maraglio 38-9
Pian del Lupo 235
Pian Piccolo 194-5
Piano Grande 195, 198
Pieralongia 162
Pignano 112
Pizzo Carbonara 137
planning 18-19, *see also individual locations*
  accessible travel 16-17
  family travel 14
Podere Case Lovara 205
Pogerola 62
Poggio San Polo 104
Ponale 36-7
Ponte Sa Barva 174
Pontone 63
Pornanino 98
Porto Venere 203, 214-15

Portofino 10, 202, 206, 217
Positano 56-7, 64-5
Pragser Wildsee 156-7
Pregasina 37
Procinto 114
Punta Campanella 52-3
Punta La Marmora 181
Punta Troia 134-5

R

Raccicano 110
Radda in Chianti 94, 96, 98, 102
Ravello 59, 67
rifugi 19, 22
Rifugio Garelli 234-5
Riomaggiore 203, 214-15, 217
Riserva Naturale dello Zingaro 126-9
Riva del Garda 36
Rocca Calascio 72-3
Rocca Ridge 78-81
Roda de Pütia 162
ruins, *see* archaeological sites

S

Sacro Monte di Ossuccio 33
safe travel 18
  language 239
Sala Comacina 32
Salinello Gorges 91
Sambuco 59
San Donato 108, 110
San Fabiano 114
San Fruttuoso 10, 206, 216
San Gimignano 95, 100-1, 106, 109, 110
San Pierto della Lenca 91
Santa Margherita Ligure 217
Santa Maria del Castello 64-5
Sant'Agata sui Due Golfi 67
Sant'Amate 41
Sant'Angelo a Tre Pizzi 66
Santo Stefano di Sessanio 72-3
Sant'Orofrio hermitage 90
Santuario della Madonna di Montenero 217

Santuario della Madonna di Soviore 217
Sardinia 165-81
   accommodation 167
   events 167
   festivals 167
   resources 167
   transport 167
   travel seasons 167
Sass Corbée 44
Sasso Piano 192
Sassolungo 148-9
Sasso piatto 148-9
Scopello 119, 126
Seceda 162
Segesta 129
Seiser Alm 142-3
Sella 226-7
Sella Massif 146
Sella Ronda 146
Selva di Val Gardena 140
Selvaggio Blu 177
Sentiero Azzurro 210-13
Sentiero degli Dei 11, 54-7
Sentiero dei Fortini 67
Sentiero del Ventrar 42-3
Sentiero della Libertà 86-9
Sentiero delle Cascate 163
Sestri Levante 203
Sicily 117-37
   accommodation 119
   events 119
   festivals 119
   resources 119
   transport 119
   travel seasons 119
Slow Food 65
Sorrento 49
Spiaggia del Fornillo 57
St Francis of Assisi 190-2
Stelvio, see Dolomites & Stelvio
Strada del Ponale 36-7
Stresa 44

Stromboli 7, 120-1
Strombolicchio 120
Su Balladorzu 170
Su Porteddu 168
Su Ruvagliu 172
Sulmona 70, 86

T

Termini 52-3
Tiscali 172-5
Torrente Rabbies 158
Torrente Valnontey 237
Tour du Mont Blanc 6, 23, 222-4
Tratto Spino 42
travel seasons 19
Traversata del Conero 198
Tre Cime di Lavaredo 150-1
Tremezzo 34
Tuònes 178
Tuscany 93-115
   accommodation 95
   events 95
   festivals 95
   resources 95
   transport 95
   travel seasons 95

U

Umbria 183-99
   accommodation 185
   events 185
   festivals 185
   resources 185
   transport 185
   travel seasons 185

V

Vagliagli 105
Val Badia 140
Val di Pejo 163

Val Vény 223
Valle del Sambuco 58-9
Valle delle Ferriere 62-3
Valle d'Orta 84
Vallone di Grauson 232
Vallunga 9, 144-7
Valnontey 226
Vernazza 211
Via dei Monti Lattari 48
Via Francigena 20, 115
vie ferrate 22, 24
villages 13
villas
   Villa Balbianello 33, 35
   Villa Carlotta 33
   Villa Dievole 105
   Villa Rufolo 59
Volastra 208
Volterra 113
Vulcano 132-3

W

weather 19
   language 238-9
websites 19
   accessible travel 17
Western & Maritime Alps 219-37
   accommodation 221
   events 221
   festivals 221
   resources 221
   transport 221
   travel seasons 221
wildlife 23, 80
wine 105, 110, 209

Z

Zans 160-1

BRENDAN SAINSBURY

Brendan has been a dedicated walker and trail-runner since his days summiting the 'fells' of the English Lake District in his youth. In the years since, he has trekked all around the world for Lonely Planet, from Cockpit Country in Jamaica to the Santa Cruz trail in Peru to the Chilkoot trail in Alaska, and contributed to more than 60 guidebooks in the process.

My favourite walk is Monte Mileto because I love mountains, Abruzzo and the magic feeling of solitude.

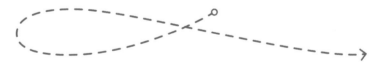

Our Story

A beat-up old car, a few dollars in the pocket and a sense of adventure. In 1972 that's all Tony and Maureen Wheeler needed for the trip of a lifetime – across Europe and Asia overland to Australia. It took several months, and at the end – broke but inspired – they sat at their kitchen table writing and stapling together their first travel guide, Across Asia on the Cheap. Within a week they'd sold 1500 copies. Lonely Planet was born.

Today, Lonely Planet has offices in Tennessee, Dublin, Beijing and Delhi, with a network of over 2000 contributors in every corner of the globe. We share Tony's belief that 'a great guidebook should do three things: inform, educate and amuse'.

Our Writers

GREGOR CLARK

Gregor is a US-based writer whose love of foreign languages and curiosity have taken him to dozens of countries on five continents. Since 2000, Gregor has regularly contributed to Lonely Planet guides, including titles on Italy and France, as well as cycling guides to Italy. Gregor lives with his wife and two daughters in his current home state of Vermont.

My favourite walk is nearly impossible to pick in a country as varied as Italy. Stromboli, Mont Blanc and Sardinia's Golfo di Orosei all come to mind – but I'll go with the Passo Gardena to Vallunga loop, a walk that encompasses the Dolomites' full spectrum of natural splendour, from the knife-edged summits of Puez-Odle to the gentle green pastures around Selva.

← MORE WRITERS -----------------------------------o

STAY IN TOUCH LONELYPLANET.COM/CONTACT

IRELAND Digital Depot, Roe Lane (off Thomas St), Digital Hub, Dublin 8, D08 TCV4

USA 230 Franklin Road, Building 2B, Franklin, TN 37064
📞 615 988 9713

 twitter.com/
lonelyplanet

 facebook.com/
lonelyplanet

 instagram.com/
lonelyplanet

 youtube.com/
lonelyplanet

 lonelyplanet.com/
newsletter